# GRACE AS TRANSMUTED EXPERIENCE AND SOCIAL PROCESS, AND OTHER ESSAYS IN NORTH AMERICAN THEOLOGY

Donald L. Gelpi, S.J.

UNIVERSITY
PRESS OF
AMERICA

LANHAM • NEW YORK • LONDON

Copyright ©1988 by

University Press of America,® Inc.

4720 Boston Way
Lanham, MD 20706

3 Henrietta Street
London WC2E 8LU England

Printed in the United States of America

British Cataloging in Publication Information Available

**Library of Congress Cataloging-in-Publication Data**

Gelpi, Donald L., 1934-
    Grace as transmuted experience and social process.

    1. Grace (Theology)   2. Theology—Methodology.
3. Catholic Church—United States—Doctrines.
4. Title.
BT761.2.G45   1987       230'.2      87-8218
ISBN 0-8191-6366-X (alk. paper)
ISBN 0-8191-6367-8 (pbk. : alk. paper)

All University Press of America books are produced on acid-free
paper which exceeds the minimum standards set by the National
Historical Publication and Records Commission.

# TABLE OF CONTENTS

## AUTHOR'S PREFACE

In the present volume, I offer the reader a collection of essays, not a series of chapters that argue cumulatively in order to establish a thesis. I have tried to write each essay in such a way that it could be read as an independent piece. Nevertheless, these six essays do enjoy a thematic unity. I enunciate that theme in the second essay, which therefore gives this collection its title. It attempts to describe divine grace, both uncreated and created, as transmuted experience and social process.

The first essay lays the foundation for the second and gives the collection its subtitle. It argues for the possibility of creating an inculturated North American theology by drawing systematically on the North American philosophical tradition. It does so by attempting to trace through the tradition seven themes which, taken collectively, suggest a concrete strategy for fostering theological inculturation in the United States. In this first essay, I attempt to describe the human condition in a Yankee idiom. In the second essay, I draw upon this same interpretation of the human condition in order to develop a new construct for understanding the relationship between nature and grace.

All the other essays in this volume elaborate in one way or another the themes enunciated in the first two. Having suggested the legitimacy of conceiving grace as transmuted experience and social process, I explore some of the theoretical and practical implications of the notion of transmutation. In the fourth essay, which attempts to probe the dynamic interplay of personal and socio-political conversion, I examine some of the consequences of conceiving grace as social process.

In the last two essays, I attempt to examine facets of a contemporary event that can lay manifest claims to having been not only a graced social process but one that has transmuted the faith experience of living Christians in significant ways. I have chosen the second Vatican council as the event to analyze. The first of these two concluding essays on Vatican II examines the ways in which the council's decrees have transmuted the graced social process we call sacramental worship. The final essay examines the council's teaching on lay spirituality. It takes the council's redefinition of the relationship between ordinary laity and lay religious as a useful point of entry into Vatican II's renewed understanding of the contribution which lay Christians make to the life of the church. In the course of reflecting on this facet of conciliar teaching, I attempt to use the construct of grace developed in the second essay of this collection in order to argue that that construct transforms what Vatican II has to say on the subject of Christian laity into a practical lay spirituality.

Because I have attempted to construct the argument of each essay in such a way that it could be read independently of the others, readers may find a certain number of fundamental insights repeated in each of them. In attempting to communicate to students the approach to the theology of grace which the following essays develop, I have, however, found that some repetition can serve the interests of clarity. The recurring themes should, moreover, help the reader to sense that the six pieces in this collection do attempt to offer a coherent approach to understanding the relationship between nature and grace.

In writing these essays, I have attempted to deal in greater depth with issues and insights previously enunciated in three other books: **Experiencing God: A Theology of Human Emergence; Charism and Sacrament: A Theology of Christian Conversion;** and **The Divine Mother: A Trinitarian Theology of the Holy Spirit.** In writing these books, I attempted to use the same theological method and to employ a consistent philosophical construct of reality. I used the method of foundational theology in Bernard Lonergan's sense of the term. I derived my philosophical approach to reality from a dialectical analysis of the North American philosophical tradition. I believe that the argument and conclusions of these three earlier studies mutually illumine one another in ways I could not explore while writing them. The constraints of time and space prevented me from calling detailed attention to the ways in which the three books make sense of one another and attempt to express a consistent theological vision. In several of these essays, I attempt to make up for this failure in my previous publications. In others, I attempt to treat in greater depth insights which I could only sketch in those earlier works.

I have undertaken these essays from a specific methodological concern. I believe that theological thought should alternate between detailed investigation of particular problems and a theory of the whole. In the three books I have just named I focused on a specific theological question. In the present volume I attempt to step back from those more detailed investigations in order to reflect on how they fit together as a whole. In the course of writing the reflections which follow I also came to realize that in my previous publications, I had fallen victim to a certain number of oversights which the present volume attempts to correct.

In this book as in previous volumes, I indulge in two literary conceits which need some explanation. I call the Holy Spirit the Holy Breath and refer to Her as She. I avoid the term "spirit" because it has too many unfortunate philosophical connotations. I have, moreover, found that I can dispense with it in pursuing foundational theology. I also believe that both the Bible and Christian tradition sanction imagining the Holy Breath as feminine. For a detailed justification of this belief, I refer the reader to **The Divine Mother.**

I wish to thank the friends and colleagues who have helped me in the writing and revision of these essays. The members of the John

Courtney Murray Group, a summer research seminar in North American theology, have read and criticized many of these pieces. I especially thank John Stacer, S.J., Francis Oppenheim, S.J., J.J. Mueller, S.J., William Spohn, S.J., and Michael Mahon, S.J. I wish also to express my gratitude to friends and colleagues at the Jesuit School of Theology in Berkeley, especially, Thomas Schubeck, S.J., Michael Buckley, S.J., Thomas Leahy, S.J., John Boyle, S.J., Harry Corcoran, S.J., Andrew Christiansen, S.J., and John Donahue, S.J. I also want to thank the editors of Spirituality Today for Permission to reprint "Thematic Grace vs. Transmuting Grace: Two Spiritual Paths." This essay appeared in a slightly edited form in that journal. The original, unedited essay appears in this volume.


Donald L. Gelpi, S. J.
June, 1988
Berkeley, California

# On Perceiving The Human Condition North Americanly:
## A Strategy For Theological Inculturation

On a clear flight from Los Angeles to Boston a lucky passenger can view some of the most spectacular scenery in the United States from an altitude of several thousand feet. The saw-toothed Sierra Nevadas, the baked salt flats of Death Valley, the twisting Colorado as it slices into the Grand Canyon, the seemingly endless expanse of the great American desert, the massive peaks of the Rockies, steaming Niagara Falls--all shrink to miniature size beneath the double windows of the smooth soaring jet. The awestruck traveler who drives across the nation can begin to savor at close quarters the vastness, the variety, the richness, the splendor of the North American landscape. Nevertheless, to know the land truly one also needs to wrestle with it at close quarters: to pant one's way to the summit of Mount Whitney, to hike Golden Canyon, to stand at Dante's View, to swim in Bright Angel creek and see the green Colorado etch its way through centuries of stone down into the roots of an ancient alpine range. Then the landscape gets into one's very life blood as the Sierra Nevadas have into mine.

The people of the United States match the richness of the land they inhabit with the diversity of cultures and nations from which they spring. A nation of immigrants, the United States has garnered its citizens from virtually every people on earth; but while this land prides itself on being called the great melting pot of races and cultures, this very boast constitutes in the eyes of many foreigners its greatest weakness. Many people from other lands equate North American culture with Hollywood westerns, Coca-cola, and capitalism. Such people smile indulgently at the suggestion that the United States has anything of genuine cultural significance to offer the rest of the civilized world.

As a people we have, however, produced more than the technology and the obscene affluence that has transformed us into a major superpower. We boast a rich literary, artistic, philosophical, and scientific tradition, despite the fact that our characteristic obsession with the future and indifference to the past frequently blinds us to our own cultural heritage.

The second Vatican Council has challenged theologians to engage in inculturated theological thinking. An inculturated theology derives its basic concepts and symbols from the culture in which a local church roots itself. Such a theology also seeks to transform that culture according to the mind of Christ.

In this essay I will attempt to argue that as North American philosophy has developed, it has produced a distinctive way of viewing the human condition. I will also begin to devise a strategy for exploiting theologically this characteristically Yankee anthropology.

Many speak of North American philosophy as though it suddenly

1

mushroomed into life at the end of the nineteenth century, but we trace our speculative roots all the way to Jonathan Edwards (1703-1758). Pastor, polemicist, revivalist, this puritan divine still ranks in the minds of many as the greatest speculative theologian this nation has produced.

The American enlightenment engendered few original thinkers, but it shaped decisively the political institutions of our republic and created many of the myths and tenets of North American civil religion.

Historians of thought in this country often portray American transcendentalism as a movement that flourished during the decade of the eighteen thirties. In point of fact, however, the movement lasted well into the twentieth century and survives to this day in organizations like the Sierra Club and the environmentalist movement.

The early American transcendentalists each elaborated some kind of doctrine of religious intuition, even though they understood intuition in a variety of ways. Ralph Waldo Emerson (1803-1882) popularized a platonized secular gospel of creative intuition. In the eighteen forties he bequeathed intellectual leadership of the movement to Theodore Parker (1810-1860). Parker spoke of a paradoxical kind of intuition. He actually believed that the human spirit possesses faculties so constructed that they intuit within subjectivity the objective truth of God's existence, of human immortality, and of the universal principles of morality. Orestes Brownson (1803-1876) during the eighteen fifties and sixties elaborated a robustly incarnational doctrine of intuitive religious enlightenment.

In the eighteen sixties Chauncey Wright (1830-1875) and Charles Sanders Peirce (1839-1914) launched a vigorous speculative assault on transcendental intuitionism. Wright defended a straightforward positivism. Peirce, on the other hand, laid the speculative foundations for American pragmatism. The cogency of their attack led Francis Ellingwood Abbot (1836-1903), one of the last of the speculative leaders of the transcendentalist movement, to seek for ways of reconciling an Emersonian transcendentalism with the logic of science.

Although Peirce formulated the pragmatic maxim, William James (1842-1910) launched pragmatism as a movement. James, Peirce, and later John Dewey (1859-1952) each developed a distinctive brand of pragmatism. James moved toward a doctrine of radical empiricism; Peirce toward a metaphysical realism; Dewey toward an instrumental naturalism.

When he died, Peirce left his papers to Josiah Royce (1855-1916) whom he regarded as the person most likely to bring to fruition the metaphysical synthesis Peirce himself was constructing when he died. Born in a California gold rush town, Royce at James's intervention joined the Harvard faculty in 1882. He espoused a metaphysical idealism and contributed significantly to both logic and the philosophy of religion.

2

George Santayana (1863-1952) studied under Royce and like Dewey defended a brand of atheistic naturalism. Less the busy instrumentalist than Dewey, Santayana's naturalism aspired to a disillusioned, self-mocking mysticism. The metaphysics he formulated in the latter half of his life strongly influenced the thought of Alfred North Whitehead (1880-1947).

A native Englishman, Whitehead did his most creative philosophical thinking while teaching at Harvard University. He absorbed a variety of American philosophical influences and described his thought as systematization of insights derived from James and Dewey. The dean of process philosphers, he can boast a significant number of disciples to this day, as process speculation advances into a fourth generation of creative ferment.

Needless to say, not all North American philosophers interpreted the human condition in exactly the same manner. Philosophy thrives on argument, and argument presupposes real disagreement. Nevertheless, as philosophical thought in this country developed, certain broad areas of consensus began to coalesce. Taken together those areas suggest a way of interpreting our human lot and destiny in a distinctively Yankee manner.

More specifically, any student of North American philosophy will find that its architects tend to sniff suspiciously at all forms of dualism. Several of them find fault with European substance philosophy. They not only focus on human experience but also tend increasingly to use the term "experience" itself as a central and unifying category. They tend to assimilate religious and esthetic experience. They tend to insist on the radical finitude of the human mind and on the dialogic character of human thought. Their minds turn spontaneously to the future and concern themselves with the consequences of beliefs and actions. Finally, one discovers within American philosphy a tension between a naturalistic and a supernaturalistic vision of human destiny.

In the course of this essay I will attempt to reflect on these seven strains within the North American philosophical tradition. And in the process of doing so, I will try to develop a strategy for deriving from the American philosophical tradition an anthropology that promises to foster an inculturated North American theology.

(1) **The Repudiation of Dualism.** Dualistic sytems of thought conceive interrelated realities in such a way that their relationship to one another loses all subsequent intelligibility. Philosophy has harvested a cornucopia of dualistic conceptions of reality. Substantial dualism splits human nature into two essentially different substances--one spiritual, the other material--and then finds that it can no longer explain coherently how two substances can be united in a single person. Operational dualism divides human powers of operation into spiritual and material faculties and finds itself thereafter unable to explain coherently how the material powers of the human soul move the spiritual to act. Subjectivism sunders

human evaluative processes from the realities they interpret in such a way that one can no longer conceive the possibility of a realistic grasp of truth. Individualism opposes single persons to society in such a way that social responsibility fades into irrelevance.

As the speculative tradition in this country developed, its architects displayed recurring dissatisfaction with dualistic systems of thought. Increasingly they insisted instead on the relational character of all reality.

Already in the writings of Jonathan Edwards one discovers a critique of operational dualism. In his **Treatise Concerning Religious Affections** Edwards resisted the attempt of Charles Chauncey and of other rationalistic critics of the first Great Awakening to divide the faculties of the human soul into the higher spiritual faculties of reason and of will, on the one hand, and the lower, material faculties of sense and emotion, on the other. The opponents of the Awakening were using this distinction in order to discredit what they called the mindless emotionalism of the first American revival. Edwards in his defense of the Awakening insisted instead on the centrality of affectivity to authentic Christian religion and practice. He described the will as affectivity brought to the peak of its exercise.[1]

Although Ralph Waldo Emerson defended an unabashed Platonic dualism, among the New England transcendentalists Orestes Brownson deplored the dualistic opposition of matter and spirit as one of the great banes of Christian thought. In his **New Views of Christianity,** published in 1926, the **annus mirabilis** of the transcendentalist revolt, the young Brownson argued that Jesus had actually come to reconcile spirit to matter. Under the sway of ideas popularized by William Ellery Channing, he also argued that the dualistic opposition of matter to spirit could only be overcome by acknowledging the human race's essential divinity. After his conversion to Roman Catholicism, a more mature Brownson would reject this particular solution to the problem of dualism as heretical, but he would continue to grope for a wholistic interpretation of the human condition.[2]

Moreover, as he drew closer to Catholicism Brownson protested vigorously against dualistic interpretations of human social relationships. He decried individualism in all its forms. Study of the French thinker Pierre Leroux convinced him of the social character of human life and of the mediatorial function of love. He even went so far as to equate love with life itself. Through love, he saw, we enter into communion with other persons and realities. And he began to understand that love can bridge the gap between the divine and the human. He came to regard Jesus as the one providentially chosen by God to lead all people through love into social communion with one another and with God (WOB, IV, 149-159).

Brownson also rejected all forms of subjectivism. In an article in his **Quarterly Review** he wrote: "The true point of departure of philosophy is never in **Being, das reine seyn** of the Hegelians, whether of the subject or of the object; but in **life,** which is the manifestation of Being. And in **life,** according to what we have established, **the subject and object, me and not me, are one and indissoluble."** Life results from the interaction, the intercommunion of the me and not me. Sensibility, intelligence, imagination, willing --all constitute ways of communing with something or someone other than myself. Moreover, through an intuitive faith in the

Word made flesh we commune with the divinity itself (WOB, I, 58-71, II, 42ff, IV, 149-159).

In speaking of the action of divine grace Brownson also carefully avoided dualistic theological language. He rejected the subjectivism of "inner light" piety. Instead he insisted that God must be discovered in the concrete, sensible reality of Jesus and in the concrete sacramental reality of the Church (WOB, V, 327ff, III, 553, VII, 291-297, VI, 116-133). He described grace as "theandric life" and pointed to the incarnation as its supreme exemplification. Moreover, through the action of the Holy Spirit in the missionary church theandric life spreads geographically, and it intensifies through divine illumination (WOB, XII, 485).

One finds an analogous concern to avoid dualistic patterns of thought in the "scientific theism" of Francis Ellingwood Abbot. Although Abbot unlike Brownson rejected incarnationalism, early in his religious career he proclaimed that the motto of the American republic, **"e pluribus unum",** holds the key that unlocks the secrets of the universe. In his book **Scientific Theism,** which Peirce praised highly, Abbot insisted on the fundamentally relational character of all reality. His doctrine of relationism portrays universals as relationships that bond the cosmos together. In his final work, **The Syllogistic Philosophy,** he returned to the same theme. He described each person as a "unit-universal" that synthesizes the concrete and sensible with the universal and relational. Every "I" emerges from a "We." The universe develops organically. Being unifies knowing and doing, and all organically interdependent, finite selves subsist in relationship with one another in the all unifying reality of God.[3]

John Dewey's naturalistic instrumentalism also mounts a strong critique of dualistic thinking. He believed that isolated realities petrify and condemned the fallacious attempts of philosophers to separate the real from the ideal, subjectivity from objectivity, means from ends.[4] Dewey portrayed reality in dynamic terms, as an event. We come to know events by having cognitive transactions with them, and we use cognitive symbols to lead human experience to shared consummatory satisfactions. Ideals function cognitively as ends-in-view, as potentially realizable satisfactions. Like Abbot and Brownson, then, Dewey discovered in the dynamic relational character of reality a speculative antidote to the poison of dualism.[5]

Dewey's political philosophy also mounts a strong polemic against individualism.   He defined true individuality as potentiality, as the capacity for growth and development.   He proposed both instrumentalism and open-ended, shared inquiry as the best means we have discovered so far for achieving full individuality in social communion with one another. Instrumentalism regards the symbols of thought as tools for leading human experience to shared consummations.   Dewey also deplored the social dualism implicit in **laissez-faire** liberalism.   The authentic defense of freedom, he insisted, engages individuals in the collaborative enterprise of

creating the conditions in which to realize a thoroughly socialized and responsible individuality.6

Process philosophy also attempts to overcome the dualistic isolation of interrelated realities by insisting on the relational character of the real.  Whitehead called his system a "philosophy of organism."   In a Whiteheadian universe, every reality that comes into existence atomizes what he calls "the extensive continuum," a unified network of relationships that bind the universe into an organic whole.   Conceptual relationships knit together the realm of possibility, and creativity links conceptual possibilities dynamically to the realm of actuality.   As a consequence in the world of process philosophy, every reality creates itself to be what it is in a dynamic, self-adjusting relationship with every other reality.      Indeed, Whitehead regarded relationship as more fundamental than essence.  By that he meant that only as a consequence of their mutual interrelatedness can entities transform themselves into the kind of reality that they will eventually become.7

We can, then, discover in the North American philosophical tradition two persistent and interrelated tendencies.   On the one hand, American philosophers tend to rebel against dualistic portrayals of the human condition.  On the other, they appeal to the relational character of reality as a speculative antidote to dualism.

Moreover, we can already begin to discern an inkling of a strategy for perceiving the human condition North Americanly.   Conceive humanity in organic, relational terms that anchor each individual solidly in its spatio-temporal environment.   Avoid language that establishes a spiritual hierarchy among human powers of operation as well as every other form of philosophical dualism.  Focus on the continuities that shape experience by insisting on its relational character, but remain nevertheless sensitive to the discontinuities that divide individuals and groups by setting them into contradictory and irreconcilable relationships.

(2) **The Assault upon Substance.**   In the history of western philosophical speculation, different thinkers have formulated diverse definitions of the term "substance."  Aristotle looked upon a substance as the reality to which the subject of a logical proposition refers; but he defined a substance as "that which exists in itself and not in another as in a subject of inhesion." He thus contrasted substances and accidents. The latter inhere in substances, and therefore do exist in something other than

6

themselves.

Toward the end of the nineteenth century, one discovers a growing reluctance on the part of several North American philosophers to invoke the term "substance." They tend, however, to derive their definition of substance, not from Aristotle, but from John Locke. Locke looked upon a substance as an unknowable substrate undergirding the sense qualities we actually experience.

A hard-nosed positivist, Chauncey Wright dismissed the notion of "substance" as scientifically useless. The category "substance," he argued, reflects the structure of language, but not the structure of reality. It reifies the logical subject of a sentence into a subsisting substrate in which its predicates are supposed to inhere as "accidents."[8] Indeed, Wright questioned the scientific utility of all metaphysical categories and dismissed metaphysics itself as "the science of the supernatural, of the non-phenomenal."[9] He rejected outright both theology and metaphysics because "the object-matters of their research were not questions of sensible experience."[10] Peirce would mount a telling critique of Wright's assault on both metaphysics and religion, but Wright's rejection of substance philosophy would find important echoes in the thought of James and Whitehead.

In **Pragmatism** William James pressed the speculative atttack against substance philosophy on somewhat different grounds from Wright. James described his understanding of pragmatism as a method in the following terms:

> The pragmatic method is primarily a method of settling metaphysical disputes that otherwise might be interminable....The pragmatic method in such cases is to try to interpret each notion by tracing its respective practical consequences. What difference would it practically make to anyone if this notion rather than that notion were true? If no practical difference whatever can be traced, then the alternatives mean practically the same thing, and a dispute is idle.[11]

Accordingly, James objected to the notion of "substance" on the grounds that the existence or non-existence of substances makes no practical differences, since in practice we deal not with substances but with accidents. James's objection envisages especially Locke's definition of substance, but it also scores a pragmatic point against neo-scholastic substance philosophers who would concede that substances are never experienced as such and that their actual existence must be inferred by a metaphysical argument. James, however, regarded unexperienceable metaphysical realities as practically and therefore as philosophically trivial.

7

Moreover, as we have already seen, other North American philosophers have suggested speculative alternatives to the notion of substance. Dewey conceived of reality more as an event than as a substance. Abbot preferred to conceive individuals as "unit-universals" rather than as substances. Royce conceived individual selves as ideas driving to concreteness through action. Moreover, this tendency to search for speculative alternatives to the category "substance" culminated finally in Whitehead's theory of "prehensions."

Whitehead dismissed the category "substance" as an instance of the "fallacy of misplaced concreteness." The fallacy consists in treating high-level philosophical abstractions as though they were subsisting, concrete actualities. Whitehead's criticism envisaged primarily Locke's definition of substance. But his philosophy of prehension suggests a way of conceiving individual realities in a way that contrasts with the thought of both Aristotle and Locke.

Whitehead defines a "prehension" as "a concrete fact of relatedness." Every prehension consists of five elements: the subject of the prehension, its initial datum, its objective datum, its negative prehensions, and its subjective form. Whitehead conceives the subject of a prehension as an emerging, atomic drop of experience which perishes in a fraction of a second. The subject emerges from its intitial datum, which Whitehead defined as the state of the universe at the instant the subject begins to emerge. In a Whiteheadian universe, as we have already seen, each emerging subject must define its essence in a relation of opposition to every other existing reality. It does so by taking into itself some portion of the physical universe, excluding other portions, and then incorporating into its concrete physical reality some novel possibility or possibilities. By relating positively to some actualities and possibilities and negatively to others, the emerging subject defines its particular perspective on the universe, its objective datum. The subject's negative prehensions, the relationships of exclusion that eliminate from the emerging subject specific actualities and possibilites, help define its objective datum. Finally, the way the subject reacts or responds evaluatively to the data it experiences endows it with a subjective form (PR, 221).

Of what is each emerging drop of experience composed? Of feelings. Physical feelings endow experience with concreteness, actuality, and causal efficacy. Conceptual feelings, or feelings of pure possibility, endow experience with vividness and presentational immediacy. Propositional feelings interrelate possibilities and actualities. Every developing drop of experience atomizes the extensive continuum and perishes in a fraction of a second as the emerging subject achieves concreteness through decision.

How does a world of prehensions differ from a world of substances? Or, to put the same question in different terms, what issues divide substance from process philosophy? The two systems disagree on at least eight identifiable issues.

8

1.    Process philosophy reverses the most fundamental presuppositions of substance philosophy. Substance philosophy equates Being, reality, with essential immutability. In a world of substances to the extent that anything changes it lacks complete reality. Process philosophy, however, rests on a very different assumption. Process philosophy equates reality and mutation. In the world of process theory things exist, enjoy reality, only to the extent that they change. Once they cease changing, they perish and are transformed into past facts.

2.    Substance and process philosophy understand the subject of change differently. Substance philosophy identifies the subject of a change with the unchanging reality that underlies it. Process philosophy holds that the subject of a change emerges from the change.

3.    Substance philosophy believes that reality is composed of essentially stable principles of being. Substances change accidentally, but in an accidental change the substance perdures and preserves its substantial essence. Process philosophy, on the other hand, envisages each individual reality as a concrescent "drop" of experience. The term "concrescent" implies that (a) in every drop of experience the feelings that constitute it grow together (in Latin the verb **concrescere** means "to grow together") and (b) as the feelings that comprise an experience grow together they become more concrete.

4.    Substance philosophy believes that action follows essence. In other words, the actions of a substance express its fixed substantial essence. Process philosophy, by contrast, holds that essence flows from action. Each individual drop of experience must transform itself into a certain kind of reality through decision.

5. Substance philosophy holds that essences, what things are, can be defined through genus and specific difference. Humans, for example, are defined as rational animals. They belong to the genus animal but are distinguished from other animals by the specific difference of rationality. Process philosophy, however, questions whether such definitions adequately express the essence of things, what they are. In process theory the essence of anything results from its history. Definition through genus and specific difference fails as a consequence to express adequately the essence of anything. In a world of processing experiences an adequate definition would have to recapitulate the history of whatever it defined. Moreover, if we reify essences defined according to genus and specific difference we fall into the fallacy of misplaced concreteness.

6.    Substance philosophy discovers two kinds of relationship in reality. Transcendental relations link act and potency. Potency is defined as the capacity to change. Act as the intrinsic determination of a potency. Predicamental relations modify substances by changing the way they are ordered to one another. As a consequence in substance philosophy, predicamental relations "follow" substance in the sense that things must be what they are substantially before they can enter into relationship with

anything else.

Process philosophy, however, views relationship in very different terms. Process thought avoids the language of act and potency. As a consequence, we find no transcendental relations in a process universe. Moreover, process theory understands "predicamental" relations very differently from substance theory. In a world of processing experiences relationship gives rise to essence. Each drop of experience atomizes the extensive continuum. It can therefore decide the kind of reality it will eventually become only in consequences of its relationship to every other entity.

7. In a world of substances, things exist in themselves and not in anything else as in a subject of inhesion. In a world of processing experiences every reality is "objectified" in every other. Things therefore exist in one another.

8. In substance philosophy the quantification of matter individuates. In process thought decision individuates. Each emerging drop of experience must decide concretely the kind of experience it will become. Individuals are therefore distinguished from one another qualitatively, not quantitatively.

On each of these issues save one, I myself believe that process philosophy moves in a sounder speculative direction than does a philosophy of substance. We need not equate being and immutability and would be better advised to identify reality and process. We can legitimately conceive every reality as an instance of experience. The subject of a change does emerge from the change. We do through decision determine ourselves to be this kind of reality rather than that. In order to understand fully the essence of any reality we would have to recapitulate its entire history. When two realities interact they mutually interpenetrate one another and therefore quite literally exist in one another. We would be better advised to understand the achievement of individuality as a process of self-definition rather than in purely quantitative terms.

Nevertheless, the claim of process philosophy that every reality stands in relationship to every other sounds to me inflated. Realities relate only to the extent that they are actually ordered to one another. That order must be positive and actual. They must attend to one another, actually interact. Negative relations do not count as either positive or actual but as merely conceptual relations. If then we attempt to show the universal relatedness of any given individual by saying with Whitehead that it is related positively to some things and negatively to everything else, we then reify negative relationships and succumb to the fallacy of misplaced concreteness.

Moreover, substance philosophy can mount a telling criticism of process theory on a different point. A substance explains individual unity and real continuity within change. The same substance endures through all its accidental modifications. In process speculation an individual reality, like a person, is composed of a society of overlapping, atomic occasions of experiences that each perish in a fraction of a second. The same subjective aim links all the members of a society. Within the society atomicity remains the ultimate fact of facts. As a consequence, in process theory if I am to speak of an individual person like Woodrow Wilson I must first decide whether I mean the pure possibility like Woodrow Wilson, the entire society of occasions that make up Woodrow Wilson, or a particular occasion of Woodrow Wilson. There may be those who find here an adequate account of individual unity and continuity within experience. However, I do not count myself among them.

A critical examination of the philosophical assault on substance philosophy undertaken by some North American philosophers yields then mixed results. It produces some telling criticisms of substance theory. Substance philosophy does tend to reify the grammatical structure of Indo-European languages. It has in the past sometimes divorced reality and experience. It has misconceived the nature of the real, the subject of change, the relationship between essence and action, and individuation. It has naively reified its abstract definitions of reality and failed to deal adequately with the mutual inexistence of developing experiences. The fact, however, that substance philosophy does explain certain facets of experience more adequately than process theory should caution the prudent thinker against dismissing substance philosophy out of hand and against buying process theory lock, stock, and barrel. Indeed, as we shall see, process metaphysics labors under several other serious speculative deficiencies. If, then, an inculturated North American anthropology desires to avoid narrow Yankee chauvinism, it must attempt to benefit from the best insights of both systems.

(3) **The Focus on Experience.** Concern with the dynamic structure of experience surfaces early in the North American speculative tradition. Speculative concern with experience begins as a descriptive exploration of religious experience. In the late nineteenth and early twentieth centuries it gives rise to a generalized theory of experience and eventually in the thought of Whitehead to a metaphysics of experience. Let us reflect in turn on each of these developments.

(a) **The Structure of Religious Experience.** In his **Treatise Concerning Religious Affections** Jonathan Edwards explored eloquently and sensitively the experienced complexities of Christian conversion. During the nineteenth century Emerson attempted in his own way to probe descriptively the experience of creativity in order to understand its religious significance. James's **Principles of Psychology** has endured as a classic in no small measure because of its descriptive account of different facets of human experience. Moreover, **The Varieties of Religious Experience** placed the category "experience" at the heart of the psychology of religion.

James defined religious experience in highly individualistic terms as "the feelings, acts, and experiences of individual men in their solitude, so far as they apprehend themselves to stand in relation to whatever they may consider divine."12   James's religious psychology therefore consciously excluded consideration of the social, institutional, cultic, or historical dimensions of religious experience. As we shall see, Josiah Royce would subsequently and quite correctly chide him for the inadequacy of his approach.

James believed that personal religious belief systems express the temperament, the individual emotional bias of the person who espouses them.   In **The Varieties** he distinguished three kinds of religious temperaments: the healthy-minded, the soul-sick, and the converted. Healthy-minded persons possess "a temperament organically weighted on the side of cheer." They tend as a consequence to overlook or to deny the evil and suffering present in the world.  The "sick soul" by contrast lives obsessed with the problem of evil.  The sick soul has crossed the pain threshold: the intensity of personal suffering has over-sensitized such people to misery, failure, misfortune. The healthy-minded show few if any religious hesitations. Soul sickness breeds agnosticism, melancholy, apathy, loathing, exasperation, doubt, and even despair.  If the healthy-minded exaggerate the goodness of life, the sick soul overemphasizes its misery. Converts move beyond both healthy mindedness and soul sickness through an experience of religious rebirth. Viewed psychologically, James suggests, conversion shifts the center of personal interest.  Religious ideas which once hovered on the periphery of consciousness now become central. Conversion also engages the will through commitment and through the sanctifying living out of the consequences of conversion.  The presence of psychological factors within conversion did not in James's mind rule out the possibility of divine agency within the conversion process.  James himself believed that we have primary experiential access to God through the activities of the unconscious psyche (VRE, 155-298).

As we shall see, Peirce would disagree vehemently with James's apparent attempt to reduce religious and metaphysical beliefs to mere projections of temperamental attitudes.  He would complain that such a position confounds psychology and logic. He would, however, in his account of hypothetical thinking discover a place for affectivity in the initial formulation of any belief.  Subsequently, Josiah Royce mounted under Peirce's tutelage an even more telling criticism of James's phenomenology of religious experience.

Royce's own descriptive account of religious experience took issue with the emotive, individualistic bias present in James's. Royce conceded that individual experience can yield genuine religious insight, but he emphasized far more than James the cognitive and social dimension of human religious behavior.

Royce believed that religious insights grasp the human need for salvation and understand the means of achieving it.  Salvation for Royce means reaching the ultimate goal of life.  We can miss that goal if we choose to.

12

Royce believed that individuals need salvation but that they cannot save themselves. Every individual seeks self-possession, integration, a peace which lifts one beyond the turmoil of life. We find salvation, however, not in solitude but in communion with others. The religious community, therefore, provides the locus of grace and healing which religious individuals need, even though it too needs saving.[13]

Moreover, Royce insisted in opposition to James, that in the social redemption of individuals reason plays an important role. Reason either analyses or synthesizes. Royce believed that religious reason synthesizes: it endows religious experience with unity and an integrating sense of purpose. It provides the religious seeker with a conception of God that allows the mind to recognize a divine act of self-revelation if and when it occurs. The reasoning religious mind also recognizes the moral claims of religion. The religiously committed must conform their individual wills to God's will. We do that most effectively, Royce believed, by consecrating ourselves to some cause. Loyalty to some cause inserts us into a saving community of grace. Loyalty to the cause of loyalty itself binds one in committed fidelity to loyal people everywhere and to the God whose saving will grounds and unifies the community of the loyal (SRI, 165-210).[14]

Massive and disastrous evils, Royce believed, overwhelm finite human minds. He insisted, however, that even suffering can on occasion yield a religious insight. It does so when the suffering is encompassed by some larger reality that endows it with a meaning it does not have in and of itself. Sin can be redeemed through forgiveness; pain can give rise to new life. (SRI, 213-214).

Although **The Varieties of Religious Experience** contains many useful insights into the ways in which affectivity conditions religious behavior, Royce's phenomenology of religious experience surpasses James's in nuance and complexity. By recognizing that individual experience opens only one of many doors to religious insight, Royce created a broader, more comprehensive frame of reference for interpreting religious experience than James, but one that can incorporate James's best insights into individual religious behavior. Nevertheless, James corrects Royce on one important point. Royce, a metaphysical idealist, found the concept of an unconscious mind unintelligible. James the psychologist knew the reality and power of the unconscious psyche and regarded it as a privileged point of access to the divine.

North American philosophy does not, however, focus narrowly on religious experience. It also concerns itself with the most generic traits of experience. Let us turn to this second strain in our speculative tradition.

(b) **The Generic Traits of Experience.** Although early philosophical speculation in this country focused strongly on human religious experience, interest in the dynamic characteristics of experience in general surfaces fairly early. Orestes Brownson in his "analysis of the subject" explored, for example, the varieties of human sensibility. He distinguished perception, memory, presentiment, and imagination. Through perception we recognize sensible objects. In that recognition the mind is already actively engaged. Sensible stimuli trigger memories. Presentiment yields a vague, confused, global feeling for the unity and wholeness of experience and provides the experienced background for more vivid perceptions. Presentiment also orients experience toward the future. It endows experience both with a global feeling for the order and stability in nature and with a sense of personal continuity. Imagination, according to Brownson, engages every kind of perception. It yields a heightened sense of the significance of the things we experience. Through imagination we grasp the real. When imaginative experience intensifies it becomes ecstasy or trance. Willing, Brownson believed, permeates all human activity, including cognition, for we must will to think. "Willing," however, in the strict sense of the term designates responsible human decisions (WOB, I, 71-129).

Already in Brownson's freewheeling descriptive analysis of human experience we can discern tendencies which other North American thinkers will echo. He avoids the language of faculty psychology and refuses to distinguish human powers on the basis of their formal objects in the manner of scholastic and neo-scholastic thinkers. Instead Brownson insists on the continuity that pervades human evaluative responses. They blend into one another and mediate a cognitive grasp of the continuities present in the world about us. With his characteristic suspicion of dualistic forms of thinking, we find in Brownson no clear distinction between the material and spiritual powers of the soul.

Peirce too reflected on the dynamic structure of human experience but at a much higher level of abstraction than any other North American thinker. Peirce held that anything that appears within human experience can be reduced to one of three categories: quality, fact, or law. Peirce defined a quality as an instance of "particular suchness." Qualities endow experience with a sense of pure possibility.[15] The category "fact" designates brute, physical interaction (CPCSP, 1. 322-336). The category "law" designates habitual tendencies, which endow experience with regularity and continuity (CPCSP, 1. 337-353).

James in **The Principles of Psychology** advanced far beyond either Peirce or Brownson, however, in describing the complexities of personal experience. Moreover, James the psychologist realized more vividly than Brownson had that any modern description of human experience needs to take into account the results of scientific investigations of the human psyche. His studies in psychology had sensitized James to the organic basis of human cognitive processes. He discovered a certain number of describable characteristics in conscious human experience. Humans always feel consciousness as personal, as belonging to oneself, as "mine." Human consciousness changes constantly: we never have identically the same idea twice. Consciousness displays continuity: it flows like a stream. "Like a bird's life, it seems to be made up of an alternation of flights and perchings." In the flights of consciousness we experience relationship; in its perchings we experience substantives. The flow of consciousness includes feelings of expectancy and absence, familiarity and newness, tendency and logical relation. Consciousness deals with things other than itself, although we also can reflect on ourselves and on our own thought processes. Finally through the focusing of attention, consciousness selects among different possible objects of cognition.16

In the course of **The Principles** James explored with similar sensitivity and descriptive detail the experience of sensation, perception, the focusing of attention, self-awareness, memory, the sense of sameness, universal insights, association and dissociation, time perception, space perception, the perception of likeness and difference, the motives for associating one thing with another, the sense of a "thing," feelings of voluminousness, reality perception, belief, inference, instinct, decision, and action.

James's descriptive exploration of experience in general in **The Principles** like his descriptive exploration of religious experience in **The Varieties** focuses primarily on individual experience. John Dewey, by contrast, emphasized the social, transactional character of human experience. He attempted his most ambitious phenomenology of experience in a late work, **Art as Experience.** Dewey believed that ordinary human experience reaches heightened consciousness in artistic experience. He therefore looked to artistic experience to cast significant light on the dynamic structure of experience in general.

Artistic experience, Dewey observed, emerges from vital organic processes and expresses human feeling and passion. Artistic creativity interrelates dynamically concrete sensibility and perceptions of ideals. Art opens experience to the mystery, complexity, and uncertainty of life. Art emerges from experience and expresses the dynamic quality of experience. Experience flows. It flows from something to something. Pauses within the flow only serve to punctuate and define the quality of the movement. A qualitative unity pervades every experience, a unity which eludes abstract conceptual expression. Art attempts to communicate that qualitative unity, to express a unified way of perceiving the real. In artistic perceptions feelings, emotion, and affectivity conspire to reduce an experience to a felt harmony. The achievement of that harmony results from a process, from the artist's interaction with a world, an environment, that supplies a symbolic medium capable of expressing the artist's felt perceptions of the real (AE, 35-44).

The interactive patterns which structure dynamically both human experience in general and artistic experience in particular display alternating moments of activity and receptivity. An excess of either disrupts perception. Esthetic perceptions grasp reality appreciatively. They result from mind play, from imaginative explorations of the texture and complexity of experience and of reality. The artist, however, does not contemplate reality passively like a spectator. Rather artists achieve insight by interacting with a chosen artistic medium: with paint, stone, sound, gesture, language. Artistic feeling always concerns itself with

15

something. The transformed artistic medium expresses an appreciative perception of reality by unifying symbolically the materials that express it. The intenser the emotion, the more effective the artistic expression. Only those emotions which can transform some artistic medium reach artistic expression (AE, 48-60).

Expressed meaning derives in part from past experiences, but the expressed meaning must be evoked by some present event and must mature subconsciously before coming to conscious expression. Artistic creation begins with an initial emotional siezure, moves through a period of active gestation, and culminates in final expression in the finished art object. The art object objectifies esthetic feeling. As a consequence, artistic enjoyment differs from immediate sensible satisfaction. It diverts sensibility from immediate satiety to embodiment in a symbolic medium (AE, 70-79).

Art selects those facets of its subject that it desires to express. All art therefore to that extent abstracts, including representational art (AE, 93-96). Artists create their own languages, which differ from one art object to another. As language art communicates. It involves the triadic relationship of interpretation in which someone tries to communicate something to someone else. What is communicated constitutes the fundamental reality of art; and artistic form defines the way that reality is communicated. In art, the form and the content of what is communicated cannot be separated (AE, 106-114).

The medium in artistic communication functions instrumentally. It focuses the creative artist's experience and mediates between the creator and those who perceive the finished art object. Moreover, just as the creative artist must interact with the instrumental medium that expresses an artistic insight, so too those who experience finished art objects must interact with them in order to understand and appreciate them. All artistic experience therefore defines a specific segment of the spatio-temporal universe (AE, 187-229).

Logical thinking reproduces at a higher level of abstraction the same dynamic patterns which structure artistic thinking, even though the meaning of an art object differs significantly from the meaning of logical sym ols. Logical symbols do not communicate in their own right the way artistic symbols do. Art objects signify in virtue of the unique quality each work possesses, a quality that clarifies and concentrates meanings present less intensely and in scattered form in other experiences. Art expresses meanings; logic states them, defining terms, formulating them into propositions, and elucidating their consequences. Logical statements set forth the conditions under which certain results may be obtained. Artistic and poetic expressions of meaning do not by contrast point to some experience not presently in evidence. They constitute rather an experience that means something in its own right. The art object means something to the creative artist who made it, and it bears meaning to those who perceive it (AE, 82-86).

16

Logical thinking, however, reproduces the transactional, artistic creation. Logical inquiry transforms experience by the symbolic forms it creates and uses. It seeks to eliminate arbitrary and ungrounded interpretations of reality. It attempts to transform indeterminate, problematic situations into determinate ones subject to rational control. Inquiry advances experimentally, by testing the consequences of different hypothetical interpretations of reality until all but the correct interpretation have been eliminated. It thus transforms an initial hypothesis into a validated judgment.17

We have examined the efforts of representative North American thinkers to reflect on the generic traits of experience. This impulse culminates in Whiteheads attempt to formulate a metaphysics of experience.

(c) **Toward a Metaphysics of Experience.** Brownson, James, Peirce, and Dewey each develop distinctive but convergent phenomenologies of experience. In the thought of Alfred North Whitehead, however, the term "experience" begins to acquire metaphysical meaning. Some thinkers use the term "experience" restrictively. They confine it to mean sensory experience, or to mean knowledge of the data for thought before that data is understood or judged, or to mean only conscious (as opposed to unconscious) evaluations. Dewey expands the term "experience" to include any human evaluative response logical or prerational, conscious or unconscious. By "experience" Dewey means the way that we respond evaluatively to reality. Dewey, however, contrasts experience with its object. We experience nature; the way we respond to nature sensibly, affectively, intuitively, and inferentially provides the stuff of experience itself (EN, 3a-4a). Whitehead by contrast broadens the term "experience" even further. He does so in his reformed subjectivist principle, which states that "apart from the experiences of subjects there is nothing, nothing, nothing, bare nothingness" (PR, 167). For Whitehead, then, any reality whatever can be described as an instance of experience. The category "experience" moreover designates not only the way we experience things but the things themselves that we experience. All reality divides then into what is experienced and into the way experienced reality is experienced. By equating "experience" and "reality" Whitehead transforms the former into a descriptive transcendental category, universally applicable in intent.

Does the preoccupation of North American thinkers with a descriptive exploration of experience suggest further strategies for perceiving the human condition North Americanly? I believe that it does.

A contemporary North American perception of the human condition could legitimately begin by endorsing Whitehead's reformed subjectivist principle. The principle as we have just seen effectively transforms the descriptive term "experience" into a transcendental category, into a category universally applicable in intent. But in my own opinion one would be ill advised to endorse as well Whitehead's dipolar construct of

17

experience. We have already reflected on some of the inadequacies of that construct. It so atomizes experience that one cannot subsequently explain its individual unity and continuity. That deficiency is linked to another. In the final analysis Whitehead elaborates a nominalistic construct of experience devoid of any real generality. As a consequence Whitehead cannot adequately account for the fundamental reality which his system seeks to explain: namely, the experience of process. Whitehead tries to construct experience from utterly determinate facts and completely particular but utterly inefficacious possibilities. He postulates that the juxtaposition within experience of a determinate fact and an inefficacious possibility will result in change, in the transmutation of experience. Why, however, should such a juxtaposition produce any effect whatsoever? To this question Whitehead's system offers, in my judgment, no adequate response.

In my opinion, one would be better advised with Peirce to conceive human experience in triadic rather than in dipolar terms. The qualities of which Peirce speaks I discover experientially in human evaluative responses abstracted from the realities they respond to and from the selves who respond. I discover the experience of fact in physical action and reaction. I discover the experience of law in the developing, habitual tendencies that shape experience. When those tendencies function autonomously I experience them as selves. When they do not function autonomously, I experience them as mere laws. When selves display capacity for conversion, I call them human persons.

We shall reflect on other advantages of conceiving human experience in triadic terms later. Here it suffices to notice two important consequences of this modification of Whitehead's construct of experience. First, it avoids the nominalism of Whitehead's position by endowing experience with real generality. Second, it allows one to combine some of the best insights of both substance and process philosophy into the dynamics of change. Let us reflect on both of these consequences in turn.

Peirce's phenomenology of experience avoids nominalism by introducing the category "law", which endows experience with real generality. When we understand a law we understand neither a particular event nor an abstract possibility but what would happen given this or that set of circumstances. Laws endow a processing universe with its moving principles. They cause process to happen. Moreover, while they themselves can develop they also endow experience with unity and continuity. Laws unify the facts they ground and endow those facts with significance. In so doing laws also lend continuity to the course of events. In this respect laws resemble substances, but as elements constitutive of experience laws, unlike substances, do not exist in themselves only but in any experience they affect positively. Moreover, laws lack the fixed essence of classical substances, for they can develop into habits of increasing complexity and can thus endow experience with continuity **within development.** Moreover, in overcoming the atomicity present in Whitehead's construct of experience laws orient experience to the future.

18

Because they perish in the fraction of a second, Whitehead's atomic drops of experience know an immediate past and an infinitesmally brief present but no real future.

The introduction of the category of law into experience forces a modification of Whitehead's philosophy at yet another point. As we have seen Whitehead not only conceived experience as a series of atomic drops, he believed that each drop of experience drives toward concreteness. In a triadic construct of experience, decisions (or facts) do endow experience with concreteness. We decide to do this rather than that. Decisions, however, also fix beliefs, create new habits, and reinforce old ones. In the process, they also endow experience with real generality.

Having revised Whitehead's reformed subjectivist principle with a new triadic construct of experience to replace the inadequate dipolar one it presupposes, one could then draw freely on the North American philosophical tradition in order to expand descriptively Peirce's three categories with insights from other thinkers which complement his own. Brownson correctly insists that human evaluations form a continuum. James offers sound insights into individual experience. Dewey's descriptive analysis of experience as organically based, environmentally conditioned, transactional and instrumental has much to recommend it. Although Dewey does not invoke Peirce's three categories in his description of experience, they can be legitimately invoked to endow his phenomenology with greater conceptual precision. As we shall soon see, however, Dewey's handling of the religious dimension of human experience leaves much to be desired. Here the insights of Edwards, Brownson, Peirce, and Royce can be used to amplify descriptively an important dimension of experience whose subtleties eluded Dewey himself.

We have examined the tendency of North American speculation to focus on experience. We turn now to a correlative tendency, its assimilation of religious and esthetic experience.

(4) **The Assimilation of Religious and Esthetic Experience.** Not only do North American thinkers tend to view the human condition in experiential categories, they also tend to assimilate religious experience to the encounter with beauty. The similarity between religious assent and the consent to beauty dominates the thought of Jonathan Edwards and Ralph Waldo Emerson. But Peirce, Royce, and even John Dewey also echo their insights in significant ways.

Edwards was led to compare religious and esthetic experience by reflecting on his own religious conversion. He testifies that his conversion led him to:

> ...a new sense, quite different from anything I ever experienced before...From about that time, I began to have a new kind of apprehensions and ideas of Christ, and the work of redemption, and

19

the glorious way of salvation by Him. I had an inward sweet sense of these things that at times came into my heart; and my soul was led away in pleasant views and contemplations of them. And my mind was greatly engaged, to spend my time in reading and meditating on Christ, and the beauty and excellency of His person, and the lovely way of salvation, by free grace in Him....After this my sense of divine things gradually increased, and became more and more lively, and had more of that inward sweetness. The appearance of every thing was altered; there seemed to be, as it were, a calm sweet cast, or appearance of divine glory, in almost every thing. God's excellence, his wisdom, his purity and love seemd to appear in every thing; in the sun, moon, and stars; in the clouds and blue sky; in the grass, flowers, and trees; in the water and all nature; which used greatly to fix my mind.18

Edwards the pastor and preacher of religious revivals found similar affective patterns in the converts with whom he dealt. He wrote his **Treatise Concerning Religious Affections,** as we have seen, in order to defend the authenticity of the first Great Awakening against the jibes of rationalistic, liberal ministers. In it he explained twelve signs for distinguishing authentic from inauthentic religious emotions. Authentic conversion, he argued, begins with a transforming consent to the divine beauty incarnate in Jesus and ends in moral beautification in His image.[19]

Edwards believed that God in creating the world took as His chief end the revelation of His own divine glory. (By a "chief end" Edwards meant the end on which God lays the greatest importance.) Because God has ordered all created reality to himself, Edwards argued, God in fact created the world simply in order to share with it His own divine excellence. God, he believed, wills the greatest good for all His creatures. They discover that good in apprehending God's excellence. That excellence revealed itself in a special way in the incarnate Word, but the same divine excellence overflows into creation itself and delights the converted heart sensitized to perceive its beauty. When we encounter "excellence" in Edwards' sense of that term we experience beauty.20

Moreover, Edwards believed that cordial consent to God causes the believer to participate in God's own beautifying excellence. Religious conversion engages and transforms human sensibility. We perceive beauty affectively because in esthetic perceptions we apprehend the true and the good simultaneously and in a manner that inevitably engages the heart. We grasp beauty not with the mind alone nor with the will alone but simultaneously, with both, in a total response of intelligent loving sensibility. For by the term "will," as we have already seen, Edwards meant human affectivity brought to the peak of its activity (RA, 96 97).

20

God works in us the consent to divine excellence manifest in Jesus and in nature through the supernatural illumination of the Holy Spirit. That consent takes us out of ourselves in ecstatic self-consecration to God. Gracious affections focus principally on the moral excellence of God. Neither mindless nor fanatical, they spring from an understanding of the significance of divine revelation and yield a growing conviction of the reality of divine things. They effect a permanent change in character, inspire humility, and motivate the imitation of the attitudes of Jesus Himself. Gracious affections display a growing sensitivity to the movements of the divine Breath and a balance freed from the distortions of egotism and neurosis. They inspire a growing appetite for divine things. And they bear fruit in Christian practice (RA 253-461).

The transcendental vision of Ralph Waldo Emerson echoes a number of these Edwardsian themes. Largely at the prompting of his crochety aunt Mary Moody Emerson, young Waldo very early in life adopted a modified neo-Platonic metaphysics. He divided the universe into a material, sensible realm of change and an eternal, immutable, spiritual realm of Being, Goodness, and Truth. In his sermons to his apathetic Unitarian congregation in Boston he tried to convince them that the plodding cultivation of virtue would elevate them from the ephemeral material universe in which they lived to the transcendent realm of spirit.By the eighteen thirties, however, Emerson had transformed these early beliefs into a transcendental gospel of creativity. Inspired by English romanticism he had come to believe that we ascend to the realm of spirit in the moment of creative ecstacy. Indeed the transcendental Emerson believed that each individual has immediate and present access within subjectivity to the creative power of the divine Over-soul, his transcendental name for the eternal realm of spirit. Every human achievement, therefore, in science, art, literature, politics, religion, trade, or even manners ultimately expresses the "Beautiful Necessity" of the divine spiritual laws that govern the universe. Moreover, like Edwards, Emerson portrayed the creative encounter with the divine as cordial consent to divine beauty.[21]

Although other North American thinkers do not focus on the similarity between religious and esthetic experience with the intensity of both Edwards and Emerson, mamy of them echo a number of their insights. Josiah Royce's philosophy of loyalty illustrates the tendency of which I speak. By loyalty Royce means: "....the willing and thoroughgoing devotion of a person to a cause. A man is loyal when, first, he has some cause to which he is loyal; when, secondly, he willingly and thoroughly devotes himself to this cause; and when, thirdly, he expresses his devotion in some sustained and practical way."22 More directly to the present point, while authentic loyalty never expresses emotion alone, it engages the affections. It demands self-control and practical devotion. It challenges individuals to transcend narrowly ego-centric concerns for ideals and realities that can make absolute and ultimate religious claims. Loyalty binds individuals to one another in community. It motivates them to suffer and even to die if necessary for the cause they espouse. It also gives the loyal a plan of life, something to live for (PL, 3-48). Clearly, although

Royce does not insist that loyal assent to a cause culminates in the consent to beauty in the way that Jonathan Edwards does, his description of loyalty echoes in many ways Edwards' portrayal of Christian conversion as cordial, practical, and selfless consent to moral excellence.

Even John Dewey acknowledged that religious experience involves something very close to the perception of beauty. Dewey discerned a religious element in human moral striving. He distinguished "religion" from "the religious." Religion, in his sense of that term, "supernaturalizes" the religious, confines it to the realm of the sacred, makes unverifiable truth claims, roots itself in mysticism, and separates the religious from lived experience. When, however, the religious dimension of experience is interpreted naturalistically it adjusts one to life and its conditions. Correctly understood, "the religious" does not inhabit a separate sacred realm. It permeates life. It engages the imagination without naively reifying its contents. It also engages intense moral feelings which are "accentuated and supported by ends so inclusive that they unify the self." When life takes on a religious dimension, therefore, morality is "touched by emotion" and acquires invigorating zest. In other words, by engaging both emotion and imagination "the religious" lends an esthetic character to human moral striving.[23]

Finally, as we shall see in greater detail later on, Peirce too in his "Neglected Argument for the Reality of God" rooted the consent to the divine in the beauty and spontaneous attractiveness of the idea of God.

This propensity of speculative minds in this country to assimilate the consent to God to assent to the beautiful suggests further strategies for perceiving the human condition North Americanly. Anyone who reflects on the experience of Christian conversion in the light of this strain in the North American speculative tradition will, I believe, be led to conclude that Christian conversion begins in a repentant confrontation with the dark side of the psyche and culminates in a beautifying, affectively motivated consent to the divine beauty incarnate in Jesus and in people who resemble him. It also culminates in Christian practice. It inserts one in loyal fidelity into the Christian community. It effects a permanent change of character and dedicates one to the life-long process of putting on the mind of Jesus in response to the illumination of His Holy Breath. It does yield an experience of supernatural grace. It engages the creative imagination and endows human moral striving with new zest and integration. When authentic, it has all the characteristics which Dewey ascribes to "the religious."

**(5) The Finitude and Dialogic Character of Human Reason.** American philosophers tend to portray the human mind as radically finite and falllible. Moreover, as speculation in this country advances, this conviction gives rise to a further belief in the fundamentally dialogic character of human reason. Let us reflect on the interplay of these two ideas within the North American philosophical tradition.

22

Emerson the transcendentalist, as we have just seen, believed during his "saturnalia of faith" in the late eighteen thirties that every individual has access within subjectivity to the infinite, creative Oversoul that animates and governs the universe. In his later thought, however, he insists, not on the virtual infinity of human creative potential but on its radical finitude.

Three events conspired to bring about this shift in his understanding of the human condition. First of all, he began to sense the limitations of his own powers. He talked about creativity so much that critics eventually challenged him to use his creativity to harp on some other theme. Second, he found the fruits of his proclamation of a gospel of creativity frankly disappointing. He seems during the late eighteen thirties to have assumed that he needed only tell people about their potentially infinite capacity for creative intuition in order to unleash an outburst of cultural creativity in the United States. When people walked away from his lectures scratching and shaking their heads and when the expected explosion of creative energy failed to materialize, he began to acquiesce in the finitude of individual human minds instead of asserting their infinite creative potential. Finally, the death of his little boy at he beginning of the fourth decade of the nineteenth century left him emotionally deflated and pricked the bubble of naive optimism on which his transcendental gospel floated. In **Representative Men** he would argue that every individual creative impulse is skewed by bias, by an excess of energy that focuses it on a specific creative enterprise to which individuals have been metaphysically predestined by the Oversoul (CWRWE, IV). For the mature Emerson, therefore, finitude, not unlimited potential circumscribes every human individual creative insight.

William James also portrayed the human mind as both finite and fallible. He described the science of psychology as the study of "finite, individual minds" (PP, v-2). His description of the workings of the human psyche underscores the fallibility of human beliefs. Any relationship to the mind at all, he asserted, motivates people to affirm the reality of an object. Humans, he found, will cling to beliefs no matter how contradictory when those beliefs are closely linked to pleasure and pain and when they motivate important actions, hold emotional interest, or feed pet idealisms (PP, 299-319). Remarks such as these would lead C.S. Peirce to distinguish sharply between the psychology of belief and normative, logical insight into how one ought to think. Nevertheless, like James, Peirce too would finally defend the fallibility and finitude of the human mind. James himself recognized, of course, that only certain beliefs enjoy logical validation. As a psychologist he also knew that in the concrete free association often supplants logic in human thinking and that inference can serve purposes ulterior to truth (PP, 325-348). Our perceptions of the world, he felt, filter out large segments of reality (PP, 573-582).

In 1868 C.S. Peirce launched a systematic philosophical attack on the intuitionist doctrines of North American transcendentalists. He criticized them for ignoring both the historically conditioned character of thought and the fact that thought must be symbolically mediated. The failure of intuitionism, he argued, called attention to certain "incapacities" in the human mind:" 1. We have no power of introspection, but all knowledge of the internal world is derived by hypothetical reasoning from our knowledge of external facts. 2. We have no power of intuition, but every cognition is determined logically by previous cognitions. 3. We have no power of thinking without signs. 4. We have no conceptions of the absolutely incognizable" (CWCSP, 5.264-317).

Moreover, Peirce's studies of the symbolic structure of inferential thinking had led him to espouse a position of "contrite fallibilism." We can discover no privileged, indubitable starting point for human speculation; rather we begin thinking about any problem in medias res. We can expend only limited resources on any problem we investigate. We must formulate our hypotheses about reality (Peirce called hypotheses "abductions" or sometimes "retroductions") before we know for certain that we have amassed sufficient data. Though deductive reasoning advances with logical necessity, the deductively reasoning mind can lay no claims to infallibility. Even validated inductive inferences can be invalidated by the discovery of new data or by the creation of a more adequate explanatory frame of reference (CWCSP, 5. 213-410). Peircian fallibilism, however, claims finally to hold out hope, not despair, to inquiring minds. It asserts that the human mind ready to acknowledge its own fallibility and finitude has a much better chance of reaching the truth than one that does not.

For Peirce, then, thinking boils down to the fixation of belief. He defined belief as a proposition for whose consequences one is willing to assume responsibility. He distinguished four fundamental ways of fixing beliefs. The way of tenacity counsels stubbornness: believe whatever you want and ignore the evidence to the contrary. The way of authority seeks to legislate beliefs. Preferable to tenacity in that it engages other minds than one's own, the way of authority has never succeeded totally in its attempt to legislate belief. The way of taste fixes beliefs on the basis of personal preference. Peirce himself preferred a fourth and final way of fixing beliefs. He called it shared, systematic inquiry and argued that it avoids the anti-social character of tenacity, the dangers of authoritarianism, and the irrationality of spontaneous tastes (CWCSP, 5. 358-387).

For Peirce, then, sound reasoning eschews the "spirit of Cartesianism." It does not seek for truth in the solitude of one's study but in active dialogue with other minds intent on answering the same question. Peirce's portrayal of human reason as social and dialogic was, moreover, destined to exert a profound influence on the thought of another important North American thinker, Josiah Royce.

Royce began his philosophical career obsessed with the fallibility of the individual human mind. In his first major book, **The Religious Aspect of Philosophy,** he used the method of relentless doubt to extricate himself from the morass of moral and religious agnosticism. Later, as the mature

Royce studied Peirce's thought, he not only came to endorse Peirce's social construct for human reason, but he also developed it in interesting and creative ways. He became convinced that the dialogic character of human reason entails that humans must reach the truth in communities of interpretation dedicated to that enterprise. Moreover, he also believed that communal awareness differs qualitatively from individual consciousness. As he mused over these insights he became fascinated with an important and complex question: what conditions must be fulfilled for communities of individuals to achieve shared awareness as communities? He formulated his answer to this question in **The Problems of Christianity.**

Royce distinguished eight conditions for the possibility of reaching community consciousness:

1. **Identification with Some Founding Event.** Shared experiences create community. In smaller communities like the family, the experiences can be shared directly. In large communities with a history and geographical spread, the members cannot share experiences with such directness. Larger communities must as a consequence come to initial shared awareness as communities by identifying with some historical event that founds the community. Think of the American Revolution or the death and resurrection of Jesus.

2. **Consensus Concerning the Originating Event.** The significance of the event that originates a community needs to be interpreted by its members. Contradictory interpretations of that event shatter a community and diminish its shared awareness. Think, for example, of the fragmentation of Christian consciousness which occurred at the time of the reformation. A community will therefore successfully achieve shared consciousness to the extent that its members agree concerning the meaning of the event that founds the community.

3. **Consensus Concerning the Community's History.** A community is separated by its history from the event which founds it. That history conditions the way it interprets the founding event. Communities will, then, achieve shared consciousness to the extent that its members also agree on the significance of the events that shape the community's history. Shared consciousness of its historical origins endows a community with a present sense of identity.

4. **Projecting a Common Future.** The achievement of an initial sense of historical identity provides a community with a solid basis for projecting shared future goals. Shared goals yield shared consciousness of a possible shared future.

5. **Achieving the Projected Goals.** Communities come to full self-consciousness as communities when they they not only plan for the future but actually execute those plans.

6. **Adequate Leadership.** The practical achievement of shared goals

in community demands a certain type of leader, one who values the gifts of each member of the community and who can orchestrate those gifts in such a way that they contribute to enhancing the shared life of the community.

7. **Freedom.** The process of historical self-interpretation as well as the projection and achievement of shared goals must advance in freedom. Oppression diminishes shared consciousness.

8. **Atoning Love.** The fallibility, finitude, and spontaneous egocentrism of individuals entails that members of a human community will with moral certainty betray the communities to which they belong through venality, malice, and self-seeking. Betrayal fragments a community and diminishes its shared awareness. Only those communities will survive betrayal which forgive in advance the treachery of individual members. The reconciliation of traitors back into the community enhances community consciousness.24

John Dewey's instrumentalism develops C.S. Peirce's social construct of human reason in a different direction. A "contrite fallibilist" like Peirce and Royce, Dewey endorsed shared and open systematic inquiry as the most adequate way to fix one's beliefs, but the instrumental orientation of his theory of knowledge led him to explicitate the purpose of shared inquiry. We reason, Dewey argues, about unresolved situations. In order to resolve problematic situations, we need first to distinguish which aspects of the situation are settled and which need resolution. Inquiry ends when the problematic elements in a previously unresolved situation have been brought under control. For example, the builders of the Panama Canal faced a problematic situation when massive loss of workers to yellow fever threatened the success of the project. The situation was finally resolved when systematic inquiry finally traced the disease to a mosquito bite and effective means were taken to get rid of the insects.

Perhaps no facet of the philosophical tradition in this country challenges traditional Catholic perceptions of the human condition more than its insistence on the radical finitude of the human intellect. Ever since the thirteenth century Catholics, following Aquinas, have tended to portray the human mind as virtually infinite, as open to the whole of Being. Scientific studies of the way human beings actually think tend, however, to call into question the human mind's virtual infinity and to reinforce belief in its radical finitude. If then we are to perceive the human condition not only North Americanly but truly we would do well to acknowledge that any given mind views the world from a limited but potentially expandable angle of vision. We should let the unavoidable fallibility of hypothetical and inductive reasoning bring us to a "contrite fallibilism." We should acknowledge that open, shared, systematic inquiry provides the best means of fixing human beliefs. We should recognize the symbolically mediated, social, dialogic character of human reason. We should work to bring into existence communites of inquiry whose shared consciousness heightens our own individual awareness. We should recognize that all inquiry seeks to transform problematic situations into determinate ones.

Moreover, the social, dialogic character of human reason offers another motive for rejecting Whitehead's dipolar construct of experience. Such a construct must explain human knowledge as the interrelation of concrete percepts and abstract concepts. Unfortuanately, however, as Royce correctly argues in **The Problem of Christianity,** such a construct of cognition cannot adequately explain the social dimensions of cognition. More specifically it cannot explain the act of interpretation in which one person explains something to somebody else. Only a triadic construct of experience allows for an act of interpretation to occur. In other words, having interpreted individuals as societies, Whitehead's dipolar construct of experience cannot subsequently explain the social dimensions of human cognition.

American thinkers not only focus on the limitations and on the dialogic character of human thought; they also show a special predilection for predicting consequences. Let us now examine this sixth strain in the North American tradition.

**(6) Concern with Consequences.** Ever since the nineteenth century much of European philosophy has focused almost obsessively on history, on the past. American philosophers, by contrast, exhibit greater interest in the future, sometimes narrowly so. Eventually concern with the future engenders and fuses with a concern with logical consequences.

The future orientation of North American thinking springs from fairly deep cultural roots. Both the first colonists and the immigrants who have persistently swarmed to our shores believed that they left the Old World for the New. In crossing the ocean they left the past behind in order to begin a new life.

The first puritans came to New England precisely because they wanted to complete the Calvinistic reformation of the Church of England in a land uncorrupted by centuries of tradition. They founded Massachusetts in the conscious intent of breaking with a corrupt past.

The desire for freedom from the burdens of history also helped motivate revolutionary fervor. In his **Dissertation on the Canon and the Feudal Law,** written on the eve of the American revolution, John Adams invoked the puritan dream in order to exhort his fellow citizens to revolution. The protestant reformation had, he argued, destroyed the despotic pretensions of the canon law of the Roman church. Monarchical tyranny still remained, however, as a threat to the final realization of the protestant dream. Only by overthrowing the monarchical tyranny of the feudal system would the work of the reformation be finally achieved in an America finally purified of this last corrupt remnant of history.

The millennial aspirations of popular revivalist piety have also reinforced North American preoccupation with the future. In the eighteenth century Jonathan Edwards interpreted the First Great Awakening as a clear sign from God that He had chosen America as the place to begin the millennium, the thousand years of peace and prosperity predicted in the Book of Revelation. Millennial aspirations also colored American revolutionary hopes. In **Common Sense** and **The Crisis** Tom Paine predicted that this nation would know a new era of peace and prosperity once the scourge of royalism had been harried from the land. The God of Reason, he proclaimed, had predestined it so.

The early transcendentalists all manifested a bias toward the future. Having located all value and truth in the transcendent realm of spirit, Emerson denied both to history as such. Theodore Parker aspired to an absolute religion untouched by the taint of the past. Orestes Brownson in the eighteen thirties longed for the Church of the Future. Once he converted to Catholicism, however, Brownson discovered the values of tradition with a vengeance.

In the thought of Peirce and of Royce, moreover, we discover a counterbalancing philosophical tendency. As we have already seen, Peirce's fallibilism displays strong sensitivity to the historically conditioned character of all human symbolic activity, a sense which Royce's theory of the conditions for the possibility of community consciousness explicitates and deepens. Peircian logic does, however, also deal with the future in its concern with consequences. Peirce originally formulated the pragmatic maxim as a method for making ideas clear. In its original formulation the method states: "Consider what effects that might conceivably have practical bearings, we conceive the object of our conception to have, then our conception of those effects is the whole of our conception of the object" (CWCSP, 5. 358-387).

Jamesian pragmatism, however, transformed Peirce's concern with consequences into an obsession with the future. James tended to interpret the history of philosophy as a clash of temperaments (P, 19). He looked to the pragmatic maxim not so much as a way of resolving past debates but as a way of reducing them to insignificance (P, 44-45). As an attitude Jamesian pragmatism looks "away from first things, principles, categories, supposed necessities" and toward "last things, fruits, consequences, facts" (P, 47). Like a good Emersonian transcendentalist, a Jamesian pragmatist thinks prospectively not retrospectively (P, 75), looks not backward but forward (P, 86).

In the thought of John Dewey the concern with consequences takes a somewhat different turn. It led him to oppose any dualistic separation of action from thought or of ends from means. Humans think for a purpose, Dewey argued: namely, in order to achieve practically shared consummatory experiences that may serve as the basis for further consummations (EN, 78-165).

Even in Royce's metaphysical idealism we find a characteristically North American concern with consequences. Royce's theory of knowledge distinguishes the internal from the external meaning of an idea. By "external meaning" Royce meant "that about which we judge." By "internal meaning" he meant the judgments we make viewed as subjective processes. He portrayed the internal meaning of an idea in dynamic terms. Our judgments, he believed, search out reality. Ideas drive to concrete embodiment, toward complete and unqualified determination in some sensible reality. Action effects the correspondence of internal and external meaning as the will immanent to an idea finds concretion in actuality.25

The concern of North American thinkers with consequences offers some interesting leads to an inculturated perception of the human condition. It suggests that a North American perception of the human condition must discourse about more than the metaphysical essence of humanness. It must offer people a practical program of action for becoming human. It should approach the enterprise of humanization with a logic of consequences and offer an empirically verifiable account of human nature. But it should, with Peirce and Royce, counterbalance any concern with the future with an equal sensitivity to the past and to the values ingredient in the cultural heritage of this nation and of the human race.

We have yet to examine a seventh and final strain in North American speculation: the conflict within it of naturalism and supernaturalism.

**(7) Naturalism vs. Supernaturalism.** Almost from the inception of speculation in this country thinkers have tended to espouse one of two irreconcilable interpretations of the human condition. Some perceive it in supernaturalistic terms. Others perceive it naturalistically.

As the tradition evolves, the term "supernatural" assumes different meanings. At the start of the debate the term means "that which transcends utterly the powers and aspirations of human beings acting on their own initiative." By the turn of the century "supernaturalism" means the same as "theism."

As North American thinkers have debated the pros and cons of naturalism as opposed to supernaturalism, they have focused on three important issues: the nature of the human condition itself, the character of human moral striving, and the existence of God.

In describing human nature both Luther and Calvin adopted an Augustinian rhetoric of human depravity. They both held that human nature had been so corrupted by sin that in and of itself it could perform only morally depraved acts. They also both insisted on the absolute sovereignty of grace. They held that only the graced individual could perform virtuous acts. In either case they ruled out freedom of choice. Either the human will succumbed necessarily to vice by its natural depravity or chose virtue in response to a necessitating impulse of supernatural grace. Both thinkers explained natural depravity by original

29

sin, by the disobedience of Adam and Eve to God's command not to eat of the tree of the knowledge of good and evil. Calvin, moreover, defended an Augustinian doctrine of predestination. God's predestining will, he held, predetermined antecedently every human choice whether for good or for ill.

In the latter part of the eighteenth century, liberal theological thought rebelled against these classic protestant doctrines. Instead of decrying the natural depravity of human nature, the liberals celebrated its natural integrity. They denied original sin and its corrupting consequences. Jonathan Edwards rose to the defense of protestant orthodoxy in two major treatises. In **Freedom of the Will** he argued that the human will could be predestined by God to choose in a certain way and nevertheless act freely. In **Original Sin** he argued that we experience the consequences of the fall of our first parents in the all too common human reluctance to accept the gospel. In the initial confrontation between naturalism and supernaturalism in this country, therefore, the antagonists in the debate attempted to interpret the human condition itself by posing an artificial choice between Calvinism, on the one hand, and the religion of the enlightenment on the other.

In the middle of the nineteenth century Orestes Brownson would discover the artificiality of that option and recogize that the council of Trent offered a middle ground between those two positions. Trent, like Luther and Calvin, defended the sovereignty of divine grace, but it eschewed an Augustinian doctrine of depravity and held with the great medieval scholastics that despite the corrupting consequences of original and personal sin, humans could perform naturally good acts. Trent also rejected Augustinian predestination and defended human freedom under grace. Moreover, like the **philosophes** of the enlightenment, Catholic theology defended the capacity of human reason to prove the existence of God and to discern the natural basis of moral behavior.

The religious creeds of Jefferson, Franklin, and the other **philosphes** who helped engineer the American revolution had this in common: they all attempted to reduce Christianity to its pure philosophical essence. Franklin converted to deism while reading a Presbyterian defense of orthodox Calvinism against the attacks of the deists.26 He believed that a benevolent and providential creator had made humans to worship and serve Him and had endowed them with reason and the natural capacity to act virtuously. Moreover, Franklin held that enlightened self-interest

motivated all naturally virtuous behavior. In 1727 Poor Richard advised his fellow Americans:

> **Self love** but serves the virtuous Mind to wake,
> As the small Pebble stirs the peaceful lake;
> The centre mov'd, a Circle straight succeeds,
> Another still, and still another spreads;
> Friend, Parent, Neighbor, first it will embrace,

His country next, and next all human race;
Wide and more wide, th' o'erflowings of the mind
take every creature in of every kind (PBF, II, 5).

Franklin thought that virtue pays off in prosperity. It means good business. Treat other people fairly, and wealth will certainly crown the patient cultivation of bourgeois rectitude (PBF, I, 115, 262, III, 306-308, 352, 397-398, 480, IV, 325).

Jefferson like Franklin espoused a species of deism. He reduced religion to the natural cultivation of virtue. He discovered the basis of morality in an innate moral sense of duty to others "which prompts us irresistibly to feel and succor their distresses."27 He recognized the presence of blindness, imperfection, and injustice in human society, but he believed that with proper education people will follow the benevolent impulses which "nature hath planted in our breasts" (WTJ, I, 278).

In **The Nature of True Virtue**, a posthumously published work, Jonathan Edwards undertook to refute the deistic claim that true religion boils down to the natural cultivation of virtue. He defined "true virtue" as the cordial consent of being to Being in general. He described true virtue as cordial because he believed that it must spring from a well ordered affectivity. He argued that benevolence to God and that alone rectifies the human will. By "Being in general" Edwards meant God. True virtue, he insisted, rejoices in the divine excellence. As we have seen, he discovered that excellence revealed in Jesus and in people who resemble Him through faith and Christian practice. Heartfelt consent to God also means that one must consent to every other reality on the terms that God Himself has determined and revealed. Consent to God ensures therefore that saints also consent to one another and to the world in the manner that God has decreed. Consent to God in this sense universalizes human consent and enables it to transcend "private affection." Actions, then, which are ultimately motivated by self-love may, in the manner of Franklin, masquerade as virtue. Edwards decried such pretense as self-serving hypocrisy.

Emersonian transcendentalism further naturalized American civil religion. In a sense, Emerson would have endorsed Edwards's definition of "true virtue." He certainly believed that our wills are rectified by consent to the "Beautiful Necessity," the transcendent Oversoul, that rules the universe. He claimed to discover that consent in the moment of creative insight. Chauncey Wright, George Santayana and John Dewey, however, shifted the speculative confrontation between naturalism and supernaturalism to new terrain by transforming it into a debate about the very existence of God. Wright believed that religious beliefs express only irrational, subjective feelings. He therefore dismissed the proposition "God exists" as "not proven." Dewey and Santayana professed forms of philosophical atheism.

Santayana avowed a humanistic sympathy for religion. He believed, however, that instinctive fear creates the gods and regarded prayer as the soliloquy of the impotent.28. Nevertheless, he expressed an appreciation for the primitive poetic character of religious thought, as long as one recognizes that religious myths and songs express only beautiful human fictions and do not describe gods to be adored (LR, III, 46). He also believed that religion contributes something important to the life of reason: it begins to teach the human spirit to contemplate ideals (LR, III, 9-12).

Moreover, the later Santayana attempted to transform this disillusioned assessment of religious faith into an equally disillusioned secular mysticism. Santayana endorsed Emerson's platonism but denied his theism. In the twilight of his own life Santayana believed that individuals find what "religious" meaning they can in the contemplation of non-existent, ideal essences which find expression in poetry, art, philosophy, and scientific thinking, but the naturalistic platonist recognizes, Santayana insisted, that the beautiful ideals which the human spirit intuits and contemplates in solitude can lay no claim to reality.29

Dewey endorsed Santayana's atheis  but eschewed his paradoxical, platonic mysticism. As we have seen, Dewey's naturalistic atheism attempts to replace religion with the religious. More the busy instrumentalist than the disillusioned, would-be mystic Dewey reduced religion to morality touched by emotion. He defined "God" to mean the active uniting of the ideal and actual poles of experience (CF, 8-9, 13-14, 17-23).

The North American philosophical tradition offers, however, some interesting speculative alternatives to Wright's agnosticism and to Dewey's and Santayana's atheism. The young Royce, as we have seen, used systematic doubt to extricate himself from religious and moral agnosticism. In **The Religious Aspect of Philosophy** he argued to the existence of God from the possibility of error. The fact that we can err presupposes the distinction between truth and error. That distinction demanded, in Royce's mind, the existence of a divine All Knower whose omniscience measures the propositions. The proof fascinated James for several years, but he eventually (and in my own opinion correctly) rejected it as invalid.

James responded to Wright's agnosticism differently. James professed "supernaturalism," by which he meant "theism." He responded to Wright's charge that the existence of God lacks empirical verification by an empirical study of human religious experience. In **The Varieties** he concluded that such an empirical investigation sanctions the belief that religious people actually experience a relationship with some kind of transcendent reality. The religious person, James wrote, "becomes conscious that this higher part (of the self) is coterminous and continuous with a **more** of the same quality, which is operative in the universe outside him, and which he can keep in working touch with, and in a fashion get on board of and save himself when all his lower being has gone to pieces in the wreck" (VRE, 393-394).

Peirce responded to Wright's agnosticism somewhat differently. Initially inclined to quarantine religion and science so that they would not influence one another in harmful ways, toward the end of his life he began to glimpse the possibility of marrying the two. Typically, he did so with the help of logic. He published his insights in "A Neglected Argument for the Reality of God."

The "Neglected Argument" begins with the "Humble Argument." The Humble Argument asks that one put aside as much as possible personal religious prejudices. It invites the mind to discard formal reasoning for "musement", or mind play. Let your mind play over all the different realms of human experience, Peirce counseled. Ponder the complexity, beauty, and emerging order of the world in which we live. When the healthy mind engages in such a reverie, Peirce believed, the idea that this world was created by some benevolent Being tends to emerge as a thinkable possibility. Then, the beauty, the spontaneous attractiveness of that idea motivates the healthy mind's initial consent to it. Once one has used the Humble Argument to elicit religious assent, the Neglected Argument subjects that assent to a logical analysis and identifies it as an abduction, as an exercise in hypothetical reasoning. Religious hypotheses, like scientific, need to be clarified and tested. To test religious beliefs, Peirce held, one needs to deduce the operational consequences of one's understanding of God and then test them out practically in the arena of human moral striving.

To Dewey's charge that revealed religion fosters authoritarianism, Royce together with Peirce would have responded that authority offers only one and not the best way to fix religious beliefs. One can also achieve religious consensus through shared systematic inquiry. Moreover, in **The Problem of Christianity** he argued for the perennial believability of Christianity. At the heart of Christian belief Royce found three basic and interrelated Christian ideas: the ideal of a universal community of salvation, the moral burden of the individual, and the ideal of atonement. For Royce, as we have seen, religion responds to the need individuals have for salvation, for attaining the ultimate purpose of life. Every individual labors under the moral burden of some guilt, since egotism causes individuals with moral inevitability to betray the communities that nurture them. The beloved community provides individuals with a saving realm of grace. Only the beloved community's forgiving love and willingness to suffer the consequences of betrayal while reaccepting the traitor back into its own ranks can redeem treachery and endow it with a saving meaning it otherwise lacks. These basic Christian ideas enjoy perennial credibility, Royce argued, because they speak directly to the human condition in every generation (PC, I).

Finally, we note in passing that Whitehead responded to Santayana's atheism by transforming the latter's realm of essence into the primordial nature of God. Whitehead read Santayana with appreciation and espoused an analogous form of Platonism. Like Santayana Whitehead believed that the essences which we experience enjoy reality but lack actuality. Whitehead called these essences eternal objects; but unlike Santayana he located them in the mind of God. In his primordial nature Whitehead's God establishes an order among all the eternal objects by deciding which he would prefer to see ingredient in actuality. God's experience of the world as it actually is endows Him with a consequent nature. God viewed in his impact on the world process also enjoys a superject nature. Whitehead's theory of the three natures of God presupposes his dipolar construct of experience. We need not, then, dwell on the theory here, since we have already found reason to question that construct's interpretative adequacy. I mention it, however, as an important philosophical response to Santayana's platonic atheism.

Does the debate between naturalists and supernaturalists in this country suggest any further strategies for perceiving the human condition North Americanly? It certainly suggests that theologians in this country would be well advised to endow traditional theological categories like grace, original sin, and even God with experiential meaning. It suggests that in discussing the relationship between nature and grace theologians in this country, while avoiding naive optimism about human nature, should avoid the rhetoric of human depravity and acknowledge freedom under grace. They should also acknowledge the human capacity to fix personal beliefs about God naturally. We think about God naturally when we abstract from His historical self-revelation in Jesus and the Holy Breath. Moreover, Peirce's Neglected Argument offers a plausible account of how one might go about fixing one's religious beliefs in accord with sound canons of logic.

The work of James suggests that North American theologians should also not hesitate to approach religious questions empirically. Moreover, in dealing with incarnational religion, an empirical theology will have to deal with two sets of data: with the data supplied by natural human experience and with the data of revelation. The latter is supplied by the history of salvation, by those events that disclose to us in normative ways the saving reality of God. Edwards's definition of true virtue also promises to yield some important insights into the dynamics of Christian conversion, as does Royce's demonstration of the perennial believability of the Christian message.

We have been musing dialectically on the development of the speculative tradition in this country in the hope that we might be able to derive from it a characteristically North American way of perceiving the human condition. We have traced seven themes through the tradition. We have discovered in each of them hints of techniques for elaborating an inculturated North American account of our human lot and destiny. Let us try to draw together in summary fashion the major conclusions we have reached. Others, of course, might evaluate our tradition differently and derive from it some other construct of the human. The one I will propose seems to me, however, to speak in a Yankee idiom.

As we have seen, an inculturated North American perception of the human condition might well begin by endorsing Whitehead's reformed subjectivist principle. In other words, it might begin by postulating that all reality, both created and uncreated can be understood as an instance of experience. We have also found good reason to prefer a triadic construct of experience to the dipolar construct that Whitehead himself proposes. A triadic construct avoids the nominalism present in Whitehead's position, explains the fact of process better, interprets better the social dimensions of experience, and endows individual experience wih unity and continuity. It allows also one to draw on the best insights of both process and substance philosophy. In our reformulation of the reformed subjectivist principle, therefore, experience is made up of three kinds of feelings: qualities, or evaluations; facts, or interactions; and tendencies, or laws. Our account of the human condition would, then, advance in the context of a metaphysics of experience in which all reality divides into what is experienced and the way experienced reality is experienced. We experience the factual impact of our environment in sensations. We experience the laws that shape experience in affective and inferential perceptions.

Having established a context for dealing with reality in general and with human experience in particular, we could then draw freely and imaginatively on the insights of North American thinkers to explore descriptively the three realms of human experience. We would have to distinguish conscious from unconscious evaluations. In describing conscious experience we would need to acknowledge an evaluative continuum stretching from sensation through affective perceptions of reality into imaginative intuitions and finally to abstract inferential thinking. With C.S. Peirce we would do well to distinguish three kinds of logical inference: abductive (or hypothetical), deductive (or predictive), and inductive (or validating). With Whitehead, we should also recognize that human evaluations endow experience with presentational immediacy. By that I mean two things: (1) through evaluation we become present to ourselves and to our world, and (2) viewed as an experience, evaluation grounds the human experience of the present moment.

Although Peirce quite correctly rejected the theories of intuition popularized by the American transcendentalists and censured them for their failure to take into adequate account the historical and symbolically mediated character of human cognition, Dewey's analysis of artistic forms of knowing offers an alternative interpretation of intuitive perceptions of reality that avoids Peirce's objections. Our construct of human experience ought then to acknowledge two kinds of human perceptions of the real: irrational, imaginative perceptions which grasp reality in judgments of feeling and logical perceptions which grasp reality through controlled inference.

Our construct of the human mind ought also to acknowledge its fallibility and its finitude. It should look to shared systematic inquiry as the best way to fix human beliefs. It should acknowledge the social, dialogic character of both appreciative and inferential forms of knowing.

It should encourage the formation of communities of inquiry, distinguish between individual and shared consciousness, and provide strategies for heightening shared awareness. Our theory of cognition should abandon the European attempt to find an absolute starting point for thought and acknowledge that all human evaluations begin **in medias res.** In describing human evaluative processes it should balance a concern with the future and with consequences by a concern with the past, with causes, and with conditions. Our construct of knowing must interrelate thought and action and provide techniques for resolving problematic situations. It should acknowledge the instrumental character of human symbols, but it should also recognize both contemplation and enjoyment as legitimate human goals.

In dealing with facts that shape experience, a North American perception of the human condition should distinguish initial facts, which evoke a stream of evaluative responses, from final facts, or the decisions which terminate evaluative responses. It should recognize also that decisions endow experience not only with concreteness, because they opt for this rather than that, but also with real generality, because they create, reinforce, or undermine habits. Our construct of experience would acknowledge too that when decisions terminate intense affective perceptions of the real they express heightened affectivity and that when they terminate logical inferences, they express a cooler, rational perception of the real.

In exploring the realm of law, an inculturated North American account of the human condition should distinguish between autonomously functioning laws, or selves, and mere laws, which function as a factor in a complex, legal reality. The laws of organic chemistry exemplify mere laws, for they describe the behavior of chemicals which have forfeited autonomy through integration into the body of a living organism.

An inculturated North American account of the human condition would also explore the analogies between esthetic and religious experience. It would understand the perception of beauty as the simultaneous, appreciative perception of truth and goodness. It would recognize the synthetic character of religious insight, that it puts one in an integrating relationship with God, with oneself, and with one's world. It would recognize that religious commitment engages human loyalties and consecrates religious converts to specific religious causes, even as it inserts them into a community of shared faith consciousness. It would acknowledge that religious experience challenges one to imaginative creativity in the living of life and that authentic religion seeks to permeate every facet of human experience.

An inculturated North American construct of the human condition would acknowledge the impact of affectivity and of temperament on human religious experience, but it would insist that only the integrally converted individual views reality with affective integrity. It would defend the position that religious beliefs involve more than the projection of

36

subjective feelings onto the world that they yield appreciative insights into a human encounter with the Holy. Our construct would recognize that human experience takes on a religious character when it becomes a search for salvation, for the means to attain the ultimate purpose of living. It would recognize that both individuals and communities need saving, but that religious communities to the extent that their lives express integral conversion before God provide sinful individuals with saving environments of grace. It would conceive the life of grace as the ongoing transmutation of experience, as growth in what Orestes Brownson called "theandric life." In evaluating the authenticity of religious affections, a North American construct of the real would, moreover, do well to include among its criteria for discernment Edwards's twelve signs of gracious affections. Moreover, with Edwards our construct of Christian conversion will acknowledge that only cordial consent to a self-revealing God ultimately rectifies the human will, even though humans can perform naturally virtuous acts.

In speaking of human religious experience, a North American construct of the human condition would also do well to avoid all forms of speculative dualism: substantial dualism, operational dualism, individualism, subjectivism, and every other perception of reality that renders real relationships among things unintelligible. Our construct will conceive reality in relational terms and will distinguish three kinds of relationships: conceptual, factual, and habitual. It will conceive reality as process and the subjects of change as emergent and self-defining. It will acknowledge the spatio-temporal character of human experience and interpret the dynamic interaction of individuals with their world as the process that allows them to define themselves to be the kinds of persons they are. Our construct of human experience will conceive individuality in both dynamic and qualitative terms, as the realization of human potential. It will encourage humans to develop their individuality in responsible social dialogues with other persons and with the world in which they live. It will acknowledge the transactional character of a human knowing. It will look to the history of a reality rather than to some abstraction to provide it with its only adequate definition. Moreover, in a universe of experiences, a North American account of the human condition will acknowledge that all finite realities exist in one another and that the universe exists in God.

Finally, any Christian theology that perceives the human condition North Americanly will endow all theological terms with experiential meaning. It will avoid the rhetoric of human depravity and acknowledge that despite their sinfulness, humans can perform naturally virtuous acts and fix their beliefs about God in abstraction from divine revelation. Such a theology will also acknowedge that that revelation judges the truth and adequacy of any natural conceptions of the divine or natural standards of morality.

I would hope that people living in other cultures would find such an interpretation of the human condition enlightening. True insights, after all, ought to transcend cultural frontiers. Moreover, inculturated theological thinking needs to avoid cultural chauvinism and incorporate into its perception of the real the best insights of thinkers from other lands. It should, however, speak like a Yankee.

I have, then, suggested only one possible way of perceiving the human condition in categories derived from this culture. I have done so partly in response to the challenge issued by Vatican II to theologians to think in an inculturated manner. I have focused on the human condition because with Karl Rahner I believe that a contemporary theology needs to build on a sound anthropology. The construct of the human which I have developed in this essay differs from Rahner's at several significant points, and it points to a different theological understanding of the dynamics of grace. The reader must judge which interprets Christian religious experience more accurately.

## ENDNOTES

1Jonathan Edwards **Religious Affections,** edited by John E. Smith (New Haven: Yale, 1968).

2Orestes Brownson, **Works,** edited by H.F. Brownson (Detroit: H. F. Brownson, 1902) IV, 3-55. Hereafter this edition will be abbreviated as WOB.

3Francis Ellingwood Abbot, **The Syllogistic Philosophy** (2 vols.; Boston: Little, Brown, and Co., 1906).

4John Dewey, **Art as Experience** (New York: Capricorn, 1958) 191-195. Hereafter this edition will be abbreviated as AE.

5John Dewey, **Art as Experience;** (New York: Capricorn, 1958) 191-195, hereafter this edition will be abbreviated AE; **Experience and Nature** (LaSalle, Ill.: Open Court, 1971), hereafter this edition will be abbreviated as EN; **Logic: the Theory of Inquiry** (New York: Holt Reinhart and Winston, 1938). Hereafter this edition will be abbreviated as LT.

6John Dewey, **Individualism: Old and New** (New York: Capricorn, 1962); **Liberalism and Social Action** (New York: Capricorn, 1963).

7Alfred North Whitehead, **Process and Reality,** edited by David Ray Griffin and Donald W. Sherburne (New York: Free Press, 1978).

8Chauncey Wright, "The Evolution of Self-Consciousness," **North American Review** (1873), 238.

9Chauncey Wright, "Masson: Recent British Philosophy," **The Nation** (November 15, 1866), 344.

10Chauncey Wright, "The Philosophy of Herbert Spencer," **North American Review** (1865), 53.

11William James, **Pragmatism** (New York: Macmillan, 1960), 42. Hereafter this edition will be abbreviated as P.

12William James, **The Varieties of Religious Experience** (New York: Doubleday), 1-32. Hereafter this edition will be abbreviated as VRE.

13Josiah Royce, **The Sources of Religious Insight** (New York: Scribner's, 1940), 3-34. Hereafter this edition will be abbreviated SRI.

14Josiah Royce, **The Philosophy of Loyalty** (New York: Macmillan, 1908). Hereafter this work will be abbreviated PL.

15C.S. Peirce, **Collected Papers,** edited by Charles Hartshorne and Paul Weiss (8 vols; Cambridge: Harvard, 1931 ff), 1. 300-321. Hereafter this edition will be abbreviated CPCSP.

16William James, **The Principles of Psychology** (2 vols.; New York: Dover, 1950) I, 224-289.

17John Dewey, **Logic: the Theory of Inquiry** (New York: Holt, Reinhart, and Winston, 938), 1ff.

18Jonathan Edwards, "Personal Narrative" in **Jonathan Edwards,** edited by David Levin (New York: Hill and Wang, 1969), 26-27.

19Jonathan Edwards, **Religious Affections,** edited by John E. Smith (New Haven: Yale, 1959). Hereafter this edition will be abbreviated RA.

20Jonathan Edwards, **The Works of President Edwards,** 10 vols. (London: 1817) I, 443-534. Hereafter this edition will be abbreviated WPE.

21Ralph Waldo Emerson, **Emerson's Complete Works** (12 vols; Boston: Houghton Mifflin, 1883) vols. I and II. Hereafter this edition will be abbreviated ECW).

22Josiah Royce, **The Philosophy of Loyalty** (New York: Macmillan, 1908), 16-17. Hereafter this edition will be abbreviated as PL.

23John Dewey, **A Common Faith** (New Haven: Yale, 1963).

24Josiah Royce, **The Problem of Christianity,** (2 vols.; Chicago: Gateway, 1968) II.

25Josiah Royce, **The World and the Individual** (2 vols.; New York: Dover, 1959) I, 47-262.

26Benjamin Franklin, **The Papers of Benjamin Franklin,** edited by Jared Sparkes, (12 vols.; Boston: Hilliard, Gray, and Co., 1840) I, 74-75. Hereafter this edition will be abbreviated PBF.

27Thomas Jefferson, **The Writings of Thomas Jefferson** (20 vols.;

Washington: Thomas Jefferson Memorial Association, 1904) XIV, 139-140. Hereafter this edition will be abbreviated WTJ.

28George Santayana, **The Life of Reason** (5 vols.; New York: Collier, 1962) III, 24-25.  Hereafter this edition will be abbreviated LR.

29George Santayana, **The Realm of Essence** (New York: Scribner's, 1927).

## Grace as Transmuted Experience and Social Process:
### Salvation in a New Paradigm

In **The Structure of Scientific Revolutions** Thomas S. Kuhn argues persuasively that breakthroughs occur in the positive sciences through paradigm shifts. Paradigms offer laws, theories, applications, and instrumentation that both allow one to explain some unexplained scientific facts and promise to explain others. Paradigms either organize or reorganize facts in need of explanation into data for scientific investigation. Paradigm shifts redefine a field of investigation by offering new laws, new theories, new applications, new instrumentation. The shift from Ptolemaic to Copernican astronomy or from Newtonian to Einsteinian physics exemplifies the kind of scientific advance Kuhn describes.

Paradigms, Kuhn argues, allow the pursuit of "normal science." They create the accepted frame of reference for addressing and solving problems. When anomalous facts begin to accumulate, facts which a given paradigm cannot explain, the stage is set for a paradigm shift. At first the practitioners of normal science resist the shift. But in a successful scientific revolution, the new paradigm finds some vocal supporters who eventually convince the rest of the scientific community of the advantages of the novel paradigm. Full acceptance, however, often takes time, as unconvinced defenders of the old paradigm die off and a new generation of scientists is introduced to the new approach.

Models function within paradigms, but paradigms include more than models. Scale models reproduce the structure of what they represent in proportions larger or smaller than life. Mathematical models quantify the realities they represent and enable investigators to measure them precisely. Imaginative models mediate between a vague, appreciative insight into a problem and the formulation of its hypothetical solution. They provide speculative thinking with an organizing root metaphor. In the early stages of atomic research, for example, the decision of scientists to imagine the structure of the atom as a miniature solar system allowed them to begin to formulate hypotheses about the way sub-atomic particles behave. New scientific paradigms will then ordinarily propose new models, but they include other things as well: new instrumentation, new operational procedures, and a new panoply of categories. They offer a new way of approaching unsolved problems, an approach sufficiently unprecedented as to attract supporters and sufficiently open-ended as to leave unanswered questions for the practitioners of the new paradigm to resolve.1

Theology does not employ the precise measurement of positive science. Theologians engage in scholarship rather than in controlled experimentation. Poor theology can degenerate into self-deception and wishful thinking. Nevertheless, a certain number of empirical checks do define the scope of responsible theological thinking. Sacred history provides the first factual check on theological speculation. Theological theories seek to interpret religiously significant events. Historians reconstruct chronicles of past events on the basis of existing data. They then attempt to provide a causal explanation of why things happened in the way they did. Sacred history tells the story of religiously significant events which verify or falsify theological theories. For example, prior to Vatican II, scholastic manuals of theology tried to show that Jesus of Nazareth defined the canonical essence of all seven sacraments of the Church. Contemporary questors for the historical Jesus and historians of Christian worship would today challenge the historical verifiability of such an account of the institution of the sacraments.

Religious practice offers another empirical check to theological thinking. Different theological explanations of the significance of religious events lead to different practical consequences. The Teutonic captivity of contemporary Christian theology, its domination by German patterns of thought, has rendered it acutely sensitive to the factual claims which history makes on theological speculation. The German love of transcendental a prioris, however, has blinded more than one contemporary Christian thinker to the need to explicitate the practical consequences of theological hypotheses. Nevertheless, for those theologians willing to learn from American pragmatism or from liberation theology's concern with praxis, the predictable practical consequences of theological theories do offer an empirical norm for opting among them. Quietism, for example, was correctly condemned for its deleterious effects on the practice of Christian prayer. Pelagianism was rejected in part because it undermined the kind of faith dependence on God which Jesus demanded of his disciples.

Not only does theological thinking advance with the kind of empiricism proper to scholarly (as opposed to strictly scientific) thought; but we can also discern in the development of theological thinking paradigm shifts analogous to those which occur in positive science. New theological paradigms emerge for a variety of reasons. They may arise in response to unresolved speculative tensions in a religious community, or they may result from a shift in the philosophical presuppositions that motivate theological speculation, or scientific advances may call those same presuppositions into question.2

New theological paradigms offer new ways of going about the business of theology. They draw on unexploited speculative sources, employ new methods of thinking, reformulate old beliefs in new contexts, create new linguistic tools for communicating the gospel, and change the way religious persons perceive God, the world, themselves. When, for example, the first Christian apologists decided to explain the Christian message in categories borrowed from Graeco-Roman philosophy, they effected a major theological paradigm shift that revolutionized Christian belief. The speculative implications of that revolution have taken centuries to assess. Indeed, the assessment continues even today. Moreover, since the days of the apologists other revolutions have transformed paradigmatically shared Christian perceptions of reality.

Think, for example, of the impact on the practice of Christian theology made by the Protestant reformation, by the Catholic counter-reformation, by historical-critical method, by ecumenical dialogue, and by Vatican II.

The development of a Christian theology of grace also illustrates the way paradigm shifts modify religious perceptions. With rare exceptions, from the second to the thirteenth century, Christian theologians perceived the world Platonically. A Platonic metaphysics, anthropology, and theory of knowledge all colored theological perceptions of the way grace operates. More specifically, the Platonic doctrine of participation provided the accepted speculative paradigm for understanding the gracing of human experience. In a philosophical world in which every reality participated in a transcendent form located in the mind of God, grace too was spontaneously understood as a conscious participation in the divine, not through reason but through faith in the God historically revealed in Jesus and the Holy Breath.3 Divinization, or the process of transformation in grace, tended to be conceived somewhat dualistically as the spiritualization of the human person, as assimilation into the eternal and transcendent realm of pure spirit.

As Christian theologians of the thirteenth century began, however, to understand and appreciate the full force and implications of Aristotle's refutation of a Platonic doctrine of participation, they were forced to reconceive the workings of divine grace. In a world full of Aristotelian substances, the essential forms of things reside not in some transcendent divine mind but in the things themselves. For the Christian Aristotelian accidental (and therefore essential) transformation, not Platonic participation, provides the correct paradigm for interpreting the dynamics of grace. In order to be able to perform graced acts the natural faculties of the soul need to be elevated to the supernatural order. The supernatural differs essentially from the natural. Christian Aristotelians speak therefore of the infusion of grace as human substances are equipped by God with supernatural powers of operation different in kind from the powers they possess in virtue of their natural essence.

From the thirteenth to the twentieth century most theologians of grace found in the paradigm of accidental transformation an adequate way of conceiving the dynamics of grace. As theological speculation absorbed existential polemic against ontic, objectifying forms of thinking, Christian teachers began, however, to abandon a scholastic metaphysics of grace for an understanding of grace as transforming interpersonal encounter.

In the present essay I would like to suggest yet another possible paradigm shift in theology, one that promises new resources for understanding the dynamics of graced transformation. I propose that we attempt to rethink the dynamics of grace in categories derived from the classical North American philosophical tradition. The Second Vatican Council has challenged theologians to rethink and proclaim the gospel in inculturated categories. The reformulation of Catholic doctrine in the light of insights derived from the classical North American philosophical tradition would enable theologians in this country to respond more effectively to that challenge and would also bring about a paradigm shift in American Catholic thinking analogous to that effected by the first Christian apologists. For such a reformulation would offer hitherto unexploited speculative resources for understanding Catholic belief and practice. It would raise new questions, offer new methods of thinking, employ new linguistic tools, and promise to revise North American Catholic perceptions of the gospel.

I propose, then, that we conceive of the dynamics of grace as transmuted experience and social process.4 Like the Platonic paradigm, the one I will propose allows us to speak of grace as a kind of participation; but my construct of grace interprets participation in a way that avoids the unacceptable dualistic and metaphysical implications of a Platonized theology of grace. My construct also recognizes with Christian existentialists that an interpersonal ecnounter with God lies at the heart of graced transformation. In contrast to existentialism it refuses to stigmatize logical thought as ontic and objectifying, for the human mind can construct a logically rigorous account of reality which conceives the real in relational rather than in objectifying terms. Moreover, like medieval theologians my construct also ambitions something like a metaphysics of grace. Grace does change the shape of reality. Indeed, since the gracing of human experience culminates in bodily resurrection, we may even say that grace transforms us physically. As Christians we look forward in hope to a whole world recreated in grace. At the same time, the approach I will suggest resists speaking of grace as either accidental or essential transformation. In the new paradigm essences may be legitimately conceived to function only as modes of sensation and perception, not as principles of being. Because my approach eschews classical philosophical categories, it speaks of neither substances nor accidents. As a consequence, while my construct of grace conceives of it as transforming, it does not describe that transformation as an accidental change. We shall explore these insights in greater detail presently. Here it suffices to note that while the new construct of grace borrows from the other three it adapts their insights to its own purposes.

My argument divides into two parts. First, I will explain some of the important philosophical insights that result from a paradigm shift to a North American perspective. Second, I will show how that shift forces us to reconceive our theological understanding of the dynamics of grace.

### (I)

The theology of grace which I will attempt to sketch in this essay draws on insights of Jonathan Edwards, Ralph Waldo Emerson, Orestes Brownson, C.S. Peirce, William James, Francis Ellingwood Abbot, Josiah Royce, John Dewey, and Bernard E. Meland, but it finds its immediate inspiration in the reformed subjerctivist principle of Alfred North

Whitehead. That principle states that "apart from the experiencing of subjects there is nothing, nothing, bare nothingness."5 In effect, the reformed subjectivist principle affirms that we should conceive any reality whatever as some kind of experience. It thus transforms the term "experience" into a transcendental category, a term applicable in intent to any reality.

No universal philosophical principle, including the proposition that Being divides into act and potency, enjoys speculative self-evidence. The truth or falsity of the reformed subjectivist principle rests, therefore, on its applicability and adequacy. It must interpret some realities in the sense in which it is defined. It must not fail to interpret any reality, for as a principle it aspires to universal applicability. The truth or falsity of the reformed subjectivist principle, will, therefore, depend in no small measure on the way one chooses to define the term "experience." I myself do so in a manner that differs significantly from Whitehead.

A "weasel word," the term "experience" has been so variously defined and used that it invites both equivocation and misunderstanding. Moreover, to the best of my knowledge, never until Whitehead made the suggestion has "experience" been used transcendentally. In the interest of clarity, therefore, let us contrast a transcendental use of the term "experience" with other more familiar uses.

"Experience" in popular parlance means a skill or expertise acquired through more or less prolonged exposure to some reality. We use "experience" in this first sense, for example, when we insert into an advertisement for new employees: "Only experienced personnel need apply."

The term "experience" has been used in a restricted sense as knowledge acquired through the senses, memory, and imagination. In this technical philosophical sense, "experience" is replaced by understanding, judgment, and decision as the mind advances from insight to an inferential grasp of reality and to practical decisions about it.

An analogous use of the term "experience" defines it as the raw material, the data of knowledge subsequently transformed into understanding, knowledge, and decision, whether the data in question be the data of the senses (as in the second meaning of "experience") or the data of consciousness. The latter consists of the operations of the mind before they are understood, judged, and decided upon, but once again understanding, judgment, and decision cannot be called "experience."

A fourth technical sense of "experience" broadens it to include every evaluative response: sensory, affective, imaginative, inferential. In this fourth sense, "experience" designates any way in which we respond cognitively to reality, but it does not include the realities themselves that are experienced.

A fifth sense of "experience" restricts it to conscious cognitive acts. In this understanding of the term, the existence of unconscious cognitive acts is either ignored or denied.

"Experience" used as a transcendental category includes all of the preceding sense of the term but goes beyond them. It recognizes the skill and familiarity born of exposure to certain kinds of reality as a certain kind of experience but not as the only kind. It concedes that knowing the data of sense and of consciousness exemplifies specific kinds of experience, but it extends the term to include every evaluative response whether conscious or unconscious. Finally, in contrast to the fourth sense of "experience" defined above "experience" used as a transcendental term includes within itself not only every manner in which reality is grasped evaluatively and cognitively but the realities themselves that are grasped. The latter stand within experience and make it into a certain kind of experience. All reality therefore divides descriptively into what is experienced and the way experienced realities are experienced. Since in such a philosophical paradigm Being is defined as some instance of experience, I cannot properly be said to have experience but to be an experience. In so speaking, of course, one abandons ordinary language and the philosophical presuppositions latent within it, but paradigm shifts always discombobulate accepted linguistic patterns.

While I accept Whitehead's innovative suggestion that we transform the term "experience" into a transcendental category, I, nevertheless, define the term differently from him. Whitehead's philosophy of organism offers a dipolar construct of experience. I conceive of experience, especially of the higher forms of experience, as triadic. I define experience as a process made up of relational elements called feelings. We can identify three generic kinds of feelings: evaluations, interactions, and tendencies. Evaluations provide the how of experience. Interactions and tendencies provide the what.[6]

Evaluations include sensations (like seeing, hearing, tasting, touching, smelling, kinetic and visceral feelings, the feeling of orientation in space); imageless affections (like fear, rage, envy, guilt, craving, sympathy, affection, admiration, love, ecstasy); images (like memories, fantasies, archetypes); and classifications (whether descriptive, inferential, common sense, mathematical, scientific, scholarly). In human experience all these different kinds of evaluative responses form a continuum. Sensations are already tinged with affective significance. Affections are linked by free association to images. Imagination clarifies affective responses and provides the matrix for abstract rational thinking. Abstractions are linked by inference. Unconscious evaluations condition conscious evaluative responses. This continuum of evaluation constitutes an identifiable realm of experience. I call it the realm of quality.

We sense interactions. We see, hear, feel, taste, touch, smell the physical impact of our world on us and our physical retaliation on it, the physical impact of one part of our body on another. The decisive physical impact of things on one another taken in itself and apart from the sensations which present such interactions and the selves that interact defines a realm of experience distinct from evaluation: namely, the concrete realm of action and reaction. I call this second realm of experience the realm of fact. Some facts, like the events I sense, initiate evaluative responses. I call them initial facts. Other facts like personal decisions terminate evaluative responses. I call them final facts. Final facts express the evaluations they terminate. When a final fact is sensed, it is transformed into an initial fact in the endless flow of experience.

Selves interact. I define a self as an autonomous tendency to react or respond evaluatively and/or decisively. Only selves which initiate activity function autonomously. Not every experienced tendency enjoys autonomy, however. When, for example, I ingest food, the chemicals I take into my body cease to function autonomously once they become part of me, even though specific chemicals within the body do tend to act in specific ways. We call the study of such tendencies organic chemistry. I call the tendencies which shape experience whether autonomous or not "laws." Laws then define a third realm of experience distinct from the realms of quality and fact but dynamically related to both. For every law is a general tendency to react or respond either evaluatively or decisively. And laws, tendencies, result from the decisions that express evaluative responses. When, for example, I fix my belief decisively about any reality, I create in myself a tendency, a habit, to respond in a certain way.

Selves, therefore, emerge out of dynamic interaction with one another. Each self defines itself into a certain kind of autonomous tendency through ongoing interaction with its world. Every spatio-temporal self finds itself bounded and limited by other selves that circumscribe it. Because it began at a particular moment in space and time, because it must define itself in opposition to other selves with whom it never achieves perfect unity, and because it consists of a limited number of acquired tendencies to react and respond in specific ways, every spatio-temporal self remains irreducibly finite. The character of every finite self is defined, not by some essential, metaphysical form, as substance philosophy suggests, but by its total history. To understand any spatio-temporal self fully one would have to recapitulate its entire story. The only essences to be found in a world of experiences consist of evaluations, qualities, abstracted from the realities they grasp and the self who does the grasping.

In a world of interacting experiences, reality takes on the character of social process; for in such a philosophical construct not only is reality conceived in dynamic relational terms, but experiences, being only relationally distinct, exist in one another. Facts, interactions, link interpenetrating selves socially. Evaluations allow them to become socially present to one another, for we become present to our world and it to us in our evaluative responses to it. Through evaluative response we also become present to ourselves. Moreover, in a world of experiences things exist in one another to the extent that they interact; for interacting realities experience one another. Experienced realities stand within the experiences they shape and help make them what they are.

In a world of mutually inexistent experiences change is understood not as essential transformation, but as transmutation. Substance philosophy equates reality and immutability. It therefore postulates that underneath every accidental change a stable substance lies that gives the changing thing its reality. In a world of experience, by contrast, the real is defined as process. When any particular process ends, it ceases to exist. Moreover, since every changing experience is composed of relational elements called feelings, change rearranges the constitutive relational structure of a developing experience. The subject of the changing experience, the self that changes, does not, however, underlie the change, it emerges from it.

The term "transmutation" names such a change technically. An experience undergoes transmutation when a new feeling is integrated into it in such a way as to modify the experience's constitutive relational structure. To put the matter technically, an experience undergoes transmutation when it develops in continuity with a prior experience while integrating into itself some novel feeling or feelings. The term "transmutation," therefore, means change but change conceived on an esthetic model. When, for example, an artist adds a dab of color to a painting, the result goes beyond the old painting plus the new dab. The added color changes the way the other colors relate to it and to one another. The whole painting changes because the felt, constitutive relationships of the colors that comprise it shift. In a world of transmuted experiences, something analogous happens in every change. The inclusion of a new feeling changes the entire experience into a different kind of experience. The difference in questions is relational not essential. Transmutation allows a self to relate to reality differently.

We call some selves persons, not things. The term "person" designates a dynamic, relational reality, subsisting in its own right as an autonomous center of responsive evaluation and decision. Persons also enjoy vital continuity and a capacity for responsible self-understanding, for decisions that flow from that same self-understanding, and for entering into responsible social relationships with entities like themselves. Things too function autonomously. And living things enjoy vital continuity, Things, however, do not possess a person's capacity for responsive and responsible behavior. In other words, persons differ from things in their capacity to undergo conversion.

The term "conversion" designates a certain kind of decision and its consequences. Converts decide to take responsibility for their subsequent growth and development in some area of their experience. Areas of personal experience differ from one another in the laws that govern them. Human affectivity and imagination follow irrational laws.

Inferential thought follows the laws of logic. Prudential thinking expresses habits of responsible choice made in the light of personally accepted values and realities that make absolute and ultimate claims. Religious behavior flows from habitual attitudes of faith. We may then distinguish four forms of personal conversion corresponding to four distinct habitual tendencies in the emerging self: affective, speculative, moral and religious. We must add a fifth: socio-political conversion. The socio-politically converted individual takes responsibility for seeing to it that one's environment and the social strucures that shape it express values and ideals compatible with converted behavior.

Conversion transmutes personal experience. Here we must distinguish initial from ongoing conversion. By initial conversion, persons pass from irresponsible to responsible behavior. Through ongoing conversion they accept the practical consequences of initial conversion. For example, initial affective conversion, the decision to take responsibility for one's healthy emotional development, does not automatically and instantaneously cure every neurosis. One may find that subsequent to one's initial decision to grow affectively in healthy ways, one still has to confront and bring to psychic integration unhealed affective conflicts. That healing process is effected by ongoing conversion.

We experience both macroscopic nature as well as human nature directly in events and personal actions that simply prescind from the historical self-revelation of God in Jesus and the Holy Breath. Natural evaluations and decisions build natural habits into the human personality.

Affective, speculative, moral and political conversion can all occur naturally. Neurotic conflict may, for example, force me to an affective conversion that has nothing to do with God's historical self-revelation. A natural, humanitarian love of truth and justice may motivate a speculative, moral, or political conversion that has nothing to do with God.

When affective, speculative, moral and political conversion have occurred naturally, religious conversion transmutes them in the technical sense defined above. Religious conversion always results from the action of divine grace. The religious convert always assents positively to some historical event of gratuitous divine self-communication. We call such assent faith in the broadest sense of that term. Faith, then, broadly understood, divides nature from grace, and religious conversion transmutes experience by integrating into it the decision to live in faith dependence on a self-revealing, self-communicating God.

Religious conversion also transmutes sinful impulses. We build sinful tendencies into our characters when we act in ways that we believe contradict the will of God. Since faith submits to the revelatory self-communication of God on the terms that that revelation demands, the obedience of faith reverses prior sinful decisions. We call that reversal repentance.

Religious conversion transmutes experience, then, by introducing into its felt relational structure the world transforming, world transcending reality of God as well as new decisions, evaluations, and tendencies born of faith. In the process religious conversion also transvalues natural and sinful experience.

The term "transvaluation" designates a specific kind of transmutation. Transvaluation modifies evaluative response. It transmutes, therefore, the realm of quality. The introduction of any new value into experience -- a new sensation, emotion, image, or inferential concept -- would also transmute the realm of quality in some way. "Transvaluation", therefore, designates a very specific kind of transmutation. Let us try to undetrstand its specificity.

Human persons judge reality in two ways: affectively and intuitively, on the one hand, and logically and inferentially on the other. We express intuitive judgments in prophecies, lyrics, stories, and judgments of discernment. We express inferential judgments in logical propositions. We can distinguish three irreducible kinds of inference. Abductive or hypothetical inference classifies initially data in need of explanation. Deductive inference predicts the operational consequences of a particular hypothetical classification of data. Inductive inference verifies or falsifies such deductive predictions and decides the extent to which the assumptions which lie at the basis of a given hypothesis obtain in reality. We will reflect in greater detail on the importance of these distinctions below. Here it suffices to note that we gather interrelated inferences into different frames of reference. For example, among narratives we distinguish myth, epic, ballad, parable, romance, realistic fiction. Each constitutes a distinct narrative frame of reference.

The commitment of faith opens experience to a religious frame of reference. Religious realities and values make morally absolute and ultimate claims. Religious events disclose God, and God confronts the religious convert as supremely beautiful, good, and true, as a reality not only worth living but if necessary worth dying for, as a reality to be clung to in every circumstance. Christian conversion demands, therefore, that every natural or sinful reality be re-evaluated in the light of God's historical self-communication in Jesus and His Holy Breath. That reevaluation process transvalues natural and sinful feelings, for transvaluation, as we have seen, occurs when senations, affections, images, or concepts which functioned in one frame of reference begin to function in a novel frame of reference in such a way that they retain some of their former meaning even as they acquire new connotations in the new frame of reference. For example, prior to conversion to Christianity one could legitimately understand oneself as a "person." But that term will begin to take on new meaning when one begins through faith to enter into relationship with a tripersonal God and with a divine person made flesh.[7]

The preceding speculative construct of experience expresses the paradigm shift to inculturated theological thinking proposed at the beginning of this essay. Other constructs could no doubt be derived from dialogue with the North American philosophical tradition. The one I have formulated conceives grace as participation in God but interprets participation as the mutual inexistence of socially interacting experiences. "Inexistence" here does not mean non-existence but existence in some reality other than oneself. Through faith, I exist in God and God exists in me in a new way because through our interaction, through God's revelatory self-communication to me and my response in faith to God, the two of us experience one another differently. Grace changes experience physically but that change is here interpreted as transmutation rather than as essential or accidental transformation. In a world of socially interacting experiences, grace results from an interpersonal encounter with a tripersonal God that sets one in a new kind of interpersonal communion with other selves, but that interpersonal communion too is here understood as a transmutation and transvaluation of natural and sinful feelings. Moreover, as we shall see, not every graced experience consists of interpersonal communion, for among the experiences of grace we must include not only prophetic confrontation with the diabolical, the demonic, and the satanic, but also the suffering of atoning love. Finally, in a world of relationally distinct experiences which exist in one another through autonomous, dynamic interaction, all reality including the dynamics of grace must be conceived as social process. What consequences for a theology of grace flow from the adoption of such a theological construct?

## (II)

Theologians of grace have traditionally and correctly distinguished uncreated from created grace. The term "uncreated grace" designates the reality of God in its capacity to transform human experience through faith. "Created grace" designates the difference that that transformation makes in human experience. In a world of mutually inexistent experiences, both created and uncreated grace must be understood as a social process. Let us reflect on the implications of the preceding statement.

a. **Uncreated grace:** The construct of experience developed in the preceding section of this essay is derived from reflection on human experience, but it can be applied analogously to the God Christians worship. The Christian God reveals himself historically in the missions of Jesus and of His Holy Breath. Any statement we make about the reality of that God must therefore be derived from reflection on those missions and must actually interpret them. Christians believe in a God whose creative and redemptive wisdom orders all things sweetly. Jesus incarnates that wisdom and thereby reveals to us the mind of God. Wisdom engages evaluative responses. Because the Christian God responds evaluatively, we must allow the presence within the Godhead of a realm of quality analogous to that present in human experience.

Moreover, in the Old and New Testaments, not only the gracious enlightenment of humans but every divine evaluative response is attributed to God's Holy Breath.8 In Her mission to Jesus, therefore, the divine Breath stands historically revealed as the cognitive link between Father and Son, as the very mind of God.

Besides responding evaluatively the Christian God acts decisively. The Father creator who sends His Son into the world confronts the believer as an aboriginal source of creative efficacy. The Son who obeys the Father's every command and the Breath's every enlightenment confronts the believer as a divine principle of obediential efficacy. He therefore stands historically revealed as the one through whom both Father and Breath act. We must then allow the presence of decisive acts within the Christian Godhead, acts that constitute a realm of fact analogous to the one in human experience.

Moreover, within the triune God we discover three distinct selves: Father, Son, and Breath. Within salvation history they each stand revealed as functioning autonomously. The Father sends the Son who with the Father then sends the Breath in eschatological abundance. The Breath inspires the Father's creative wisdom and enlightens the incarnate Son as well as those who believe in Him. Moreover, the Son's relationship to the Father can only be described as interpersonal. If then the three members of the divine triad enjoy co-equality within the Godhead, their relationship to one another must be described as an interpersonal communion.

The Christian Godhead can also be described as an eternal process. Because the Father sends the Son into the world, we know that from all eternity the Father generates the Son. Because both Father and Son send the Breath into the world, we know that from all eternity the Holy Breath proceeds from both of them. If then the Christian God also enjoys unity then the reality of the Godhead exemplifies all the characteristics of the higher forms of experience. It is a process which integrates three kinds of feelings: qualities, facts, and laws.

Christian theologians have attemppted to expplain the unity of three persons in one God in a variety of ways. Some have held that the divine unity, being an absolute mystery, cannot finally be explained. Others have argued that the three persons all enjoy the same simple divine substance which functions as a principle of activity common to all the divine persons. Others still have argued that the unity of the divine persons consists in their perfect mutual inexistence. (The council of Florence endorsed this third explanation.) A fourth position equates the unity of the divine persons with their vital identity. All of the above explanations lie within the realm of Christian orthodoxy. Three heretical accounts of the way the divine persons relate within the Godhead have been correctly condemned. Modalism identifies the Son and Breath with the person of the Father. Arianism unifies the Godhead by denying divinity to Son and Breath. And tritheism shatters the unity of the

Godhead into a collectivity.

We certainly experience the reality of God as mysterious, but if we say that God is absolutely mysterious, we must also hold that He is absolutely unintelligible. An absolutely unintelligible God would also be absolutely unrevealable. Since, then, God has in fact revealed Himself in history and since we do know something about Him we must set aside as unacceptable obscurantism any theological attempt to avoid explaining the divine unity by appealing to the absoluteness of the divine mystery.9

Moreover, if we can legitimately conceive of God as an experience, then we must also conceive the divine reality as the supreme exemplification of experience, as that experience than which none greater can be conceived. As the experience of everything experienceable God would also enjoy supreme intelligibility. The mystery of the divine experience would, then, result from its infinity and inexhaustibility. It would flow from the fact that divine experience contains all other experiences and is contained by none of them. Moreover, nothing any finite reality experiences and understands about the supreme and infinite divine reality will ever exhaust what we can know about the Godhead. In other words, the mystery of God results from the confrontation of a finite human experience with the supreme and inexhaustible intelligibility of the divine experience, not from God's intrinsic unintelligibility.

Moreover, if we are willing to describe the Christian God as an experience, we cannot explain the divine unity by identifying the three persons with a substantial principle of activity common to all three. For one thing, the term "substance" does not function in an experiential construct of reality. Things subsist in such a construct, but subsistence is defined as the capacity to function autonomously rather than as existence in oneself and not in another as in a subject of inhesion. The closest thing to a substance in a world of experiences would be the selves that people it. The three divine selves in the Godhead are, however, the very realities whose unity is in need of explanation.

If then one conceives reality as experience, as I have suggested, and if within that frame of reference one seeks to understand the divine reality itself as an experience, one cannot consistently explain the divine unity by appealing to a substantial principle of activity common to the three divine persons. One can, however, with the council of Florence speak of their unity as a type of mutual inexistence.

In a world of experiences everything exists in something else to the extent that the two experiences experience one another, for what is experienced stands within experience and helps make it a certain kind of experience. In a world of experiences, the mutual inexistence of the divine persons, far from an anomaly, exemplifies instead a state of being common to every reality. Indeed, the divine persons differ from other realities not because they exist in one another but because they do so with such a supreme perfection that a greater unity among persons cannot be conceived. When human persons interact in love over a period of time, they begin to resemble one another as they acquire shared beliefs, attitudes, and habits of responding. In other words, human persons who exist lovingly in one another for a significant time come to enjoy a similarity of life. The divine persons, however, being the supreme exemplification of mutual inexistence exist in one another from all eternity not with a similarity but with an identity of life. How does this come about?

The incarnate Son offers us our only historical evidence of the way the divine persons relate to one another within the Godhead. In the gospels the Son relates to the Father who sends Him and to the Breath who enlightens Him with a perfection of obedience that transforms His life and death into an act of perfect self-donation. Mutual self-donation, then, provides an historically derived theological rubric for understanding the way the divine persons relate to one another within the Godhead. It also explains the divine unity. The divine persons give themselves to one another so perfectly that their mutual, loving self-gift creates an identity, not a mere similarity of divine life.

Not only then may we conceive of the Christian God as an experience but we may also legitimately conceive of the Godhead as the supreme exemplification of interpersonal communion in love. That communion results from the eternal procession and mutual self-donation of the divine persons to one another in supreme and perfect love. Moreover, the fact that the divine experience subsists as an eternal social process provides the pattern, the norm for the historical gracing of human experience. We become graced by being drawn socially into the experience of interpersonal communion shared by the divine persons. Through the obedience of faith we learn to give ourselves lovingly to them and to those they love. We do so in imitation of the loving mutual self-giving that unites them in an identity of divine life. As a consequence, in a world of mutually inexistent experiences, created grace must be understood on an analogy with uncreated grace, namely as a social, spatio-temporal process that transpires within an eternal divine process whose eruption into history transmutes natural and sinful feelings into an experience of social communion in hope, faith, and love.

b. **Created grace:** Every orthodox theology of grace recognizes the transformative character of created grace, the change which an encounter with God in faith effects in those who believe, but the change effected in the creature is conceived differently under different theological paradigms. If then we understand created grace as transmuted experience and social process, how should we conceive its dynamics?

l. **The gracious transmutation of natural hope:** Christian hope transmutes and transvalues natural human hope. Natural hope dwells in the heart, not in the head. It expresses an appreciative insight into the past and present forces that are shaping the future to which one aspires.

Hope grasps reality in fallible, irrational judgments of feeling analogous to fallible, rational, logical judgments. Natural hope thrives on images, on visions of personal satisfaction, and of a world preserved or transformed by human initiative. True hopes paint an accurate picture of the dawning future: false hopes, a deceptive one. Some hopes ambition specific goals. Others yearn for ultimate satisfaction, for a satisfaction unmarred by any form of dissent. Vague hopes inspire mysterious visions that express inchoate stirrings of the human heart.

Natural hope prescinds from the historical self-communication of God in Jesus and the Holy Breath. It springs in part from affective conversion, from confrontation with the dark, shadow side of the psyche. The repression of the negative affections (like anger, fear, guilt, envy) gradually draws the human psyche into a maelstrom of personal conflict, violence, and eventually despair. "Nervousness" gives way to more serious personality disfunctions. If not attended to, the latter breed increasingly violent antisocial behavior that eventually requires hospitalization. At the end of this spiralling descent into the hell of despair lie suicidal tendencies and actual deeds of self-destruction. As hope dies, the imagination ossifies. It becomes prey to rigid, obsessive, and neurotic patterns of behavior, but when repressed negative feelings are raised to consciousness and healed through confrontation, forgiveness, reconciliation, gratitude, and authentic self-appreciation, the positive affections -- sympathy, love, esthetic appreciation -- find greater freedom of play. The imagination acquires new flexibility and realistic scope, and natural hope is born.

Despair isolates. Hope draws one into creative. imaginative communion with one's world and with other persons. Similarly, the wounded heart in need of healing finds it in communion with others who support, forgive, encourage, and accept despairing individuals desperately in search of hope. Whether in its nurture or in its fulfillment, natural human hope draws one to participate in and to foster communities of mutual encouragement and support.

Christian conversion transmutes and transvalues natural human hope through an encounter in faith with the risen Christ in the power and anointing of His Breath. We may identify two important dynamics in the graced transmutation of natural, personal hopes. First, Christian hope reorients natural hope to the future God has promised. It does so by informing natural hope with those images that inform the shared hope of Christians: the heavenly banquet, the new Jerusalem, the victory of the Lamb, final resurrection. Second, natural hope is healed of sinfulness and of human egocentism through the transvaluation in faith and love of its spontaneous images and attitudes. That process of transvaluation bears fruit in the experience of initial and ongoing repentance which mystics call the dark night of sense.

In a world of mutually inexistent experiences the cultivation of Christian hope involves more than the personal healing of individual hearts. It demands as well the transformation of oppressive environments into environments that nurture Christian aspiration. Hope dies in individuals when the heart is overwhelmed by the diabolical, the demonic, and the Satanic forces that shape the world in which individuals and communities live. The diabolic twists meaning into a lying counterfeit of truth. The demonic suffuses the world with violence and conflict that deprives it of significance. The Satanic pretends to righteousness while hypocritically incarnating the forces of antiChrist.

Natural human hope can set individuals and especially communities of hope in loyal, prophetic opposition to the diabolic and demonic forces operative in the world. Natural hope needs then to be nurtured not only by personal affective conversion but also by a political conversion that inspires collaborative opposition to the forces of selfish and sinful egotism that create environments of despair. Dissent, rejection, violent opposition, manipulation, exploitation -- all shatter and fragment experience and thereby breed defeat, discouragement, and the death of hope. Hope by contrast thrives on shared consent, on common aspiration to the same realities and values, and on a shared practical faith in a common future.

Christian conversion transmutes and transvalues political conversion by suffusing the quest for justice with religious fervor and by demanding that the search for a just social order also incarnate gospel values. It sets the Christian community in prophetic opposition not only to the diabolic and demonic forces in human society but also to the Satanic forces as well. It pits us against the forces of antiChrist. It demands that shared visions and collaborative efforts to bring about a just social order that incarnates the mind of God and of Jesus.

Moreover there is a sense in which the shared hope of the Christian community takes precedence over individual Christian hopes. The resurrection of Jesus and the illumination of His Breath provide Christian hope with its ultimate ground. Christians yearn collectively for the establishment on this earth of the divine reign proclaimed by Jesus and for the ultimate transformation of all creation in the image and power of the risen Christ. That shared hope takes practical form in the creation of Christian communities of hope dedicated to the establishment of the reign of God's justice on earth. Such communities of hope create the matrix of grace in which the hopeless can find healing and the courage to share in concrete realistic, and practical ways the common hope of Christians.

2. **The gracious transmutation of belief:** In a world of mutually inexistent experiences, individuals may choose to fix their beliefs through mindless and stubborn, personal dogmatism, through an appeal to authority, or through private esthetic preference; but given the fact of human finitude and fallibility, shared systematic inquiry offers the most adequate means of fixing personal beliefs naturally.

Through shared inquiry communities come to self-awareness as communities. For a community of any size or duration to achieve shared communal awareness, its members need to identify with the founding event from which the community takes its rise. The community also needs to reach a consensus about the significance of that event and of the intervening history that links the community to it. Communities retrieve their histories both appreciatively, through spontaneous memories, narratives, and lyrics, and inferentially, through scholarly history. Shared consensus about its origins and subsequent development endows the community with a sense of its present identity. For communities like individuals derive their reality from their total history. In consciously reappropriating that history a community comes to understand its distinctive character as a community.

In order to achieve full shared consciousness, communities must, however, deal not only with their past but also with the common future to which they choose to aspire. For hope too shapes shared communal awareness. Indeed, a community reaches new self-understanding as a community when it achieves a consensus concerning the way its beliefs and hopes ought to shape both the ultimate and immediate future to which it aspires. The shared consciousness born of such consensus is further augmented when that same community acts corporately to realize the common goals for which its members yearn collectively. Corporate action, however, requires corporate leadership. Effective corporate leadership evokes and coordinates the community's best talents and human resources in the interests of reappropriating its origins, projecting a common future, and bringing that future to successful realization.

The natural fixation of personal belief ought, then, to transpire in communities of interpretation and shared inquiry engaged both in the ongoing reappropriation of their histories and in the projection and practical achievement of shared ideals, beliefs, and aspirations. Natural speculative conversion seeks to ensure the responsible fixation of personal beliefs through participation in such a community of interpretation.

Christian conversion transmutes natural speculative conversion into the responsible search for personal and ecclesial self-understanding in a Christian community of religious inquiry and practical witness to gospel realities and values. It transforms the natural search of human communities for shared consciousness as communities enter into a sharing of the charisms of the Holy Breath. That sharing creates the faith consciousness of the Christian community as such and of its individual members. Let us reflect on how this comes about.

Experience, as we have seen, develops through social transaction. And a charism of the Holy Breath transmutes every moment in the growth of experience. How does this occur?

Through sensation we become initially present to ourselves and our world. The gift of tongues and similar gifts of prayer yield an initial felt sense of standing in a present, faith-motivated relationship with the world-transcending, world-transforming reality of God. In prayer we sense and touch the presence of God and are touched by it.

The imageless feelings that transmute sensations into perceptions of the laws or tendencies, operative in experience exercise a judgmental function within experience. As we feel our way into different situations we judge them affectively and prudentially. The charismatic anointing of the Holy Breath transmutes natural prudential judgments of feeling into the discernment of spirits in faith.

The lyric and narrative voices explore and clarify intuitively affective perceptions of reality. Through story and song the human heart comes to new insight into the complexity of life and of reality in general. The charism of prophecy transmutes such natural intuitive perceptions into a divinely inspired vision of the actions and saving intentions of God.

Poets, storytellers, and prophets declaim truth. Teachers explain truths and offer logical and persuasive reasons for accepting them. Teaching therefore engages logical inference and argument in ways that the intuitive grasp of reality does not. Teaching may advance naturally in abstraction from God's historical self-revelation in Jesus.. The charismatic anointing of the Holy Breath transmutes natural teaching into the attempt to understand in faith the saving action of God in human history.

Finally, individuals with natural gifts of leadership can inspire others to dedication to common projects. Action-oriented charisms like administration, helping, pastoral leadership, care for the poor transmute the shared activity of the Christian community into the realization in faith of its shared hope to do the deeds that incarnate divine love.

A charism of the Holy Breath transmutes each moment in the growth of experience. No single individual believer, however, possesses all the charisms. Individual Christians will, as a consequence, experience the gracing of every moment in the growth of experience only if they are willing to participate in a charismatic community of faith in which the gifts of others compensate for the charisms one lacks personally. Since the charisms ensure that experience develops in receptive dependence upon God, individual Christians are nurtured to mature faith through openness to the charismatic impulse of the Holy Breath throughout the church universal.

The sharing of the charisms ensures that the Christian community's search for self-understanding transpires in faith. Prophets and teachers of wisdom summon Christians to ongoing repentance and belief that opens them to the charismatic anointing of the Breath. Gifts of prayer teach Christians to trust in the abiding presence of the Triune God. Teachers of instruction help the community retrieve its heritage and come to a conscious sense of identity in faith. Prophets and teachers orient the community in faith and hope to the future God has promised. Discerners advise pastors and leaders to make wise decisions about community projects. And those with action gifts orchestrate the collaborative efforts of the Christian community to establish the reign of God on earth.

Those facets of the shared experience of Christians untouched by the Breath's charismatic anointing develop either naturally or sinfully. The shared self-awareness of Christian communities as Christian can, however, advance only in faith. Indeed, in a world of mutually inexistent experiences, Christian faith consists in the first instance in the authentic sharing of all of the divine Breath's gifts of sanctification and of service in such a way that the Christian community learns collectively to put on the mind of Christ. Individuals come to faith through participation in the social process of charismatic sharing that creates the Christian community's collective faith consciousness, for the authentic sharing of all the charisms of the Holy Breath in faith transmutes the shared consciousness of the Christian community into an ambience of grace that evokes and nurtures the faith of individuals. Moreover, individual faith comes to fruition as individual members of the Christian community learn to help create such an ambience of grace by incarnating the mind of Christ in deeds of service formed in docile obedience to the charismatic anointing of the Holy Breath.[11]

In other words, in a theology of grace as transmuted experience, Christian faith consists in the first instance in the social process by which the Christian community achieves ecclesial self-consciousness through the sharing of all the charisms of sanctification and of service. In the second instance it consists of the achievement of personal self-understanding as a Christian through active participation in such a charismatic community of faith.

3. **The gracious transmutation of love:** Natural human love takes a variety of forms: the needy love of young children, the bonds of affection that draw families together, the joys of friendship, the intoxications of romantic love. Christian love transmutes all such natural loves by creating a community whose life together incarnates the atoning gift-love historically revealed in the crucified and risen Christ. Christian charity demands that every form of human love imitate Christ's love. Like his love it must simply be there. It must forgive in advance any hurt, forgive while the injury is being done, forgive before there is any sign of repentance. The quality of divine love revealed in Jesus stands as a constant challenge to the finitude and egocentrism of natural human loves. In the process it transvalues them and transforms them into expressions of the divine love incarnate in Jesus.

Christian charity makes very specific moral demands. It demands that those who commit themselves to living for others as the children of God in the image of Jesus must labor to bring into being the kind of faith community to which He summoned His disciples. Jesus, however, sought to gather around Himself a group of people who trusted in the providential care of His Father so totally that they were thereby liberated to share their possessions with one another as a sign that they draw their life from God rather than from the things of this world. The true children of God should not therefore heap up possessions but labor in order to have something to share with others. Jesus also demanded that His disciples share their goods on the basis of need, not of merit alone. In sharing its goods the Christian community excludes no one in principle and welcomes saint and sinner alike. It shows special concern to reach out to the alienated and marginal. It seeks, therefore, to bring into existence a universal community open in principle to anyone, especially to those whom others refuse to accept. Because Christian sharing expresses faith in God, it takes place in a community of worship. In that community mutual forgiveness in the name and image of Jesus provides the test of the authenticity of prayer. Sharing possessions in faith dependence on a providential God also expresses and acknowledges the fact that, being sinners forgiven by a self-sacrificing God, Christians reach out to others with a forgiveness that seeks to imitate the indiscriminate and gratuitous perfection of God's own love. Moreover, in the post-Pentecostal Church in which each believer shares a portion of the Holy Breath, faith sharing encompasses not only the sharing of worldly goods but the sharing of oneself in charismatic deeds of service that incarnate the love of Christ. Christian charity makes then these basic moral demands.

Christian charity blends the needy love of a child, the gift love of Christ, and the contemplative love of the mystic. Every follower of Jesus bears the wounds of sin. All suffer limitations. No disciple loves authentically, therefore, who constantly condescends to others out of an impregnable sense of personal strength. All need love, and authentic charity blossoms in the mutual give-and-take of love within a community of mutual sharing and mutual forgiveness. Moreover, despite their sinfulness and limitations, Christians look to the Holy Breath to inspire in them the same kind of selfless divine love incarnate in Jesus. Finally, as believers are increasingly transported by the divine beauty incarnate in Christ and Jesus-like people, Christian love matures into the contemplative love of the mystic bound in service to God and to the world through the knowing that is loving.

Like faith and hope, therefore, Christian charity designates in the first instance a social process, the process of gratuitous self-sharing in community in the name and image of Jesus. Moreover, the Christian community when in process of transformation in charity provides a matrix of grace in which individuals can begin to learn how to transvalue their finite, egocentric natural loves in the all-embracing, forgiving love of Christ. Moreover, like hope, charity contributes to the shared faith consciousness of the Christian community by translating both the practical consequences of faith and the aspirations of hope into shared deeds of love and mutual service.

Finally, faith, hope, and love viewed as personal acts commit individuals to a dynamic process of graced socialization that draws them both individually and collectively into contemplative communion with the three divine persons, into the love that bonds them in that perfect unity of divine life that expresses the perfection of their mutual self-donation in love.12

4. **Gifts of sanctification and the moral life:** Christian conversion transmutes human experience by setting it in a life-giving relationship with the triune God. Converted consent to the historical self-communication of God endows human experience with a wholly novel capacity to respond in faith. As it transvalues human affectivity, belief, and action, it transforms them into Christian hope, faith, and charity. In other words, the transmutation of experience effected by Christian conversion changes the convert into a new creation.

After authentic Christian conversion, therefore, human moral striving occurs in a wholly different context: namely in the context created by faith. That fact transmutes the search for moral integrity into something different from natural moral striving. The reality of the Christian God and the attitudes, beliefs, and quality of love incarnate in Jesus provide the consenting convert with a new and more adequate context for understanding human moral striving than anything natural reason can contrive. More specifically, Christian conversion transmutes and transvalues the natural quest for justice into the Christian search for holiness in which the mind of Christ rather than mere natural moral reasoning provides the ultimate norm for judging prudentially the rightness or wrongness of human decisions. As a consequence, Christian moral sanctity is effected by ongoing docility to the sanctifying gifts (**dona**) of the Holy Breath which teach us to put on the mind of Christ.

In a world populated by experiences, moreover, the term "mind" embraces every evaluative response. It designates the entire realm of quality. "Putting on the mind of Christ" involves, as a consequence, the monitoring of sensations, the healing of disordered affections, and the charismatic transvaluation of both intuitive and inferential perceptions of the real. We also learn to put on the mind of Christ by actually living in His image, for every habitual tendency that structures human experience results from a decision. We therefore acquire the same attitudes, visions, and beliefs as Jesus when we live for the same realities and values as He.

Jesus summoned all men and women to live as children of God in His image. Those who obey that call labor to bring into existence communities of faith sharing, of unrestricted love, and of divine worship in the service of atonement. Those communities seek to transform natural and sinful social structures until they incarnate gospel values. The dynamic social process of personal transformation in a charismatic community of faith, worship, and prophetic witness, transmutes human moral striving into the search for Christian holiness.

Moreover, as in the case of hope, faith, and charity, the collective holiness of the Christian community creates an ambience of grace that nurtures the personal search for sanctity. The living example of Jesus-like people and the beauty incarnate in their lives draws the hearts of individuals to live likewise. Moreover, the sanctity of the Church acquires enhanced sacramental visibility in communities dedicated to holiness.

When, therefore, we understand grace as transmuted experience and social process, we can in a sense explain the origins of the Christian community by appeal to the dynamics of conversion. As Christian conversion transmutes and transvalues human hearts, minds, and actions, it brings into existence a community of shared religious aspiration, belief, and love that provides an environment of grace which nurtures in those who live within it an ever deepening union with God. At the same time the graced longings, convictions, and mutual charismatic service of individual believers creates the very environment of faith that nurtures them in their personal quest for God. This sounds paradoxical, that the very individuals who under the inspiration of grace create the Christian community, should simultaneously relate to the community as the source of their own graced development.

Two facts explain the paradox. First of all, the environment of grace which we call the church exceeds the charismatic contribution to any one of its members. In other words, while each finite individual under the inspiration of the Holy Breath contributes something to the shared life of the total Christian community, nevertheless, each individual believer still needs to learn from and be corrected by the hope, faith, love, holiness, and charismatic service of the other members. Second, the shared life and consciousness of communities transcends the lives of the individuals that compose it. Individual consciousness, for example, results from the ability to distinguish one thing from another and to grasp the relationship among distinguished realities. The shared awareness of communities by contrast results from a complex process of investigation, planning, and practical collaboration. Communities come to a shared sense of indentity when through historical investigation they come to understand collectively the events that created them and the historical processes that have brought them to a particular moment in their common history. On the basis of that shared sense of identity, communities need then first to decide on the future they intend to share and then to collaborate in the effort to transform their common dreams into an actuality. Individuals who participate in the complex processes of dialogue and practical collaboration that create the shared awareness of the communities to which they belong, experience a heightened personal awareness as they learn to think of themselves no longer as isolated individuals but as members of this or that community. Nevertheless, the shared conscious life of the community as such differs in quality from the consciousness of the individual members who comprise it precisely because it roots itself in complex processes of social interaction that transcend individual life processes. When grace informs the social processes that create a community, it functions as an environment of grace for its individual members, eventhough it could never exist apart from their collaborative efforts.

The social process we call the church, however, exists in another complex social process we call the world. Church and world approach reality from a different set of presuppositions. The church as church perceives reality with the eyes of faith. The world viewed precisely in its worldliness abstracts from the fact of devine revelation and therefore perceives reality naturally, with secular eyes. The processes of abstraction which produce secularity need not result from human malice. The finitude of the human mind prevents it from dealing simultaneously with every reality. The more complex each problem, the more the human mind must focus narrowly upon it in order to master it. The focusing of human attention creates different frames of reference for dealing with reality: common sense, positive science, scholarship, artistic and literary perceptions of the nautre of things. In each of these frames of reference, human thought often enough advances in complete abstraction from religious or Chritian faith. Sometimes in addition the institutionalized attitudes, beliefs, policies, and actions of the world also contradict faith. When that happens the church must either enter into conflict with the world or allow the world to corrupt it. Even mere secularity can pose a severe challenge to the integrity of faith when it forbids believers the right to re-evaluate secular realities and values in the light of faith.

When, moreover, we view the church and the world as instances of experience and as social processes that transpire within one another we are forced to recognize as folly any attempt on their part to ignore one another. The church must deal with the world, the world with the church. Both have something to teach one another. Both have the right to challenge one another when one encroaches illegitimately on the territory of the other.

Any attempt to deal with the larger, impersonal intitutions that structure the life of both the church and secular society demands socio-political conversion. Those who have undergone socio-political conversion take responsibility not only for the motives and consequences of their own personal decisions but also for the decisions that shape the policies and actions of large institutions. Socio-political converts attempt to ensure, to the extent that they can, that such policies and actions express and foster integral conversion before God. As gospel values begin to transmute and transvalue socio-political conversion, they transform it into the Christian search for social justice, deprivatize the Christian search for holiness, and force the church both individually and collectively to confront in faith the economic, social, and political issues of its day.

Clearly in a theology of grace as transmuted experience and social process, hope, faith, charity, and ongoing moral sanctification cannot be understood adequately as essentially different habits that modify natural substances. Rather they consist in feelings that mutually interpenetrate one another and thereby endow Christian experience with its specific character. Hope animates faith, charity, and the search for holiness and justice. Faith clarifies hope and motivates charity, Christian moral striving, and the search for a just society. Charity and Christian moral practice express hope and faith. Hope, charity, and the search for sanctity and justice heighten faith consciousness. Moreover, through mutual inexistence the hope, faith, love and ongoing sanctification of individuals all participate in the collective faith, hope, love, and sanctity of the Christian community and vica versa.13

## (III)

We have been attempting to think the dynamics of graced transformation in a new paradigm that responds to the challenge of Vatican II to pursue inculturated theological thinking. We have characterized gracious transformation as transmuted experience and social process. Such a conception of grace contrasts with other more traditional paradigms.

When grace is conceived platonically, transformation in faith is understood as assimilation to the transcendent realm of Spirit. Then the gracing of human experience takes on dualistic connotations, since the realm of spirit differs essentially from the material realm of space and time. The Platonist equates Spirit with reality, truth, goodness, immutability, and eternity and matter with illusion, deception, unreality, and fleeting satisfaction. A Platonic paradigm for understanding the dynamics of grace tends, as a consequence, to undervalue or misprize the physical, the temporal, the historical, but when we conceive of grace as transmuted experience and social process, interaction with revelatory events of grace offers privileged access in faith to the divine process that co-exists with every spatio-temporal process and whose free self-disclosure in history endows human social interaction with an enhanced complexity and integration. Grace conceived as transmuted experience and social process promises then no escape from history to the secure, unchanging, transcendent realm of spirit. It plunges one into the historical process we call experience and looks to eventual absorption into an eternal process unmarred by the dissent of sin. Moreover, when we conceive reality as experience, we can describe the dynamics of graced transmutation without ever invoking the categories "matter" or "spirit." We can as a consequence avoid the unfortunate dualistic connotations of a platonized theology of grace.

A theology of grace as accidental transformation suffers less from otherworldliness and more from preoccupation with individuals and from an operational dualism. A theology of grace as essential transformation must explain most fundamentally how individual substances acquire supernatural powers of operation essentially different from those they possess by their essence or nature. Grace must, then, first be infused into the individual soul so that it can then act in ways that express its essential transformation into a supernatural reality. Moreover, in this paradigm for understanding the dynamics of grace, believers are oriented to Being and implicitly to God by an essential orientation of their individual intellects and wills, which grace subsequently transforms. Being spiritual these faculties link one in a privileged way to the immaterial, eternal, immutable reality of God.

A theology of grace as transmuted experience and social process insists by contrast that individuals acquire a specific character not by possessing some fixed essential nature but by choosing to become a certain kind of self through social intercourse with other selves that exist dynamically within an individual experience and make it into a specific kind of experience. Moreover in a world of experiences we grasp reality not only logically and inferentially but also affectively and appreciatively. We know God and the world with both heart and head and need to coordinate within religious experience these two ways of perceiving the divine reality. As a consequence we need no longer regard the faculties of intellect and will as yielding privileged access to God. Instead we may experience God throughout the whole spectrum of human evaluative response. Thinking the dynamics of grace in the new paradigm thus overcomes the operational dualism latent in a theology of grace as accidental (and therefore essential) transformation.

In a theology of grace as personal encounter, one discovers God in the experience of meaningful relationship. A theology of grace as interpersonal encounter tends, however, to describe grace as an I-Thou relationship. As a result it can in the popular imagination tend to romanticize the experience of grace by characterizing it too exclusively as a meaningful, one-on-one relationship.

A theology of grace as transmuted experience and social process corrects any romanticizing tendencies latent in a theology of grace as interpersonal encounter by discovering in the simultaneous communion of all three divine persons the ultimate pattern for the graced transmutation of human experience. It therefore conceives the dynamics of grace as a complex social process in which individual I-Thou encounters may occur but without exhausting the human experience of graced transformation in God. The social process that mediates transformation in faith enjoys complexities that go beyond meaningful one-on-one relationships. It includes loyalty to one's faith community as such. It demands also not only an encounter with some meaningful other but also prophetic confrontation with the meaningless, the demonic, and the satanic. Finally, besides the fulfillment of an I communing with a Thou, the new paradigm includes in the experience of grace the kenosis of forgiving, atoning love. In atoning love one experiences rejection, not communion.

I myself find the construct of grace sketched in this essay meaningful and theologically suggestive. It interprets my own faith experience and that of the people to whom I minister pastorally. I would hope that others would also find it helpful. It offers a speculative alternative to some of the more popular contemporary paradigms of grace. I would, however, anticipate the greatest interest in and sympthy for the new paradigm among those who have, as I, spent some time studying the North American philosophical tradition. I believe that the paradigm shift I have suggested in these paragraphs--the pursuit of an inculturated Catholic theology in dialogue with classical North American philosophers--holds great promise for re-conceiving other doctrines than the dynamics of grace. And I for one would welcome new insights into the gospel elaborated by other practitioners of the new paradigm.

## Endnotes

[1]Thomas S. Kuhn, **The Structure of Scientific Revolutions** (Chicago: Univ. of Chicago Press, 1970).

[2]Ian G. Barbour, **Myths, Models, and Paradigms: A Comparative Study in Science and Religion** (New York: Harper and Row, 1974),

[3]In the new paradigm I am proposing, the terms "matter" and "spirit" do not function. They are not needed to describe the dynamics of experience. Since both terms are fraught with unacceptable dualistic connotations, I have chosen to designate the third person of the trinity with a term that better approximates the original Hebrew word. "Ruah" in Hebrew designates breathing. The Holy **Ruah** designates the divine breathing, an empowering graced illumination from on high. With time the Holy Breath came to be recognized correctly as divine wisdom, as the mind of God, and as a divine person. I have discussed these matters at greater length in **The Divine Mother: A Trinitarian Theology of the Holy Spirit** (Washington: University Press of America, 1984).

[4]Donald L. Gelpi, S.J., **Experiencing God: A Theology of Human Emergence** (New York: Paulist, 1978).

[5]Alfred North Whitehead, **Process and Reality,** edited by David Ray Griffin and Donald W. Sherburne (New York: Free Press, 1978) 167.

[6]Gelpi, **op. cit.,** 62-97.
[7]**Ibid.,** 178-202.

[8]George T. Montague, S.M., **The Holy Spirit: Growth of a Biblical Tradition** (New York: Paulist, 1976),

[9]Paul Tillich has grasped most clearly the consequences of characterizing God as the infinite and absolutely mysterious horizon of human transcendence. Tillich finds it inconceivable that such a God could in fact be revealed in space and time. Cf. Paul Tillich, **Systematic Theology** (Chicago: Univ. of Chicago, 1967).

[10]I have developed these insights in greater detail in **The Divine Mother: A Trinitarian Theology of the Holy Spirit.**

[11]Gelpi, **Experiencing God,** 205-255; **Charism and Sacrament: A Theology of Christian Conversion** (New York: Paulist, 1976) 9-110.
[12]Gelpi, **Experiencing God,** 259-323; **Charism and Sacrament,** 168-171.
[13]Gelpi, **Charism and Sacrament,** 27-61.

# Thematic Grace vs. Transmuting Grace:
## Two Spiritual Paths

Not long ago I was attempting to convince a student of the practical importance of conceding to human beings the capacity to attain naturally to affective, intellectual, and moral conversion. I argued that any other position failed to take into account the complexities of the conversion process. The student and I shared the same approximate age. An ordained priest, he had spent many years in the apostolate before coming to Berkeley, California for theological "retooling" (or "refooling," as one of his fellow students wryly described the process of updating). My interlocutor, however, was not to be "refooled" easily. He resisted my empassioned defense of natural conversion. "How," he argued, "can natural conversion occur when pure nature does not exist in the concrete?".

At his words I could not help but smile wistfully. When I was discovering theology in the sixties, the denial that pure nature as such exists in the concrete had been hailed by American liberals as an exciting, revolutionary idea imported from the European continent. Conservatives, however, sniffed suspiciously at the notion and grumbled that it smacked of heresy. In one of its formulations the theological repudiation of the concept of pure nature had in fact come within an ace of being condemned as such by the Holy Office. Now this same theory was being cited to me by one of my own students as a self-evident truth that reduced my own hypotheses to manifest absurdity. "Thus," I mused, "fares every revolution. Yesterday's breakthrough quickly hardens into today's vested interest."

For a variety of historical reasons the denial that "pure human nature" exists in the concrete implies a particular psychological and theological approach to the understanding of the relationship between nature and grace. In the paragraphs which follow I will call the approach in question a theology of thematic grace. The theologians who defend the position to which I refer do not use my term "thematic grace," but it describes the position they espouse. The thinkers in question defend the hypothesis that every human individual longs spontaneously for the beatific vision. This longing however remains implicit and unthematic until it is explicitated and thematized by supernatural faith.

St. Teresa of Avila prized theological competence in her spiritual directors. That wise and holy lady knew that a healthy spirituality must be rooted in sound doctrine. I myself for many years found a theology of thematic grace attractive, until both personal and pastoral experience as well as reflection on its presuppositions convinced me of its invalidity. In the present essay I will try to explain why I abandoned a theory of thematic grace for an understanding of grace as ongoing and radical transmutation. And I will suggest that these two doctrines lead to different approaches to spiritual growth and development.

My reflections divide into four sections. In the first I will review as briefly and as clearly as I can the emergence and popularization of the notion of thematic grace. In section II, I will argue that despite an initial attractiveness, the idea of thematic grace finally rests on a fallacious conception of human nature. In section III, I will argue that a valid insight into human existence demands both that we rehabilitate theologically the notion of human nature and that we replace the notion of thematic grace with an understanding of grace as ongoing, radical transmutation. Finally, in the fourth section I will attempt to explore the practical consequences of my argument for an understanding of Christian spirituality.

**(I)**

Joseph Maréchal, S.J. (1878-1944) laid the speculative foundations for a modern theory of thematic grace. A philosopher rather than a theologian Maréchal attempted to reply systematically to the contention of Immanuel Kant that the idea of God is an empty, unverifiable conception.

Maréchal reached the height of his speculative career at a difficult time for Catholic intellectuals. Between 1922 and 1923 he published the first three volumes of his monumental five volume work **Le Point de Départ de la Metaphysique (The Starting Point of Metaphysics)**. At the time witch-hunts for modernists had subsided. But conservative integralists still kept a weather eye peeled for deviant speculative innovations. Catholic intellectuals had to submit to the constraints of strict ecclesiastical censorship. Maréchal's sympathetic reading of Kant's philosophy in the third volume of **The Starting Point of Metaphysics** caused alarmed conservatives to label him a "Kantian." They intended the label as a reproach. In the 1920's Kant's works were still listed on the index of forbidden books. And loyal Catholic intellectuals were expected in obedience to Pope Leo XIII's encyclical **Aeterni Patris** to defend some form of Thomism. In the eyes of suspicious integralists Maréchal's Kantian leanings left him open to the charge of heterodoxy.

Maréchal defended himself from this attack by publishing immediately the final volume of his projected five volume work. The fourth would not appear till after his death. But after careful censorship and several revisions the fifth volume saw print three years after the third, in 1926. In it Maréchal argued that a Thomistic theory of knowledge anticipates the problems raised by Kant and demonstrates the invalidity of the Kantian attempt to reduce the idea of God to an empty unverifiable philosophical concept. In Kant's analysis of the a priori structures of knowing, Maréchal argued, the German philosopher had erred by limiting his account of human cognition to an analysis of the relationship between concrete sense images and abstract universal ideas. In the process, Maréchal argued, Kant had overlooked a more fundamental a priori structure of consciousness, a structure which a Thomistic theory of knowledge supplies. For Aquinas had penetrated to the reason why we apply abstract, conceptual labels to the things we see, hear, taste, touch,

68

and smell. We do so in order to form judgments about them. Our judgments grasp reality, being, truth. To the reflective mind, Maréchal believed, the alleged human ability to ask endless questions about things and to make endless judgments about them teaches us that the human intellect of its very nature thirsts inexhaustibly after truth, after reality, after Being itself.

Those who administer IQ tests legitimately question whether the human mind can in fact ask endless questions and endlessly answer them, but Maréchal found ample support for his position in the texts of St. Thomas. His reading of the Angelic Doctor focused on aspects of Aquinas's doctrine that other Thomists had tended to overlook. Maréchal waxed most eloquent whenever he described the faculty of the intellect as a dynamic appetite for Being. In Thomistic psychology Being supplies the spiritual faculty of the intellect with its formal object. Maréchal portrayed this relation of the intellect to Being in dramatic terms. He saw the human mind as a driving appetite for Being, restlessly unable to find satisfaction in the judgmental grasp of any particular, limited, contingent reality. The understanding of this person or that event leaves the human mind unsatisfied, he argued. It spontaneously seeks more knowledge, other insights, other truths. This alleged fact teaches us that when the intellect thirsts for Being, it really thirsts for Absolute Being, for infinite Truth, for God. It yearns moreover not for some empty idea of God but for the living actuality itself. Since, moreover, the intellect provides the will with the objects of spiritual desire, within the spiritual faculties of the intellect and will there wells up naturally an insatiable longing for the divine. That longing is conditioned in the sense that nature of itself lacks the means to fulfill it, but it nevertheless springs from human nature. As a consequence, Maréchal did not hesitate (with the blessing of Aquinas) to discover in every human psyche a natural longing for the beatific vision; and, he noted, natural appetites demand fulfillment, even when that fulfillment is effected through an act of divine grace.[1]

Maréchal's seminal work has helped inspire several influential Catholic theologians. Among them Henri de Lubac, S.J. and Karl Rahner, S.J. have perhaps built most effectively on his insights in order to develop and popularize their particular theologies of thematic grace.

De Lubac marshaled his encyclopedic grasp of the Christian theological tradition in order to lend sanction to Thomistic belief in a natural desire for the beatific vision. But his thought advanced significantly beyond that of Maréchal's in its systematic assault on the concept of "pure nature." In the concrete we live, de Lubac argued, in a world transformed by grace. Theologians need not therefore construct hypotheses about the way things might have been arranged had the order of grace never existed. Rather, they must give an account of the world as it actually exists in its concrete graced condition. Moreover he rejected any attempt to conceive the order of grace as merely reproducing at a supernatural level powers and operations already present in human nature. Rather the spiritual dimension of human nature must be so conceived that by its very essence it opens onto the divine. He insisted on the continuity between the natural and the supernatural order: "Grace perfects nature." He believed that the gratuity of divine grace was sufficiently preserved if one holds that God in creating each individual assigns it a supernatural end. In impressing a supernatural destiny upon the human spirit (however that might occur) God elevates it to a purpose and a fulfillment that exceeds its natural powers.

De Lubac conceded the paradox of conceiving human nature as naturally destined to a supernatural end, but he believed that the infinite horizon of the intellect and will sets human nature apart from sub-human creatures. It instills in the human spirit a natural desire for union with God as the only reality that can satisfy the human spirit's infinite longing for truth and goodness. Since this union can be accomplished only through the action of divine grace, the soul's capacity for union should be characterized as obediential: at no point can human nature claim grace as something owed to it. Moreover, the desire for divine union can be fulfilled only by supernatural means.

Deprived of the light of revelation and left to its own devices, the human spirit will, de Lubac believed, overlook its mysterious and spontaneous longing for God. The idea of a natural longing for a supernatural fulfillment also baffles common sense, which seeks to deny it. Only the person of faith, he insisted, recognizes that: "The offer of grace expresses in the realm of moral liberty the same act of divine origin which the summons to the supernatural expresses in the ontological realm."[2]

Karl Rahner's theory of thematic grace differs from de Lubac's both in details and in complexity. A subtle and nuanced thinker Rahner has absorbed theological influences from a variety of sources, but his Marechalian roots show themselves both in his method and in the metaphysics of knowledge which he espouses.

Like Maréchal Rahner's thought seeks to blend Kantian transcendental method with a neo-Thomistic metaphysics and theory of knowledge. Rahner, however, advances beyond Maréchal in his concern with the theological implications of a Thomistic metaphysical psychology. Not content to seek for the conditions for the possibility of knowing in general, Rahner extends transcendental method into the realm of Christian belief. He seeks to grasp the conditions for the possibility of faith in Christian revelation. Among those conditions, however, he numbers a metaphysics of knowledge reminiscent of Maréchal's. Moreover, he believes that that metaphysics explains and unifies every human speculative enterprise including the enterprise of theology.

Rahner characterizes the human person as a "spirit in the world." The human spirit by the spontaneous dynamism of both intellect and will stands from the first moment of its existence oriented toward Being. This spontaneous orientation expresses the essence of spirit and endows it with a "transcendental" horizon which includes the world-transcending reality of God. The human spirit also exists in the world because, being embodied, it becomes conscious of its transcendental dimension through interaction with sensible, spatio-temporal realities. These supply the words, the categories that the human spirit needs in order to reach explicit self-awareness. Of its very nature therefore the human spirit lives in dynamic openness to a God whose historical words and deeds of self-revelation provide humans with the categories they need to grasp their inbuilt, a priori openness to the infinite, mysterious, and ultimately ineffable reality of God.

Rahner's endorsement of the main lines of a Thomistic theory of knowledge becomes even more apparent when he identifies the transcendent horizon of spiritual self-awareness, the human mind's dynamic "pre-apprehension of Being," with the formal object of the faculty called the "agent intellect." This faculty, or power of the soul, supposedly mediates between the transcendental and the categorical dimensions of the human spirit. In its dynamic pre-apprehension of any and every reality, the agent intellect endows the human spirit with an abiding essential openness to both created and uncreated being. At the same time by abstracting from sensory and imaginative awareness the concepts the mind needs to interpret itself and its world, the agent intellect provides the human spirit with the categories it needs to reach explicit self-awareness to thematize it's longing for God.3

Rahner's endorsement and elaboration of a Maréchalian metaphysics of knowledges helps provide speculative warranty for his theology of thematic grace, but he exhibits more concern than de Lubac to qualify Maréchal's belief in a natural human desire for the beatific vision. Maréchal, Rahner suggests, failed to make it sufficiently clear that the beatific vision is not owed to human nature as such. Without proper theological qualification, any attempt to speak of a natural desire for a supernatural reality could seem to call into question the gratuity of divine grace, for it fails to distinguish adequately the gratuity of creation from that of redemption. In other words it could seem to confound God's free gift of natural existence with His free gift of supernatural life.

Because the beatific vision is a work of supernatural grace, Rahner holds that the longing for it present in the spiritual faculties of intellect and will must also result from the supernatural gracing of each individual. Every human individual from the first moment of existence lives, therefore, in a "supernatural existential." That is to say, grace so transforms the essential dynamic structure of spirit that it longs spontaneously not only for God but for the knowledge of Christ that culminates in the beatific vision. As a consequence, every human being will hear the word of God spoken in Jesus either as the explicitation of its spontaneous longing for a triune, incarnate God or as a silence. Moreover, because this graced expansion of the formal object of the spiritual faculties of intellect and will is built (somehow) a priori into the psyche, a direct experience of pure human nature no longer lies within the realm of human possibility. Humans can know themselves consciously only as graced.

Rahner's metaphysics of knowledge and the theology of thematic grace it inspires colors the rest of his theology in significant ways. He characterizes guilt and sin as a denial of one's a priori orientation to God and to Christ. Being a priori, God's implicit and unthematized self-communication to humans takes place (as an offer) before it is accepted or rejected. Faith thematizes spirit's supernaturally elevated transcendentality. In other words, the historical revelation of God in Christ supplies a posteriori the categories that allow us to interpret the a priori gracing of our experience. Belief in a supernatural existential also color's Rahner's theology of mystery. Our graced pre-apprehension of God orients us to the Christian mystery as such, a mystery that infinitely transcends its particular categorial interpretations and expressions. The supernatural existential also transforms into anonymous Christians all of those non-Chiristians who follow the spontaneous graced dynamisms of spirit, for anonymous Christians on conversion to Christianity discover the categories they need in order to thematize the longing for Christ that had previously motivated their spiritual quest.4

Rahner offers the subtlest, and most nuanced account of the dynamics of thematic grace. As a consequence his theory has had considerable impact. It has been popularized in Juan Luis Segundo's four volume catechetical work **A Theology for the Artisans of a New Humanity.**5 It has also influenced the liberation theology of Gustavo Gutierrez.6 As my student's reaction suggests, it is regarded as self-evident by many theologically informed, liberal Catholics.

The reflective reader will by now have recognized that a theology of thematic grace does not float in a speculative vacuum. It rests on specific philosophical and methodological presuppositions. It presupposes the truth and adequacy of a Marechalian metaphysics of knowledge and of Thomistic faculty psychology. Indeed, in its current formulations, it stands or falls with both.

## (II)

For many years I found a theology of thematic grace attractive. It avoided the extrinsicism of the old scholastic text books which spoke of nature and grace as two parallel but otherwise seemingly unrelated realities. A theology of thematic grace appealed to experience: it invited individuals to reflect on their personal experience and judge whether or not they discovered there the dynamisms which a theology of thematic grace described. By treating all people of good will as anonymous Christians, it seemed to establish an atmosphere of religious tolerance that boded well for ecumenical dialogue not only among Christians but among world religions as well.

With time, however, both personal reflection and pastoral experience have caused me to abandon this particular theory of grace as demonstrably invalid and as spiritually and pastorally misleading. I would like to explain why.

In its present formulation a theology of thematic grace presupposes the adequacy of Kantian transcendental method. Maréchal used Kant's method in order to refute Kant himself and to elaborate the metaphysics of knowledge that gives a theology of thematic grace its present speculative warranty. De Lubac presupposed the basic validity of Marechal's position. And Rahner extends transcendental method into the realm of theology by searching for the conditions for the possibility of Christian revelation.[7]

Unfortunately for a theology of thematic grace, however, the inadequacy of Kantian transcendental method has been demonstrated philosophically. Here the reader will pardon a few brief technical observations. One cannot, however, evaluate a theology of thematic grace without examining the philosophical ideas that nourish and enliven it and give it its warranty.

Charles Sanders Peirce (1839-1914) can, I believe, lay claim to being one of the greatest philosophical minds the United States has produced. As a young man he read Kant's **Critique of Pure Reason** every day for several hours until by his own testimony he could recite long sections of it by heart. He discontinued the practice when he became convinced of the invalidity of Kant's logic and method.[8]

Transcendental method seeks through a process of personal reflection on oneself to grasp the conditions for the possibility of knowledge, morality, and esthetic judgment. Peirce's studies in logic convinced him, however, that Kant's own account of how the human mind works remains seriously flawed. Kant, Peirce contended, had assumed that there is only kind of inference, or argument: namely, deduction. A professional logician, Peirce had demonstrated to his own satisfaction that there are three kinds of inference, or argument: abductive (or hypothetical) inference, deductive (or predictive) inference, and inductive inference (or the verification or falsification of a deductively clarified hypothesis).

In other words, if the human mind is to explain any reality it must on the basis of limited data formulate a fallible hypothetical account of why the reality in question behaves the way it does. It must then understand the predictable consequences of the explanation it proposes. Finally, it must show that its predictions obtain in reality.

For example, when Charles Darwin set sail on the Beagle he did not intend to formulate the theory of evolution, but as he amassed more and more biological data, he became convinced that natural selection accounts for the origin of species. That is to say, he proposed evolution through natural selection as a hypothetical explanation of how species originate. He did not publish his theory for years partly because he knew that in order to justify it he had to show that it explained the origin of every biological species. The ability of natural selection to explain the origin of all species remains disputed to this day because the evidence that Darwin predicted deductively would materialize sometimes failed to do so.

I will spare the reader the details of Peirce's theory of logic. But I regard his position as demonstrably sound. If so, however, those who assert that they have proven **anything** by the use of transcendental method make an inflated and unverifiable logical claim. One cannot deduce a priori the universal structure of the human mind by the simple expedient of reflecting on one's own thought processes. One can only formulate a hypothesis about the way the human mind may be expected to work, an hypothesis based on extremely limited data, an hypothesis that may or may not be true.

As we have already seen, a theology of thematic grace in its present formulation stands or falls not only with the validity of transcendental method but also with the truth or falsity of Thomistic faculty psychology. Unfortunately, however, the proposition that Thomistic faculty psychology offers a true and valid account of the way the human mind actually works cannot be sustained speculatively. It suffers from internal contradictions, and it fails to interpret human cognitive behavior as it occurs in the concrete. Let us reflect on these two deficiencies in turn.

Years ago I was weaned philosophically on Missouri Valley Thomism, a systematic restatement of Gilsonian Thomism popularized by members of the graduate faculty of St. Louis University. They produced several philosophical text books widely used in Catholic circles in the fifties. Missouri Valley Thomism held the methods of transcendental Thomists suspect. In its best formulations it sought to reconcile Thomistic philosophy with the methods and results of positive science, and it showed greater concern than most transcendental Thomists for treating the philosophy of St. Thomas as a system. Study of a speculative system as a system alerts one to the points at which the system breaks down. A Thomistic account of human cognition breaks down at two significant points. It cannot explain the origin of the faculties or powers of the soul; nor can it explain the origins of intellectual knowledge.

Thomistic psychology holds that the human person is endowed with certain powers, or faculties, of operation and that the scope of these faculties is limited by each one's formal object. The formal object of a power includes not only the kinds of reality with which the faculty deals but the aspect under which the faculty in question attains those objects. For example, the faculty of sight is said to grasp physical objects as colored. The intellect, however, is said to grasp the same reality as being.

In a Thomistic universe, every created substance from a mineral to a person acts through the faculties that modify it accidentally. The faculties produce and explain particular activities like moving, sensing, imagining, thinking, willing. What produces and explains the faculties themselves? The substance endowed with the faculties must. But how can a substance produce its own powers of operation when it needs them to operate in the first place? To this question Thomistic psychology offers no adequate answer. St. Thomas says the faculties are produced by the substance through a process of "natural resultance."9 Contentment with such purely verbal solutions to speculative problems contributed in no small measure to the demise of medieval scholasticism.

A second contradiction haunts a Thomistic theory of knowledge. It suffers from operational dualism. Dualistic interpretations of the world distinguish conceptually two interrelated realities, but they do so in such a way that their relationship to one another ceases to make sense. Platonic philosophy, for example, distinguished the human soul from the human body, but it conceived them as two distinct substances, one material, the other spiritual. Forever thereafter Platonists could no longer explain how a single unified human person resulted from the accidental linkage of two essentially different kinds of substance.

Aquinas with help from Aristotle recognized the folly of such substantial dualism and held that the human soul is not a spiritual substance in its own right but the form of the human body. In order, however, to preserve the spirituality and immortality of the soul, he also argued that it possesses purely spiritual faculties, namely the intellect and will. He also held that all human knowledge originates in the senses. As a consequence, he found himself hard pressed to explain the very origin of intellectual knowledge, for if human knowledge originates in the senses they must somehow move the intellect to act. But in Thomistic psychology the senses are essentially oriented by their formal object to material, not to spiritual realities. Left to themselves they cannot move the intellect any more than they can have an impact on a purely spiritual reality like God or a Thomistic angel.

In order to find a way out of this impasse Aquinas postulated the presence in the human spirit of two intellects, one active the other passive. The active intellect, he suggested, uses the image present in the imagination in order to impress on the passive intellect the intelligible species that allows it to form abstract concepts about concrete, material, sensible realities. Of itself the image in the imagination, being sensible and bound to matter, could never have such a spiritual effect, but it acquires this power when it is used by the agent intellect. The agent intellect being spiritual uses the sensible phantasm to produce a spiritual effect, just as a pencil, which in and of itself makes no intelligible marks like words, acquires the power to do so when it is used by a human mind. This analogy between the pencil and the image in the imagination limps, of course; for a pencil writes on another material reality like paper, whereas the sensible image is supposed to produce a purely spiritual effect on a purely spiritual reality, namely, on the passive intellect. One might as well speak of one angel using a slide projector to project not an image but an idea onto another angel. In other words, having avoided substantial dualism, a Thomistic theory of knowledge falls victim to operational dualism. Having divided the powers of the soul into spiritual and material faculties, it can no longer explain the derivation of intellectual from sensory knowledge.

All of this might sound far from a theology of thematic grace, except for the fact that in its present formulation Thomistic faculty psychology validates that theology. The human pre-apprehension of being and of God results in such a theology from the formal object of the human intellect, and in Rahner's theory from the formal object of the agent intellect specifically. That formal object defines the "horizon" of human knowing. It orients us essentially to God. It explains the natural desire for the beatific vision celebrated by Maréchal and de Lubac. In Rahner's thought the supernatural existential mysteriously expands the formal object of intellect and will by allegedly transforming it into a longing for Christ and the vision of God.

Contemporary psychology has long since abandoned Thomistic faculty psychology as unverifiable. From Rahner's methodological standpoint this abandonment amounts to a benighted lapse from consciousness of the transcendental to subsistence in the merely categorical, but until he or one of his disciples can offer a better validation of transcendental method than he has done heretofore or provide convincing evidence of the truth of faculty psychology, the behavioral evidence we possess lies with the psychologists.

Let us put the matter succinctly, a theology of thematic grace argues to the human spirit's openness to the infinite "metaphysically" and "a priori." If Peirce's theory of inference holds (and I for one believe that it does), then metaphysics can make no privileged speculative claims. A priori arguments offer only unverified hypotheses. As a consequence, the hypotheses of metaphysical psychology labor under the same fallibility as scientific ones and require similiar validation. By the same token hypotheses about the dynamic structure of the human mind require validation in human cognitive behavior. Alas, however, for a theology of thematic grace, human behavior provides no evidence for affirming the presence in any given individual either of an insatiable desire to grow intellectually or of an orientation toward infinite Being.

Psychological testing discovers in the human psyche not an insatiable appetite for being and for truth but a spontaneous and initially innocent egocentrism that is transformed through habit and through fear into an ego inertia that resists challenge and transformation. Careful study of human cognitive behavior discovers no other tendencies in the human psyche than those acquired in the course of a lifetime. In order to be oriented to the finite idea "Being as such" one needs the metaphysical education of a Rahner. Moreover, judged in the light of human cognitive activity the human intellect enjoys no infinite horizon but only a finite and expandable one. Humans enjoy only limited intellectual interests. They come quickly to an end of the questions they can ask and even more quickly to an end of those they can answer. They organize the limited solid information they possess into equally limited frames of reference. They can develop finite religious interests and ask finite religious questions. But they can and do elect not to do so.

Here developmental psychology offers some especially enlightening information. Jean Piaget, the dean of developmental psychologists, has argued persuasively that philosophers of knowledge can never agree because they never take the time to test their hypotheses against the way human beings actually think.10 His studies of cognitive development in children together with those of Lawrence Kohlberg, James Fowler, and other developmentalists give solid evidence for believing that the human mind advances in its thinking from one limited frame of reference to another. Until the age of approximately eighteen months children live at a sensory-motor level. They cannot even imagine a world. Until the age of eleven they cannot think abstractly. Once the capacity to think abstractly emerges, the mind joins similiar propositions together to form identifiable frames of reference: common sense, mathematics, positive science, philosophy, theology. All these frames of reference open only a limited window on the world.11 In other words, the "horizon" of the human mind from birth to death remains irreducibly finite. When healthy the human intellect seeks to expand its horizon on the world. But such expansion may or may not occur.

Nor can we assume that every human intellect enjoys essentially the same cognitive tendencies as every other. The Myers-Briggs test has provided some experimental validation of Jungian personality theory. That theory, however, distinguishes eight major psychological types with correspondingly different ways of thinking.12 In point of fact, transcendental method in its preoccupation with personal reflection on one's own cognitive structures appeals spontaneously to introverts, and with the spontaneous egotism that characterizes the finite human intellect, those who ply transcendental method tend to assume (incorrectly) that everyone thinks exactly as they do.

The fundamental finitude of the human mind also calls into question Karl Rahner's theological explanation of the human experience of mystery. That humans can and do encounter mystery in the course of their lives cannot be seriously contested. But because Rahner fallaciously assumes that transcendental method gives him privileged access to the dynamic structure of the human psyche and because he interprets that structure in categories derived from Thomistic faculty psychology, he locates openness to mystery in the powers of the spirit, and especially in the intellectual preapprehension of Being as such. A more psychologically plausible account of the experience of mystery locates it not in the intellect, finite as it actually is, but in imaginative and appreciative forms of knowing. If anything, intellectual activity dissipates the human sense of mystery. The more rational explanations the human mind possesses, the more diminished its sense of the mysterious. In point of fact we discover mystery at the precise moment when our rational explanations break down, when we come to an end of what our finite intellect can account for. Then we are thrown back on vaguer feeling, on myth, intuition, imagination, and ritual in order to deal with ourselves and our world. But both rational experiences of intelligible explanation and mythic and ritual explorations into mystery transpire within finite, human frames of reference.

Another difficulty accrues to the attempt of a theology of thematic grace to identify God with the supposedly infinite horizon of the human intellect. Paul Tillich has stated it best. Like Rahner he believed that the human spirit enjoys an essential orientation to infinite Being. Like Rahner he interpreted that orientation as an orientation to God. Tillich, however, argues quite correctly that if the very reality of God functions as the horizon of the human intellect, then that reality can never be expressed in space and time, for the horizon of the intellect being infinite can never be grasped in finite, created categories or expressed by finite, created beings. For Tillich therefore the divine Being subsists in a realm infinitely removed from any finite, created reality. Finite, created religious symbols can then only point toward the infinite, transcendent, divine horizon of the human spirit, much as an individual can stand on the Pacific shore and point toward the western horizon. The horizon itself is never seen, never grasped as such; only things within the horizon are. As a consequence Tillich found the incarnation of a divine person unthinkable. Having denied the divinity of Jesus, Tillich also found no theological justification for belief in a triune God. Rahner defends both the incarnation and trinitarian belief. But he has never explained satisfactorily how his identification of God with the horizon of the human spirit avoids the logic of Tillich's argument.13

I have been trying to explain some of the speculative motives that caused me to abandon a theology of thematic grace. I have pastoral motives as well.

A theology of thematic grace claims to interpret human religious experience, even though it argues to the dynamic structure of that experience a priori. It suggests that the Christian convert will experience faith in Christ as the conscious explicitation of an implicit orientation to God and to Christ present within the psyche prior to conversion. The converts I have dealt with have experienced nothing of the kind. They describe their conversion experience not in Maréchelian or Rahnerian categories but in terms reminiscent of Johanthan Edwards. They speak of a new and wholly different sense of God, of themselves, of the world. They testify to a new taste for spiritual things. They speak of transformation in the Spirit, of a new creation which conversion effects, of its revolutionary and transforming consequences.14

Nor can we verify universally the presence of the supernatural existential in every human person. If, as Rahner contends, the supernatural existential gives dynamic structure to every human psyche, then every time one transcends categorical thinking and raises to thematic consciousness the transcendental "horizon" of the intellect, one will discover there a longing not only for God but for Christ. Oriental mysticism ambitions just such a transcategorical thematization of the horizon of knowing. Unfortunately, however, for a theology of the supernatural existential, one does not find at the end of every mystical quest either a longing for God or a desire to know Christ. Some forms of oriental mysticism are entirely compatible with an atheistic world view. Moreover, careful study of mystical experience suggests that the longing for God and for Christ will terminate the mystical quest only if it motivated it from the start. Instead of being built a priori into the psyche, graced longing for God and for Christ is conditioned upon faith.15 In other words, even though a theology of thematic grace appeals to religious experience, when the chips are down, it fails finally to interpret the very experience to which it appeals.

I have also found that a theology of thematic grace finally creates more confusion than mutual understanding in ecumenical exchanges, for it fallaciously assumes that all people relate to God in essentially the same way. As a consequence, a theology of thematic grace fails to credit sufficiently the incredible variety of human and religious experience. It betrays well meaning Christians into projecting into the unconverted, attitudes which result only from converted faith in God. Belief in the supernatural existential also leads the same well intentioned Christians to project into the religious experience of non-Christians elements that derive specifically from a Christian conversion experience. In other words, in ecumenical exchanges a theology of thematic grace all but ensures mutual misunderstanding. Here I in no way wish to deny analogies among the religious experiences of Christians and non-Christians, but I resist facile generalizations about their essential likeness as methodologically unjustified. I would insist that similarities be validated case by case.

Finally, I have found that a theology of thematic grace tends to mute the kergymatic voice of the Church. One cannot help but wonder if both Jesus in His ministry and Peter on Pentecost would have preached as effectively as they did had they summoned their respective audiences not to repent and believe the good news but to thematize the a priori orientation to God and to Christ bult into their agent intellects. Moreover, I have found that those who espouse a theology of thematic grace often feel less need to proclaim the gospel at all. They frequently prefer to trust in the good will of the unconverted and in the implicitly graced character of their choices.

If the preceding objections can survive scrutiny, they point to the need for a different understanding of human nature than the one which gives speculative warranty to a theology of thematic grace. They also demand that our theological interpretation of the way human nature comes to be graced be correspondingly revised. To this double problem we turn in the section which follows.

## (III)

A brief summary of the argument up to this point may cast light on its subsequent course. We are examining two contrasting approaches to the understanding of the relationship between nature and grace: a theology of thematic grace and a theology of grace as radical transmutation. We have examined in some detail the first of these two theological approaches. A theology of thematic grace asserts that supernatural faith thematizes, or raises to explicit consciousness, an impulse to God built a priori into the human psyche. That impulse is characterized either as a natural desire for the beatific vision or as a supernatural existential which transforms the essential, natural orientation of the human intellect and will toward Being and toward God into a supernatural longing for the fullness of grace revealed to us in Christ.

We have traced the emergence, development, and popularization of a theology of thematic grace. We have found that it builds on a very shaky philosophical foundation. It fallaciously assumes the adequacy of Kant's transcendental method to construct a metaphysics of knowledge despite the fact that transcendental method of itself yields at best an unverified hypothesis about the structure of reality and about the way the human mind actually operates. A theology of thematic grace also fallaciously assumes that Thomistic faculty psychology offers a valid account of both human nature and the human psyche. Indeed, the very idea of thematic grace in the formulations we have examined stands or falls with the truth of faculty theory and with its claim that the finite human mind enjoys a virtually infinite horizon that orients it to Being as such. This alleged "essential orientation" of the human intellect and will to infinite Being and therefore (implicitly) to God endows belief in a natural desire for the beatific vision with speculative warranty. Faculty psychology also grounds belief in the supernatural existential which expands and elevates to a supernatural level the agent intellect's pre-conceptual grasp of Being.

As we have seen, however, the human mind in its concrete operations gives no evidence of enjoying the virtual infinity which a theology of thematic grace attributes to it. It manifests no desires or impulses beyond those limited ones it has acquired in the course of its finite history. It's "horizon" remains from birth to death irreducibly finite. In point of fact as the human mind matures it becomes increasingly focused on limited realms of value: sensations, intuition, logical thought, or feeling. In other words, within the limited span of operations and tendencies that structure it, ego inertia leads the human mind to specialize in certain evaluative skills and to neglect others. Finitude, spontaneous and initially innocent egocentric interests, and inertia characterize the spontaneous operations of the human mind rather than an insatiable longing for truth, reality, and goodness. The mind's fear, both conscious and unconscious, and its fallibility ensure that its relationship to Being always suffers from partiality and haphazardness.

Moreover, by postulating the same essential religious dynamisms in all human minds, a theology of thematic grace fails to do justice to the varieties of religious and mystical experience. It offers no adequate account for the sense of discontinuity which marks an experience of radical conversion, the feeling of being not only turned around but transformed into a new kind of person. By lulling believers into the naive assumption that everyone is oriented a priori to God and to Christ, a theology of thematic grace mutes the kerygmatic voice of the Church and tends to transform ecumenical dialogue into an exercise in mutual misunderstanding.

These deficiencies in a theology of thematic grace suggest the need to search for a viable theological alternative. A theology of grace as radical transmutation attempts to offer such an alternative. Because I espouse a theology of transmuting grace I will in the paragraphs which follow formulate it in terms that I find personally meaningful. My position develops out of the pioneering work of Bernard Lonergan, and it converges at significant points with the thought of Robert Doran, Walter Conn, and James Loder.

The two theological positions we are examining agree at several points. And clarity suggests that we identify points of agreement before we proceed to contrast the two. Both agree that the concepts "nature" and "grace" imply one another in a theological context; hence, a modification of one's understanding of either term will demand a corresponding alteration of the other. Both positions concede that the concrete world in which we live has been changed through the action of divine grace. Both positions appeal to human experience. Both reject an artificial extrinsicism in describing the relationship between nature and grace and hold that grace perfects nature, though they differ in their understanding of how this occurs. Both positions agree that grace is not owed to human nature, that the attainment of a supernatural end demands supernatural means, and that the experience of faith in this life begins a process of gracious illumination that culminates in the beatific vision.

How then do these two theologies of grace differ? They espouse different methods. They conceive human nature differently. They therefore offer contrasting interpretations of the way nature and grace relate to one another. Let us explore these three differences in turn.

a) **Method.** A theology of grace as radical transmutation espouses a foundational method. It borrows the term from the work of Bernard Lonergan but departs from Lonergan's own theological method at a significant point. In what then does foundational theology consist? Moreover, how does a theology of grace as radical transmutation alter Lonergan's own methodological presuppositions?

Foundational theology seeks to elaborate a strictly normative theory of conversion. Normative thinking attempts to explain the way things other than the thinker ought to be expected to behave. Strictly normative thinking looks to the thinker's own personal behavior. It measures the responsibility or irresponsibility of human evaluations and decisions against ideals and principles that have been personally espoused and appropriated as affectively, intellectually, morally, or religiously binding. In other words foundational theology ambitions a systematic account of healthy emotional development, of intellectual development based on sound psychological, logical, and methodological principles, of moral development that conforms to sound ethical rules and ideals, and of authentic religious growth.

Foundational theology numbers fifth among eight functional theological specialties. Functional theological specialties differ from one another in the kinds of questions each asks and in the operational procedures each employs to reach its conclusions. The first four specialties--research, interpretation, history, and dialectics--ambition the systematic retrieval of a particular religious and cultural tradition. The research theologian gathers the data relevant to the resolution of religious questions by archeological research, the editing of critical texts, or the compiling of dictionaries and similar tools employed by theologians. Interpretation attempts to explain to contemporary religionists the meaning of the data amassed by theological research. Historical theology tells the story of religious communities and of the cultures in which they develop on the basis of a sound interpretation of research data revelant to that story. Dialectical theology probes the conflicts that emerge in the history of any religious community and assesses the relative adequacy of their motives.

Foundational theology ranks fifth among the theological specialties because it needs the results of the first four in order to advance its own insights, for any sound theology of conversion must take into account the history of the religious community in which it occurs, the conflicting attitudes, beliefs, and commitments that divide that community, and the meaning of its sacred texts and artifacts. Divisions in any community of faith always betrays the presence of religious inauthenticity and the absence of conversion at some level. A strictly normative theory of conversion attempts to identify troublesome inauthenticities and to overcome them.[16]

A theology of grace as radical transmutation invokes Lonergan's theory of functional specialties. It attempts to practice foundational theology. It stands within an experience of conversion and attempts to assess the validity or invalidity, the adequacy or the inadequacy of the motives that give it shape. A theology of grace as radical transmutation departs, however, from Lonergan's thought at an important point. Like the proponents of thematic grace, Lonergan defends transcendental method and believes that it provides him with an irreformable starting point for all human speculation. As we have already seen, however, transcendental method offers only a fallible and therefore revisable hypothesis about the structure of reality and the dynamics of human cognition. As a consequence, a theology of grace as radical transmutation eschews every attempt to construct a metaphysics of knowledge based on transcendental method and recognizes instead the need to measure any proposition concerning reality in general and human nature in particular systematically against the behavior of both. By the same token, a theology of grace as radical transmutation demands that foundational theory itself advance by testing the truth or falsity of religious propositions and the adequacy or inadequacy of religious frames of reference against religiously significant events.17

b) **Human Nature.** As we have seen, a theology of thematic grace conceives of human nature as a fixed essence present in every human individual. It asserts that every human intellect and will enjoys a fixed orientation to Being and to God that expresses those faculties' innate spiritual essence. Since grace corresponds to these essentially predetermined psychic dynamisms, consistency demands that grace itself be similarly conceived. Accordingly the supernatural existential is described as an essential re-orientation of the natural dynamisms of spirit that transcends anything that humanity can conceive or desire of its own essence or nature. The supernatural existential begets in the soul a new essential orientation, a graced longing not only for God but for Christ and for the fulfillment of supernatural faith in the beatific vision.

A theology of grace as radical transmutation conceives of human nature very differently. Instead of describing the human in dated, essentialistic terms derived from medieval scholasticism, it takes a page from process theory and speaks of human beings as developing experiences. It defines experience as a process made up of three identifiable variables: evaluations, interactions, and tendencies.

The evaluations that shape human experience include: (1) sense qualities (like colors, tastes, smells, touches, sounds, visceral and kinetic feeling, pleasure, pain). (2) affective impulses (like complacency, desire, affection, friendship, love, rage, fear, guilt). (3) the images that structure intuitive perceptions (whether remembered, constructed, or archetypal); and (4) the abstract concepts that function in the three forms of logical inference. Interactions punctuate human evaluative responses as the decisive impact of environmental forces impinges on human experience and elicits from humans a more or less adequately motivated decisive response. Things bump into us, and we bump back. The tendencies that shape experience consist of the developing set of finite habits that comprise any given human self. These tendencies result from the way in which each self interacts with his or her environment. Habits endow experience with continuity, for they beget routine behavior, the inclination to act in predictable and characteristic ways. Habits also ensure that the self I am in process of becoming today develops in continuity with the self I was yesterday, the day before, and all the yesterdays of my life, for habits perdure. The new habits I learn today must be integrated into the finite set of habitual tendencies I possessed yesterday.

Although the conception of human nature which grounds a theology of thematic grace acknowledges the role of habit in the development of the human person, it conceives of those habits as accidental modifications of stable, essential tendencies built a priori into human nature and grasped in a privileged metaphysical insight by transcendental method. A theology of grace as radical transmutation, as we have just seen, renounces the claims of transcendental method as logically and methodologically unjustifiable; and it is content instead to discover in each developing human self only those tendencies which can be verified in human behavior. In other words, in an experiential construct of human nature, no fixed essential dynamisms lie beneath the habitual tendencies acquired in the course of a lifetime. Instead those acquired tendencies constitute each emerging human self.

Experience grows through transmutation. Transmutation occurs every time a novel evaluation, interaction, or tendency is integrated into a developing experience in such a way as to change its constitutive relational structure. Every new sensation, every new social interchange, every new meal, every new physical motion, every new commitment, every new act of worship, every new acquired skill adds new complexity to human experience. Like the addition of a new patch of color to a painting it brings into being a new kind of experienced reality by demanding that all the other relationships that comprise experience adjust themselves in order to accomodate the new addition. In an experiential understanding of human nature the dynamisms that structure the human psyche do not then enjoy the fixed essential orientations postulated by faculty psychology and by classical philosophical thought. They evolve as each self defines the character of its orientation toward itself and its world through ongoing interaction with its total environment.

In a theology of thematic grace every human mind of its very essence possesses a virtually infinite horizon, a dynamic appetite for Being and implicitly for God. In an experiential construct of human nature, only those dynamisms structure the human mind which have been acquired in a lifetime of symbolic behavior. Because every human mind begins at a specific moment in space and time, the sum total of the habits that comprise it remains forever finite, even though education and intellectual growth may continue to endow this or that mind with new habitual complexity. **As a consequence, (and here we touch the heart of the matter) in an experiential approach to human nature any given human mind may or may not be oriented dynamically to God.** Rather each self must acquire such an orientation either by fixing its personal beliefs on purely rational motives concerning the reality and nature of God or by responding positively and graciously in faith to some event of divine self-revelation. That revelatory event, however, does more than supply the categories that allow the mind to thematize a longing for the divine it already possesses of its very essence. Rather the revelatory event together with the faith it inspires transmute the psyche by building into it a wholly new habitual orientation toward a self-revealing God. We call such a dynamic reorientation of the self the infusion of supernatural grace. It transmutes experience by endowing it with a new capacity to relate to God both correlative to God's free act of self disclosure and impossible apart from that self-revelation.[17]

Finally, we note that an experiential construct of human nature finds validation in contemporary developmental psychology. Today, however, we stand only at the beginning of the development of developmental psychology. We can anticipate the emergence of other developmental schemes than those already proposed by Eric Erickson, Jean Piaget, Lawrence Kohlberg, James Fowler, and Daniel J. Levinson. But the developmental principle that the healthy human mind can advance from less adequate to more adequate and inclusive (though finite) frames of reference remains a sound one.[18]

c) **Relationship between nature and grace.** An experiential construct of human nature demands the philosophical and theological rehabilitation of the concept of "nature." A theology of thematic grace either demands too much of human nature or fails to do it speculative justice. It demands too much of human nature in speaking of a natural desire for the beatific vision. De Lubac concedes the paradoxical character of such a doctrine. Rahner for his part correctly recognizes that the belief that human nature can in and of itself aspire to a supernatural destiny lapses from paradox into confusion and contradiction. It confuses the gratuity of creation with the gratuity of grace. Rahner's attempt to avoid the same confusion in his own theology of grace causes him however to transform "human nature" into a residual concept. One may, however, question whether reducing the idea of nature to a conceptual residue does it full justice. Rahner holds, as we have seen, that in consequence of the fact that the human spirit's a priori pre-apprehension of Being has been graced by the supernatural existential the direct conscious experience of pure nature no longer lies within the realm of human possibility. Instead what humans are by nature must be inferred by abstracting those experienced realities whose source can be identified as supernatural. Rahner reaches this paradoxical position in consequence of several conflicting motives in his thought. On the one hand, like Maréchal and de Lubac he wishes to discover the desire for God welling up spontaneously within every human spirit. On the other hand, he feels justifiably reluctant to ground that desire in human nature alone. Moreover while he appeals to experience in order to validate the residual character of "human nature," he argues to its inavoidability transcendentally and therefore a priori.[19]

If, however, one actually consults experience instead of arguing a priori to the way it must be structured, one is absolved from the need to degrade human nature to a conceptual residue. We experience nature directly. We experience human nature directly. We do it all the time. We can identify the natural tendencies in human nature by the motives that specify the decisions that give rise to them. As we have seen, within experience evaluations, decisions, and habitual tendencies mutually condition one another. The kinds of decisions we take derive their character from the evaluative responses they terminate. I may act angrily or lovingly, imaginatively or rationally. It all depends on the angry or loving, rational or intuitive character of the personal evaluative stance which my action expresses. My actions determine the kinds of tendencies that make me the particular self I am. They create new habits, reinforce old ones, and interrelate or dissociate existing ones. I act naturally when I respond to created reality and ignore those events that reveal God to me historically. Faith, then, divides natural from gracious responses. I act sinfully when I deliberately thwart what I believe to be God's will for me. Naturally motivated decisions build purely natural tendencies into every human personality, tendencies which can be experienced and named directly and as such. Faith motivated decisions build graced tendencies. Sinful decisions build sinful tendencies.

Grace transmutes and transvalues both natural and sinful tendencies. It transmutes and transvalues sinful tendencies through repentance. It transmutes and transvalues natural tendencies by enhancing them and ordering them to a satisfaction they could never achieve in and of themselves: namely, loving union with a God who has entered human history and reveals himself in faith to those He chooses. In other words, grace perfects nature. But it does so by transmuting it and endowing it with entirely new ways of relating to God. We call the transmutation of human experience in faith created grace. And the fact that created grace transcends anything we can do or experience naturally explains the discontinuity which converts experience on coming to faith. Hope graces the repentant heart by healing it of disordered affections and binding it to a faithful God. Faith graces the human mind by teaching it to acknowledge the saving significance of religious events. Love graces human decisions by ensuring that they are informed by gospel values. The gifts of sanctification (**dona Spiritus Sancti**) ensure ongoing docility to the Holy Spirit in putting on the mind of Jesus. And the charisms of service (**gratiae gratis datae**) bind Christians to one another in a community of faith, of worship, and of mutual service. All these different forms of created grace transmute the natural elements that structure human experience.[20]

The fact that humans can and do respond with purely natural motivations grounds the possibility of experiencing a purely natural conversion at an affective, intellectual, or moral level. I use the term "conversion" in a broader sense than it often popularly enjoys. In popular parlance conversion means the espousal of a particular creed or the decision to join a particular church or sect. By conversion I mean the decision to assume personal responsibility for one's own subsequent growth and development in some area of human experience. An area of experience is delimited by the kinds of tendencies or habits which structure it. Affective, irrational tendencies differ from rational ones. Habits of evaluation differ from habits of decision. In affective conversion I assume personal responsibility for the health of my subsequent irrational, emotional growth. In intellectual conversion I assume responsibility for the truth and falsity, adequacy or inadequacy of my subsequent rational beliefs. In moral conversion I assume responsibility for the ethical character and consequences of my subsequent decisions. In socio-political conversion I assume responsibility not for my own decisions but for influencing in so far as I can the decisions that shape human institutions to just or unjust ends.

I can attain all four forms of conversion for reasons that have nothing to do with God. My neuroses can reduce me to a pitch of misery that forces an affective conversion. The deceit of others may lead me to personal responsibility in intellectual or moral matters. The natural human desire to live lovingly and responsibly in my personal and institutional dealings my fellow humans may draw me positively to all four forms of natural conversion. God's historical self-revelation in Jesus and the Spirit need have nothing to do with any of these decisions. Not that the natural convert denies divine revelation. He or she simply fails to take it into consideration in making a choice for responsible living. When one makes such a choice, one experiences a natural conversion.[21]

Authentic religious conversion can, of course, never transpire naturally. For the religious convert decides to respond responsibly in faith to some historical act of divine self-revelation and self-communication. Religious conversion always therefore results from the action of uncreated grace (God) and transmutes experience by infusing created grace (the difference in the believer an ongoing life of faith makes).

In an experiential approach to the theology of grace, the human capacity to experience natural conversion, to decide for personally and politically responsible rather than for personally and politically irresponsible behavior on purely natural grounds, constitutes what theologians in the past have called the human obediential potency for grace. For the natural capacity to opt for responsible behavior builds into the human person an ability to respond responsibly in the face of a gracious act of divine self-disclosure and self-communication. The potency in question remains obediential because nothing in human nature can force God to reveal Himself historically or claim that such a grace is owed to human nature as such.

Religious conversion seeks to transvalue affective, intellectual, moral, and political conversion to the extent that they remain only naturally motivated. Why is this so? Every conversion creates a strictly normative frame of reference. So does religious conversion; but because the realities and values with which religious conversion deals are derived from the unexpected and unpredictable eruption of the divine into human history, religious frames of reference are faith derived. The strictly normative character of religious conversion results from the fact that because religious events disclose to us a supremely beautiful, true, and good divine reality, they make morally absolute and ultimate claims. That is to say, they demand that the convert be willing not only to live but to die if necessary for the one supremely desirable reality we call God. They demand that the convert cling to God ultimately in all circumstances.

Such a claim and the transformation in God it effects can be legitimately described as radical. For it demands that all merely natural realities including natural conversion be re-evaluated in the light of the ultimate realities which religious conversion grasps and is grasped by. Humans do not naturally and spontaneously desire to die for any reason, though they may learn through love the meaning of such self-sacrifice. But religious conversion demands in addition the willingness to live and die for world-transcending realities. The paradox of dying naturally in order to live supernaturally suffuses authentic religious conversion with an unavoidable element of discontinuity. The newness of life which religious conversion brings does not emerge with easy spontaneity from natural hopes and aspirations. Radical transmutation rather than mere organic continuity names the religious game.

## (IV)

We have been attempting to describe two contrasting theologies of grace. Both stand within the pale of Christian orthodoxy. They tend, however, to inspire different brands of spirituality. In commenting on the tendencies inherent in the two theological positions I have described, however, I in no way intend to comment on the personal spiritualities of those who defend them theoretically. Rather I wish only to comment on some of the practical consequences latent in principle in either position.

By a spirituality I mean a practical way of approaching the reality of God and the process of growth in faith. In this sense one can speak of as many personal spiritualities as there are individual believers. Schools of spirituality emerge when through education personal spiritualities develop identifiable affinities.

Not every spirituality will have extensive theological motivations, but those who pursue theology systematically live under the constraint of integrating theological speculation into their own personal religious growth. They also need to allow intellectual conversion to inform religious faith with sound logical and methodological principles. They also need to allow religious conversion to transvalue intellectual pursuits by focusing thought on the ultimate significance for the rest of human life and experience of those events in which God graciously reveals and communicates Himself to His creatures. We take our theological beliefs seriously when we not only defend their truth but also accept their speculative and practical consequences. The more we do both, the more will theology inform one's personal spirituality.

The two theologies of grace we have examined differ in the things they consider important. We have reflected on some of the speculative implications of both positions. In practice each will if taken seriously also tend in principle to inspire contrasting religious attitudes and therefore contrasting spiritualities. Let us examine some of these tendencies.

1) **In the practical living of a life of faith a theology of thematic grace tends to inspire a certain complacency about one's essential orientation to God, a complacency which a theology of transmuting grace challenges.** A theology of thematic grace builds not on a foundational exploration of the dynamics of conversion but on a metaphysics of knowledge whose validity is assumed even though argued to only a priori. As a result, theologians of thematic grace talk more about the essential dynamisms of the human psyche than the complexities and varieties of converted, religious experience. Indeed, they rarely discourse about conversion at all. And when they do they offer little novel insight into its significance.

Not that a theology of thematic grace rules out the possibility of conversion. In both of the theories of grace we have examined the convert renounces sin for the obedience of faith. In a theology of thematic grace the assent of faith thematizes the essential, a priori orientation of the intellect and will to God whether that orientation results from the natural desire for the beatific vision or from a supernatural existential. In a theology of transmuting grace religious conversion radically transmutes and transforms experience by endowing it with wholly new graced tendencies entirely absent from any merely natural experience.

Moreover to the extent that a theology of thematic grace affirms the universal presence in all human individuals of a supernatural orientation toward graced union with God, an orientation that precedes the act of faith, it tends to inspire a pious belief in the implicitly graced character of all morally sincere acts. As a consequence the sincerity of a choice, the fact that it does not grow from sinful motives, can begin to be prized as a sign that it expresses at least implicitly a graced longing for divine union.

A theology of grace as radical transmutation insists by contrast that sincerity alone, the mere absence of malice, gives no clear evidence that an action is implicitly graced. Humans can act sincerely when they respond to created goods while simultaneously ignoring God's historical self-revelation in Jesus and the Spirit. Mere natural sincerity, no matter how intense, always falls short of supernatural faith. And faith marks the dividing line between nature and grace. Not that natural sincerity displeases a divine creator who takes pleasure in all natural goodness. If, however, natural moral sincerity is to become graced, it needs to be transvalued in faith. That transvaluation changes it radically by suffusing it with gospel values and with a new dependence on the prompting and illumination of the Holy Breath of Jesus, a dependence it previously lacked.

In sum, a theology of thematic grace encourages a certain complacency about one's fundamental orientation to God by assuming on questionable metaphysical and psychological grounds that that orientation expresses the essence of spirit and is built into the psyche a priori. A theology of transmuting grace discourages this or any other form of religious complacency. It demands instead constant scrutiny of one's motives in order to determine whether or not they express an intregral five-fold conversion. Similarly while a theology of transmuting grace recognizes natural goodness as a value in its own right, in rejecting the a priori gracing of experience it demands a constant concern to enhance, transform and transvalue naturally good responses by relating them to gospel realities and values in faith.

2) **A theology of thematic grace looks upon the a priori structure of the individual psyche as the most fundamental source of personal orientation to God; a theology of grace as radically transmuting finds the fundamental source of personal orientation to God in interaction with religious events and with religious communities.** A theology of thematic grace discovers the most fundamental orientation of humans toward God in the dynamic spiritual structure of the individual psyche. The individual intellect and will in consequence of their virtual infinity enjoy an essential orientation to the divine whether that orientation expresses a natural desire for the beatific vision or a supernatural existential. That orientation originates a priori, e.g., prior to any interaction with one's world. Religious events supply the categories that thematize this essential orientation. But the a priori structure of individual consciousness rather than religious events themselves provides the point where the human spirit finds its essential orientation to the divine.

A theology of grace as radically transmuting by contrast looks upon the individual psyche and the dynamisms that shape it as both fallible and finite. It looks upon the a priori's of any human cognitive act as historically acquired and on the adequacy of the relation of any given mind to Being, or reality, as varying from individual to individual. The dynamisms of any given intellect and will may or may not orient their owner to God. The mind's habitual tendencies may or may not be informed by grace or transmuted by faith. As a consequence, a theology of grace as radical transmutation fails to find in the individual psyche a necessary or privileged source of religious orientation.

A theology of grace as radically transmuting discovers our most fundamental orientation to God not in the a priori structure of subjectivity but in interaction with those events which reveal to us a self-communicating God. The religious significance of revelatory events must through the process of interaction be personally appropriated in faith, if individual experience is to acquire a graced character. The revealing event may on occasion consist of the direct action of God on the experience of some individual in solitary contemplation. More often, however, grace is mediated sacramentally through the faith witness of other persons or of a graced community of believers.

90

Moreover, belief in the fundamental fallibility of the human mind also endows a theology of transmuting grace with an enhanced concern for the social dimensions of human religious experience. Minds convinced both of their fallibility and of their conditioned historical character do not seek for reality, truth, goodness, and God primarily in the varied and undependable structures of individual human subjectivity. They seek them instead in the social corrective of shared systematic inquiry. Moreover shared religious inquiry pursued in faith and under the charismatic guidance of the Holy Spirit does more than provide graced subjectivity with the categories it needs to thematize its a priori orientation to God. Rather shared religious inquiry is prized as a sacramental event which reveals to those who participate in it God's gracious self-communication itself.

In other words, while a theology of thematic grace conceives the believer's relationship to God in terms that smack of religious individualism, a theology of grace as radical transmutation encourages a search for God in the very social sharing of gifts and charisms within a community of faith and worship. Social intercourse rather than individual subjectivity links one to the divine.

By the same token in a theology of thematic grace faith, hope, and love tend to be conceived as supernatural transformations of an individual human spirit. They thematize the individual intellect and will's essential orientation to God, whether by nature or by grace. In a theology of grace as radical transmutation, however, faith, hope, and love are conceived by contrast as social process. In such a theology human persons are viewed as mutually interpenetrating experiences who discover the reality of God in interaction with those events in which He communicates himself to us and in a special way in the shared faith consciousness which results from sharing the charisms of the Spirit in community. In such a theological frame of reference transformation in hope, faith, and love cannot be viewed primarily as the relationship of an individual to God. Rather they must be viewed as the very social process by which God reveals and communicates Himself to communities and through them to the individuals who comprise them.

3) **While a theology of thematic grace locates religious consciousness primarily in the intellect and will, a theology of grace as radical transmutation ambitions the transvaluation and transformation in faith of both the rational and irrational ways in which humans relate practically to God.** Because it roots itself in a Thomistic metaphysics of knowledge a theology of thematic grace labors under the intellectualist bias that characterizes every Thomistic anthoropology. In such a system the spiritual faculties of intellect and will are prized as those powers of the soul which give us conscious access to God. Since the will derives the realities it seeks from the intellect, of these two privileged faculties the intellect orients us most fundamentally to reality and to God. The intellect therefore provides the basic link between the human and the divine.

Other Christian philosophers and theologians have tried to temper the intellectual bias of Thomistic anthropology by exalting the will over the intellect. In the past these attempts have ordinarily remained trapped in the operational dualism that mars scholastic faculty psychology. They fail to do justice to an affective, appreciative grasp of reality and of God. A theology of transforming grace eschews faculty psychology with its talk of fixed formal objects and essential dynamisms in the psyche. It also eschews the categories "matter" and "spirit" and speaks instead of humans as developing experiences. And it discovers within experience both affective and rational forms of knowing.

Affective, or appreciative, consciousness advances irrationally. It follows not the laws of logic but those of free association and synchronicity. It expresses itself lyrically and dramatically in art, literature, ritual, and myth. It grasps the real in judgments of feeling like those which function in discernment and in artistic creativity.

Rational consciousness by contrast follows the laws of logic and of inference. It advances from description to strictly normative thinking and finally to explanation. It grasps reality through inductive inferences formulated into rational judgments.

Because it construes human persons as experiences, a theology of transmuting grace avoids the intellectualist bias which theologies of thematic grace inherit from Thomism. A theology of transmuting grace grounds the experience of mystery not in the finite intellect but in an appreciative grasp of the real. It demands that appreciative consciousness grow responsibly out of affective conversion. It also insists that rational consciousness should express intellectual conversion. It demands in other words, not only that the convert recognize the validity of both rational and irrational perceptions of the real but also that rational interpretations of reality be coordinated with mytho-poetic insight and vice versa. As a consequence, a theology of transmuting grace displays a more nuanced sensitivity to the variety and complexity of human and religious forms of knowing than does a theology of implicit grace.

4) **A theology of thematic grace celebrates the continuity of religious experience; a theology of transmuting grace anticipates both continuity and discontinuity within an experience of integral conversion.** A theology of thematic grace developed in reaction to an artificial opposition between nature and grace sometimes defended in neo-scholastic manuals. Manual theology tended to describe nature and grace as advancing on two parallel but unrelated tracks. Theologians of thematic grace protested against this extrinsicism and attempted to overcome it without confusing the two realms of nature and grace. They insisted strongly as a consequence on a continuity between nature and grace. They discovered that continuity in the a priori orientation of the spirit to God. They insisted that faith thematizes an appetite for the divine built a priori into the human psyche. As a consequence, theologians

of thematic grace can find themselves, as we have seen, hard pressed to account adequately for the discontinuities which surface in the human experience of conversion, the sense of being not only turned around but transformed into a radically different kind of person.

One may anticipate then that a spirituality based on a theology of thematic grace will tend to value continuity within religious growth and to undervalue discontinuity. It will urge individuals to become consciously what they already implicitly are rather than demand that they become a radically different kind of person. It will eschew an evangelizing rhetoric and counsel people to expect grace to fulfill their spontaneous spiritual longings.

A theology of transmuting grace recognizes the need for continuity in both natural and graced development. New habits, tendencies, ways of responding need to be integrated organically with those already acquired. A theology of transmuting grace locates the human obediential potency for grace in the capacity to undergo purely natural conversion at an affective, intellectual, and moral level. It anticipates that an authentic religious conversion will display initially an uncanny, even alien character that transcends anything available to humans in their interaction with created realities and values. The eruption of God into a naturally developing experience transmutes and transforms it into somethimg radically new and different. It does not negate or destroy the naturally good tendencies present in a convert's personality, but it does re-arrange the constitutive structure of experience in new and startling ways by setting it into a new kind of developing relationship with the world-transforming, world-transcending reality of God. Authentic religious conversion reorients human aspiration toward a God who confronts us in purification and judgment as a consuming fire and whose relentless love challenges the finitude, the spontaneous self-preoccupation, the inertia, and the self-righteousness of every human ego.

One may anticipate therefore that a spirituality based on a theology of transmuting grace will value both continuity and discontinuity in religious growth. It will counsel converts to seek personal integration and satisfaction but to anticipate religious breakthroughs that effect more than the thematizations of tendencies already present within human nature. Such a spirituality will seek to restore an evangelizing rhetoric of repentance and recommitment to Christian pulpits. Such a spirituality will with all the gospels warn believers that a love relation with the Christian God demands as much the discontinuity of dying as it does the joy of continuous human development. Instead of counseling non-Christians to look upon themselves as anonymous Christians, it will warn them as Jesus did His contempories that Christian discipleship demands radical sacrifice and the willingness to undergo purifying transformation in God, for we must die to everything that is not Christ if we are to live with and in Him.

The two theologies of grace we have examined offer believers two contrasting spiritual paths. The decision to follow either will of course be tempered for better or for worse by the other variables that shape any given individual religious experience. After all we should not expect finite, fallible humans to act with entire consistency. I have personally opted for a theology of transmuting grace. I have done so in the full knowledge that many will prefer to follow the path I have rejected. And they like me must live by the consequences of their personal choices. Which path will you choose to follow?

### Endnotes

1Joseph Maréchal, S.J. **Le point de Depart de la Metaphysique** (5 Volumes; Louvain: Editions du Museum Lessianum, 1926-1947), V.

2Henri de Lubac, S.J. **Le mystere du surnaturel** (Paris: Aubier, 1965).

3Karl Rahner, S.J. **Hoerer des Wortes: Zur Grundlegung einer Religions-Philosophie** (München: Kosel Verlag, 1936).

4Karl Rahner, S.J. **Theological Investigations** (Baltimore: Helicon, 1954) I, 297-346.

5Juan Luis Segundo **A Theology for the Artisans of a New Humanity,** translated by John Drury (Maryknoll, NY: Orbis, 1973).

6Gustavo Gutierrez, **A Theology of Liberation** (Maryknoll, NY: Orbis, 1973).

7Rahner, **Theological Investigations,** XI, 68-114.

8C. S. Peirce, **Collected Papers,** edited by Charles Hartshorne and Paul Weiss (8 Vols; Cambridge: Harvard, 1933-1960) I. 4, 2. 619-644.

9**Summa Theologiae,** I, lxxvii, 6, ad 3. I am concerned in this article primarily with Transcendental Thomism rather than with Aquinas himself. Since Transcendental Thomism acquiesces in a Thomistic philosophy of human nature, one cannot deal adequately with the issues raised by a theology of thematic grace without some attention to those facets of Aquinas's philosophy which ground it. As we shall see, the theology of transmuting grace which I will propose endorses the main lines of a Thomistic theology of grace. But it attempts to provide that theology with an updated, philosophical understanding of human experience that speaks in an inculturated North American idiom.

10John Flavell, **The Developmental Psychology of Jean Piaget** (Princeton: van Nostrand, 1963).

11Jean Piaget, **Insights and Illusions of Philosophy,** translated by

Wolf Mays (NY: World, 1971). When one concedes the finitude of the human mind, one need not deny thereby human openness to mystery or religious transcendence. Both result from specific transforming encounters with the Holy that expand and challenge the finite human ego to assent to some specific act of divine self-communication. A finite human experience of transcendence develops dynamically, through the ongoing expansion of one's experience of a divine reality that always encompasses and goes beyond whatever I can know of it. We know the transcendent reality of God in two ways: through ego processes which advance through concept, image, and affection or through the unitive knowing that is loving effected by infused contemplation. That knowledge may advance more or less consciously

12C. G. Jung **Psychological Types,** translated by H. Goodwin Baynes (NY: Harcourt Brace, 1923); David Keirsey, **Please Understand Me: Character and Temperament Types** (Del Mar, CA: Prometheus Nemesis, 1978).

13Paul Tillich, **Systematic Theology** (Chicago: University of Chicago Press, 1967).

14Jonathan Edwards, **A Treastise Concerning Religious Affections,** edited by John E. Smith (New Haven: Yale, 1959).

15R. C. Zaehner, **Mysticism: Sacred and Profane** (New York: Oxford, 1961).

16Bernard Lonergan, S.J., **Method in Theology** (New York: Herder and Herder, 1972).

17Donald L. Gelpi, S.J., **Experiencing God: A Theology of Human Emergence** (NY: Paulist, 1978) 18-51. A theology of grace as radical transmutation recognizes the capacity of natural reason to reach certitude concerning the reality of God. That certitude may be grounded in a reasoned argument, or demonstration. A theology of grace as radical transmutation finds a plausible philosophical account of how natural reason normally attains to God in C.S. Peirce's Neglected Argument for the Reality of God (Peirce, **Collected Papers,** 6. 452-493). But a theology of grace as radical transmutation insists that a graced encounter with a self-communicating God transcends and transforms any human relationship to God based on natural reason alone.

18Gelpi, **op. cit.,** 155-204.

19Rahner, **Theological Investigations,** I, 297-317.

20Donald L. Gelpi, S.J. **Charism and Sacrament: A Theology of Christian Conversion** (NY: Paulist, 1976) 8-112.

21Gelpi, **Experiencing God,** 178-185.

## Personal And Political Conversion:
### Foundations For A Theology Of Liberation

The Lord hears the cry of the poor, and in our day He has raised up prophets to plead on their behalf. The voice of liberation theology has begun to stir the hearts and consciences of Christians throughout the world. As millions face the grim fate of death by slow starvation in the deserts of Ethiopia, as the masses try to eke out a precarious existence in the **pueblos jovenes** of Latin America, as an escalating arms race converts billions of dollars into bombs rather than food, as racism, capitalistic greed, sexism, and jingoism conspire to shackle blacks, **Latinos,** native Americans, and other minority groups in this country in economic enslavement, the prophetic witness of liberation theologians prods persistently at Christian consciences benumbed by affluence, egotism, and a fatuous capitalistic gospel of greed. Few in number, often attacked and beleaguered, betrayed at times by their own rhetorical excesses, liberation theologians in north and south America, in Africa, and in Asia have with herculean effort so goaded the consciences of first world Christians that even the institutional churches have begun to heave their bulk and move massively but solidly closer toward a preferential option for the poor.

In this country liberation theology emerged from the black radicalism of the late sixties. Martin Luther King's Christian pacifism mobilized the black community to espouse a church-based, biblically inspired form of activism that placed Christian ministers at the forefront of the black community's struggle for justice. When Stokley Carmichael's northern, urban-based, and ghetto hardened Student National Coordinating Committee rejected King's doctrine of non-violence, it brought into existence a new, secularized form of black political activism that changed both the direction and the tactics of the radical black community's struggle against white, racist oppression. Instead of seeking integration with white society, the radical black community found strength in a new and militant assertion of its own blackness. Instead of pursuing King's path of non-violent resistance to white bigotry, the new militants rallied around the cause of Black Power. They also announced the right of blacks to use any means, including violent ones, to achieve their social and political rights.

The Black Muslim religion posed a second threat to the leadership of Black Christian activists. The Black Muslim church urged blacks to fuse their racial and religious identities by joining a religion with African roots that sanctioned the violent search for justice in a white, racist society.

Black liberation theology began in this country in part as the response of concerned black churchmen to reassert Christian leadership of the black political left wing. In its earliest formulation it adopted the rhetoric of Black Power, but the theological movement soon developed a healthy pluralism. More moderate voices, like that of James Deotis Roberts, attempted to move black liberation theology to a position somewhere between those of Martin Luther King and of James Cone, whose book **Black Theology and Black Power** had launched the movement in 1969. In his early works Cone aligned himself fairly closely with the aims of the Black Power movement, though his more recent writings express broader social aims. Roberts, however, on the one hand eschewed the goal of racial integration for which King had struggled, while on the other he nevertheless called for reciprocity and ultimate reconciliation between blacks and whites, but as between equals who recognize and endorse one another's differences and racial identities.

Quite understandably, black liberation theology focused at first on racism as the origin and source of all the woes and sufferings of the black community, but as black liberation theologians began to enter into dialogue with Latin liberationists, shifts began to occur in their approach to the quest for freedom and justice. The more radical among them responded to the allure of Christian marxism. An initial application of marxist analysis to the situation of North American blacks flushed out other sources of black oppression besides racism. Capitalism, classism, and sexism have joined the old enemy racism as targets of prophetic denunciation. At the same time black liberationists have begun to show a greater sense of solidarity with the oppressed of other races whether in this country or abroad.

Another strain in more recent black liberation theology questions the adequacy of the methods of Latin liberationsts to deal with all of the religious issues that confront the black community in the United States. One may, then, hope that as the dialogue between black and Latin liberationists advances, black theologians in this country may enable their Latin colleagues to hone their theological method to a finer cutting edge.[1]

A survey of the growing body of liberation theology reveals other potential areas of growth. Paradoxically, most liberationists have to date failed to address adequately a fundamental question which they cannot ultimately avoid: namely, in what does liberation consist?[2] They have insisted correctly that for the opppressed liberation means changing the social, political, and economic structures that reduce them to subhuman standards of living. But does that insistence, however justified and urgent in its appeal, do theological justice to the question of liberation?

As I have pondered this paradox, I have come to believe that foundational theology can make a contribution here to the contemporary human search for an enhanced freedom. Foundational theology probes the dynamics of conversion. Christian conversion promises to effect a new exodus, to liberate those who experience it. Any Christian theology of liberation must, then, find a way of relating the experience of conversion to the human conquest of freedom. In the present essay I would like to suggest some ways of forging the link between the two. More specifically, I would like to explore both descriptively and normatively three kinds of freedom: elementary human freedom, authentic personal freedom, and the authentic quest for socio-political liberation. I shall argue that personal conversion enhances elementary human freedom and that it authenticates the political quest for freedom in one way even as it is authenticated by socio-political conversion in another.

(I)

**(1) Elemntary Human Freedom.** I define elementary human freedom as both the ability to choose to act or not to act, to do one thing rather than another and the capacity to realize one's choice practically. Elementary freedom roots itself therefore in the human ability to distinguish alternative forms of realistically possible behavior. As a consequence, elementary human freedom flickers. It waxes and wanes in different individuals and circumstances of life as varying influences condition personal ability both to identify viable alternatives for choice and to effect them.

We may name five such influences: environmental, conceptual, perspectival, habitual, and decisive. Let us try to understand their character and how they enhance or inhibit elementary human freedom.

**a. Environment.** The embodied character of human experience roots it in a spatio-temporal environment. We date and locate our births, our careers, our dying. Human selves as a consequence achieve personal self-definition by interacting with the other selves. I call finite selves capable of conversion human persons. We call the selves that lack such a capacity things. The persons and things with whom I interact comprise my world. They confront me, make demands on me, encourage me, nurture me, contradict me, oppress me, destroy me.

My physical body belongs to the total environment from which I emerge. Indeed, every self that develops in space and time must put together a body that sustains its activity and, if it lives, its life. When human bodies function properly, when they feed regularly, rest and exercise as they should, they empower thought and reflection physically and so foster the growth of elementary human freedom by allowing us to imagine different courses of action. Sickness and disease circumscribe physically the human capacity to think and act and with it the ability to distinguish viable alternatives for choice. As a consequence, they diminish elementary human freedom. Anyone who has suffered a serious toothache knows whereof I speak.

Other environmental influences also conspire to enhance or inhibit the human capacity to distinguish and choose different paths of activity. Urban ghettos, small rural towns, deserts and wastelands offer fewer

-99-

opportunities for elite cultural enrichment than institutions of higher learning. A society which encourages the free exchange of ideas offers greater scope to the growth of elementary human freedom than oppressive dictatorships.

**b. Conceptual Differentiation.** The environments which supply the raw materials out of which we create our bodies enhance or inhibit elementary human freedom in two ways. First, the more possible objects of choice they supply, the more they enhance freedom at least potentially by making choice physically possible; the fewer the realistically possible objects of choice they supply the more they circumscribe freedom. Clearly, the prisoner in solitary has fewer alternatives from which to choose than the free citizen. Those with access to excellent libraries have more books from which to choose than those who do not. Urban businesses have more potential customers than rural. London and New York supply lovers of the stage with more productions from which to choose than smaller urban centers.

Second, our surrounding environments enhance elementary human freedom when they educate the mind to distinguish alternatives for action and foster the skills needed to act; they constrain elementary human freedom when they do the opposite. For in order to move freely in my environment I need much more than a variety of realistic possibilities from which to choose. I need to differentiate them conceptually in order to opt for one rather than another. As I differentiate more and more possibilities for choice, I grow simultaneously in both consciousness and freedom. An illiterate set loose in the most elaborate of libraries still cannot choose which book to read. Someone uninstructed in the rules of chess may move the pieces randomly but lacks the freedom to play, until through instruction the potential player becomes conscious of the way the different pieces move and the purpose of the game. We need to understand how to manipulate mathematical symbols before we can solve problems. Artists need instruction in the techniques of their medium before they can produce masterpieces. We act with greater moral freedom when we bring to problems of conscience a nuanced sense of the complexity of the situation which confronts us. Political strategists need a detailed understanding of the electorate in order to plan and execute an effective campaign. In these and similar circumstances the subtlety and complexity of one's personal conceptual responses either enhances or constrains the exercise of freedom.

**c. Perspectives.** When we face problems of considerable complexity our capacity to differentiate alternative paths of action also grows if we can approach the question that faces us from a variety of perspectives and of methods. As a consequence, not only conceptual but also perspectival variables condition the growth and decline of freedom. The tribesman who knows only traditional means of cultivating the soil lacks the freedom of the practitioners of agribusiness or of the authors of the green revolution to employ a variety of approaches, technologies, and tools to reap more abundant harvests. Similarly, in any hotly disputed question awareness of the different approaches and methods employed heretofore to reach only partially adequate solutions frees the mind to search for alternative approaches that will finally solve the problem. A literary critic schooled in different kinds of criticism will approach the interpretation of a text with greater flexibility of mind than the literal minded. Moralists who understand the issues which divide different schools of ethical reasoning will approach questions of conscience with more flexibility of mind than moral fundamentalists. The poitician supplied with a variety of strategies adapts to political challenges with greater freedom than one with a single strategy. In other words, an enhanced capacity to approach practical problems from a variety of perspectives also enhances freedom. A diminished such capacity diminishes freedom.

**d. Habits.** Besides the physical constraints upon human freedom imposed by one's body and its surrounding environment, the habits we have acquired in the course of a lifetime also impose realistic limits on the exercise of freedom. One may dream of becoming a concert pianist; but unless one has acquired the necessary skill at the keyboard, one may never tour the concert halls. The student who has never learned the discipline of research will never pen scholarly articles. The idealist who has never learned the meaning of prudence courts constant frustration in attempting to transform dreams into actuality. Only the skilled rhetorician possesses the power to motivate audiences to concerted political action. Habitual skills, then, empower freedom; their lack inhibits it.

**e. Decisions.** The decisions we take also condition the exercise of freedom. They do so in two ways. They choose the environments in which we attempt to achieve some purpose, environments with the physical capacity to either enhance or inhibit realistic choice. Students, for example, need to decide which college or university will best prepare them for their life work. Employees need to decide which job promises most advancement. Iron curtain refugees defect to the west because they find here a freer lifestyle. Decisions also build into our characters the habitual skills that make choice realistically possible. An accomplished linguist can communicate with more people than those who only speak their native tongue. Habitual practice created the musical virtuoso or the graceful athlete. Years of experience produce the shrewed politician or business executive.

We may then conclude that elementary human freedom manifests the following descriptive traits. (1) Its conditioned character limits freedom. Any human therefore who aspires to absolute freedom whistles in the wind. (2) Elementary human freedom flickers. We experience moments of greater freedom, moments of greater constraint. (3) Different people enjoy different kinds of freedom corresponding to their circumstances, skills, and wit. (4) The fact that elementary human freedom lives stretched between constraint and possibility makes it

Janus-faced. More specifically, freedom **from** constraint creates the possibility of freedom **for** some desirable course of action.


## (II)

**2. Authentic Personal Freedom.** Authentic personal freedom enhances elementary human freedom. While elementary human freedom roots itself in the capacity to distinguish realistic alternatives of action, authentic freedom roots itself in personal conversion.

**a. Conversion.** I define conversion as the decision to reject irresponsible choices and to assume responsibility for one's subsequent development in some area of human experience. We act responsibly when we measure the motives and consequences of our conduct against norms and values which we affirm as personally binding and when we do so in responsive dialogue with others, especially with those affected by our choices. We respond to others rather than merely react to them when we attempt to hear them and to view reality, including the reality of our own conduct, from their perspective. In other words, we respond to other persons when we treat them as persons with needs and responsibilities similar to our own. We take responsibility for ourselves when we decide to acknowledge our accountability to others and to the norms and ideals we profess personally. Responsibility endows human activity with authenticity. In other words, I act authentically when I live up to my responsibilities. I succumb to inauthenticity when I behave irresponsibly in spite of my professed intention to do the opposite.

I also distinguish initial personal conversion from ongoing. Initial conversion occurs when the convert first passes from irresponsible to responsible behavior. As a consequence, initial conversion ought to coincide with adult coming of age, although smaller children can be gradually schooled to take more and more responsibility for their lives. Ongoing conversion follows necessarily from initial conversion and authenticates it. Theologians who defend a theory of the fundamental option like to talk about the human capacity to dispose of oneself radically and totally. I doubt that we possess such a capacity short of death. Our decisions, even our decisions to convert initially, change us only partially. Subsequent to initial conversion, converts must continue to deal with irresponsible habits formed before conversion. They must resist the temptations to backslide. They must grow in understanding of the exigencies of personally responsible living and submit to them. Growth processes such as these deepen and enhance initial conversion and deserve therefore to be called ongoing conversion.

We shall reflect presently on the kinds of experiences which structure the different forms of conversion. For the moment, however, I have been attempting to define in a preliminary way some of the fundamental terms I employ in order to speak about conversion. Let us then begin to probe descriptively the kinds of experience which affective, intellectual, religious, and moral converts undergo.

**b. Affective Conversion.** The affectively converted individual takes responsibility for his or her subsequent emotional development. Human emotions divide initially into the negative and the sympathetic affections. We respond negatively to our world with fear or aggression. We respond negatively to ourselves with guilt and self-hatred. When we love, befriend, empathize, rejoice, we respond sympathetically.

Initially, the affective convert needs to deal principally with repressed negative feelings. Repressed negative emotions have yet to be integrated in lifegiving ways into the total structure of the emerging human personality. As a consequence, they tend to acquire an enslaving power alien to the conscious self. The more they are repressed, the more powerful such feelings become. The more the beleaguered ego resists facing them, the more it falls victim to their untamed power.

Enslavement to the negative affections begins with "nervousness," hypertension, exaggerated emotional responses to trivial stimuli. When these coping devices fail, more serious personality disfunctions ensue: withdrawal, fainting, sleepwalking, phobic and counterphobic states, drunkenness, drug abuse, self-mutilation, psychic compulsion. Unless affective conversion frees the tormented conscious ego to face and deal with unconscious rage, fear, and guilt, a third level of emotional enslavement ensues. One begins to be possessed by unintegrated negative feelings which express themselves consciously in dangerous, destructive behavior. The explosion of negative emotion is sometimes heralded by an impairment of perception, judgment, or even consciousness. After the explosion, the conscious ego experiences a temporary reduction of tension, until like a quiescent volcano the unconscious erupts again in violence, uncontrollable depression, possessed manic states. Further psychic degeneration requires hospitalization, as the conscious mind withdraws into an autistic, solipsistic world of bizarre and chaotic behavior. If the unfaced impulses lurking within the unconscious successfully overwhelm the last defenses of the beleaguered conscious ego, it sinks into a maelstrom of self-hatred and tries to find relief from its torment in suicide.[3]

As dark, repressed, negative feelings possess the human psyche, imagination dies and with it the ability to conceive lifegiving forms of behavior. The sympathetic emotions stifle in a miasma of rage, defensiveness, and self-hatred. As the ability to cope realistically with one's world falters, not only do dreams of happiness die but also the ability to create realistic strategies for shaping one's world to one's own purposes.

Affective conversion reverses this descent into the hell of

emotional imprisonment. First and most fundamentally, the affective convert takes responsibilty for facing, with whatever human help and support necessary, the dark forces that lurk in the unconscious. Rage, fear, and guilt can all play a positive role in creating a personal human identity provided they are integrated in conscious, lifegiving ways into the psyche. Stupidity, injustice, oppression, and hypocrisy should make us mad. Instead of repressing anger we need to direct it against its proper targets. We should fear persons and forces that threaten our personal survival. Healthy fear motivates humans to defend themselves against injustice and oppression. Even guilt can become lifegiving when it is acknowledged and laved in the balm of forgiveness. Great sinners can become great saints lost in the wonder of atoning love's healing consolation.

Clearly, then, affective conversion enhances enormously elementary human freedom by enabling the convert to deal systematically with repressed, enslaving emotional drives. Initial affective conversion inaugurates the process of emotional healing; ongoing affective conversion extends it to all of the dark, unexplored corners of the unconscious psyche. Since no sinful child of Adam and Eve enjoys complete psychic integration, individuals differ in both the degree and quality of their affective freedom. Nevertheless, the affectively converted find in emotional healing the release of the sympathetic emotions, the birth of hope, and a growing ability to deal realistically with their world and to shape it practically to the purposes of love.

**c. Intellectual Conversion.** The intellectually unconverted resist reflection and contemn dialogue with those with whom they disagree. They imagine foolishly that truth can be dished out on a platter. Bound to a single way of viewing reality, they display readiness to codify their beliefs and memorize an endless list of answers in order to confound troublesome adversaries. They set their faces like flint, however, against any attempt to question their own presuppositions, to weigh the pros and cons of different arguments, to confront the facts that either validate or invalidate beliefs, to recognize the limits of different frames of reference so that they can opt for the more adquate ones.

The intellectually converted take personal responsibility for the truth and falsity of their beliefs and for the adequacy or inadequacy of the frames of reference they employ in order to fix their beliefs. Intellectual conversion heals the human mind from the imprisoning constraints of fundamentalism. The intellectual convert recognizes the limitations of determining personal beliefs on the basis of personal dogmatism, of authority, or of taste alone. Sensitive to the finitude and fallibility of human understanding, intellectual converts value the experience and insights of others and acknowledge that shared systematic inquiry offers the surest method for arriving at true beliefs and for constructing adequate frames of reference for doing so.

The heart of the affectively converted expands in hope to beautiful visions of a possible future and seeks the realistic means to effect it. The mind of the intellectually converted loves the truth with passion and loathes rigidity of mind, deceit, obfuscation, and error. Love of truth breeds the intellectual virtues of honesty, integrity, and genial openness to any argument that leads to truth and does not block the path of inquiry. Love of truth also inspires curiosity, the willingness to explore unfamiliar paths of thought and to face startling and unexpected evidence. Love of truth also nurtures intellectual flexibility, a freedom of spirit to change one's views when the evidence warrants it. That same love motivates the mind to submit to the discipline of sound logic and methods of thinking.

Clearly, the intellectual convert experiences greater freedom of perception and of judgment than the unconverted fundamentalist. Like affective freedom, however, intellectual freedom differs from individual to individual in both degree and quality. Even the most insatiably curious still labor under the constraints of intellectual finitude. In the span of a lifetime the human mind can only begin to master a limited terrain of truth. Each mind develops specific methods for arriving at the truth, not all of them equally successful. As a consequence, humans grow in intellectual freedom by active participation in communities of shared inquiry and by openness to the validated results published by other such communities than the ones to which they themselves personally belong.

**d. Moral Conversion.** The morally converted individual takes responsibility for the quality of the motives and consequences of one's own personal decisions. Prior to moral conversion humans may and do attend to practical matters. Everyone by the force of circumstance must respond to the challenges and opportunities of one's world, but pre-moral practicality moves within the constraints of a crude, self-centered pragmatism. It measures success or failure by narrow, egocentric standards.

Children manifest an innocent, amoral egocentrism. As the process of socialization forces them to acknowledge the needs of others, they begin to discover moral accountability and with it the need to measure the acceptability of one's actions by their consequences not only for oneself but for others. Moral conversion heightens this sense of personal accountability. The morally converted live by values and realities that make specifically ethical claims. Values and realities make specifically ethical claims when they control our dealings with other persons, when they call us to commitment in every circumstance, and when they demand of us the willingness not only to live, but if necessary, to die for them. A recognition of the evil inherent in the arbitrary killing of innocent humans would exemplify a strictly moral attitude.

The moral convert espouses a personally appropriate vision of the way in which one ought to live and order one's life, one's dealings with others, and the world which sustains one's life. The morally converted also recognize their personal accountability for the quality and character of that vision. They recognize their need for a personal rationale for acting that expresses a defensible vision of human living. They love virtue in a way analogous to the affective convert's love of beauty and the intellectual convert's love of truth. They cultivate character: prudence in deliberating the consequences of alternative paths of action, justice in dealing with others, courage in defending the cause of right, temperance in enjoyment, personal sensitivity to the moral demands of persons and situations.

The moral convert recognizes too that vice enslaves while virtue liberates and humanizes. Unable to transcend the egocentric concerns of childhood, the vicious lack the capacity to recognize the mutual interdependence of humans upon one another. That constraining obtuseness further blinds them more or less culpably to the destructive consequences of their personal choices for themselves and others. Vices express socially undisciplined cravings that isolate the vicious from those social contacts and challenges that could free them to love some reality other than themselves.

Moral conversion also inserts one into the world of prudential moral discourse in which the advantages and disadvantages of conflicting personal lifestyles and patterns of behavior can be scrutinized and weighed for their capacity to open one to the whole spectrum of human virtue. Such moral discourse enhances moral consciousness and therefore moral freedom.

Clearly, in freeing one from the narrow constraints of blindly egocentric behavior and by opening one to mutually nurturing and responsible forms of interpersonal behavior, personal moral conversion enhances elementary human freedom. It alerts one to the destructive consequences of some personal choices and to the lifegiving potential of others.

Affective, intellectual, and moral conversion can all occur naturally. By that I mean that humans can decide for emotionally, intellectually, or morally responsible behavior in complete abstraction from God's historical self-revelation to humankind. That divine self-disclosure took unique, definitive, and normative shape in the incarnation. As a consequence, full, conscious access to God flows from the enabling illumination of the Breath of Christ, even though we find traces of Her presence in other religious traditions than the Christian.

**d. Religious Conversion.** By religious conversion I mean the decision to respond responsibly to the free, gratuitous, historical self-disclosure and self-communication of God. By Christian conversion I mean the decision to respond responsibly to the definitive, free, gratuitous, historical self-disclosure and self-communication of God accomplished in Jesus and in the illuminating power of the Breath that proceeds from Him.

Because the religious convert always responds to a free and humanly unmerited self-communication of God in love, authentic religious conversion never occurs naturally. God's graciousness enables and perfects it. Religious conversion, and especially Christian conversion, therefore, enhances elementary human freedom by creating within humans the capacity to respond not only to created realities but to the world-transcending reality of a self-communicating God.

Clearly, each moment within personal conversion extends and enhances elementary human freedom by expanding the human capacity to imagine, formulate, and evaluate the predictable consequences of different realizable forms of behavior. The different moments within personal conversion address and therefore help further liberate different realms of personal experience. Affective conversion frees up the emotions; intellectual conversion, the speculative mind; moral conversion, the practical mind. Religious conversion, especially Christian conversion, enhances even further the freedom born of the three natural forms of conversion by creating a novel context, that born of faith, within which affective, intellectual, and moral growth transpire. More specifically, religious conversion creates the possibilty of affective, intellectual, and moral growth in response to the liberating reality of God.

**f. The Dynamics of Personal Conversion.** We would, however, fail to do justice to the complex challenge posed by the human need to grow in personal freedom through personal conversion were we to ignore the ways in which the different forms of personal conversion mutually condition one another. For that conditioning extends the benefits of freedom effected by a specific form of conversion to the other forms as well.

We can identify five dynamics within personal conversion. (1) Affective conversion animates speculative, moral, and religious conversion. (2) Intellectual conversion seeks to inform affective, moral, and religious conversion. (3) Moral conversion helps orient affective, intellectual, and religious conversion to realities and values that challenge us to absolute and ultimate commitments. (4) Religious conversion, especially Christian conversion, transvalues affective, intellectual, and moral conversion. (5) Christian conversion mediates between affective and moral conversion. Let us examine each of these dynamics in greater detail for the light each throws on the conquest of authentic personal freedom.

The different qualities of freedom which each form of personal conversion engenders all have the capacity to extend human freedom by mutually conditioning one another. Affective conversion heals the heart of neurotic and psychotic rigidity and frees the imagination to dream. Rational, moral, and religious behavior deal in different ways with the same realities that the heart grasps appreciatively. The affectively converted person brings to speculation, prudential deliberation, and the exploration into God a hope and zest that vitalizes the human enterprise. The affective convert's imagination teems with fascinating possibilities. In all these ways, affective conversion **animates** the other forms of conversion by endowing them with emotional and imaginative freedom.

Affective conversion animates intellectual in two ways. First, it frees the mind from emotional attitudes that distort perceptions of reality. Repressed negative emotions cause us to overreact to the persons and things in our world as we project onto them meanings which they themselves do not signify. Paranoia peoples the world with non-existent enemies. Phobias endow heights, crowds, and other mundane realities with debilitating terror. Persons who threaten us usually symbolize for us often in unconscious ways aspects of ourselves which we fear to face but must if we are to see those who threaten us as the individuals they are. Second, affective conversion inspires the speculative mind with creative flexibility. When we formulate rational hypotheses we do not in a sense think logically. No logic supplies the mind with rules to come up with a correct explanation of the way things behave. Instead speculation begins with mind play. We must dally with unexplained facts, allow our fancies to imagine a variety of models, to imagine explanations, methods for solving some problem until the moment comes when we cry "I've go it!" and propose an educated guess about the causes of the unexplained facts that confront us.

Affective conversion animates moral conversion by freeing the conscience from prejudice and by endowing it with imaginative flexibility. Some immoral behavior roots itself in emotional disorders. Sexism, racism, and militarism, as we shall soon see, engage unconscious emotional attitudes that can betray the conscience into serious ethical irresponsibility. Neurotic attitudes can cause us to act in destructive ways toward the persons we deal with on a day to day basis. Affective conversion clarifies the conscience by uncovering the emotional roots of moral evil and healing the troublesome disorder. Affective conversion also frees the conscience to deal creatively with moral dilemmas. The human conscience lives distended between an ideal vision of the way people ought to behave and actual conduct. The healthy conscience solves moral dilemmas imaginatively. It appreciates the actual values ingredient in any ethical situation, understands clearly the moral ideal to which it is called and the principles that govern responsible moral behavior, regrets whatever in the situation falls short of the ideal, and then uses the imagination to decide not only prudentially but creatively how one might act to advance an imperfect situation the next possible step toward the perfect realization of the moral ideals and principles to which the conscience submits. In both these ways, then, affective conversion animates moral.

Affective conversion animates religious by unconvering the

emotional disorders that motivate sinful conduct and by inspiring religious hope. As we shall see, religious conversion, especially Christian conversion, demands the transvaluation in faith of natural human emotions. Nevertheless, affective conversion conditions and liberates Christian conversion in its own right. Understood in its broadest sense faith engages the entire human person: heart, head, conduct, personal and institutional transactions. Fully authentic faith demands then among other things a healthy affectivity in which to root itself. Not infrequently lack of faith springs from old emotional wounds: from being victimized by the hypocrisy of self-proclaimed believers, by manifest inconsistency and injustice in the church. Affective conversion helps bring to conscious healing emotional obstacles to faith. It also frees the human imagination to respond enthusiastically to divine beauty historically revealed.

In order to grow responsibly at an affective, moral, or religious level, we also need to understand the dynamics of emotional, moral, and fiducial development. In order to grow responsibly with our minds we need to understand how to understand. Intellectual conversion can then **inform** affective, moral, and religious growth with rational precision, with sensitivity both to a variety of ways of conceiving the same reality and to different methodological approaches to the emotional, moral, and religious questions that beset us. In the process, intellectual conversion enhances personal freedom in other areas of behavior than speculative.

The personality sciences, for example, yield many sound insights into the conditions for healthy affective development and into the causes of emotional illness. Moralists need to know the truth about moral situations before they can reach some judgment about how to respond to them ethically. Theology keeps religious faith from degenerating into a rigid fundamentalism. Scientists and scholars need to know the kinds of operational procedures that will lead their thought to correct solutions to speculative questions. Intellectual conversion teaches all of these attempts to understand human conduct to obey sound logic, to prefer more comprehensive explanatory and normative frames of reference, and to obey methods that foster true insight. In the process intellectual conversion endows human thought as well as the other forms of conversion with the kind of flexibility that leads to sound insight and validated judgments.

Both moral and religious conversion **orient** us to realities and values that make absolute and ultimate claims. Such realities and values orient us because they lure us by their beauty even as they stand in judgment over our ethical failures. They supply us with a plan and pattern of life, with a way of dealing with other persons. The endow our consciences with moral consistency. Moral conversion discovers ethical realities and values through prudential reasoning. Religious conversion discovers them through reflective faith and the gift of discernment. As a consequence, the two forms of conversion complement one another and together endow emotional and intellectual behavior with the freedom to respond selflessly.

Although moral realities and values bind the conscience, they should not be imposed on situations with the rigidity of a drill sergeant. We need to form our consciences imaginatively and creatively. When confronted with a moral dilemma, we should, however, never lie to ourselves about the ethical norms and ideals that constrain us. Those who adjust their principles from one situation to the next act pragmatically, not ethically. Nevertheless, genuine ethical ideals control the conscience by their beauty. They provide a vision of a world in which love, justice, and mutual selfless concern motivate human behavior rather than hatred, cupidity, and egotistical self-serving. Having come to clarity concerning the moral ideals it espouses, the deliberating conscience needs then to appreciate the genuine values ingredient in the problematic moral situation which confronts it. We cannot, however, appreciate any reality until we first deal with those aspects of it that threaten us. Once the conscience has dealt with threatening forces that blind it to the concrete values facing it and once it has by this means advanced to a sound appreciation of the good embodied in a problematic moral situation, it then needs to regret those elements of the situation that fall short of the ideals to which they ought to conform. The deliberating conscience then needs to use its creative imagination in order to decide how to advance the situation confronting it toward the most perfect embodiment of those ideals possible under the circumstances. Moreover, human consciences do not deduce the correct course of action with logical necessity. They decide it prudentially and with religious disernment. Prudence and discernment express judgments of the heart which seek nevertheless to conform to sound moral principles and ideals.

When it advances in abstraction from religious conversion, moral conversion develops naturally, but it ensures that personal affective and intellectual conversion advance with selfless responsibility. Moral conversion therefore introduces into the human pursuit of freedom a personal willingness to submit by choice to ethical constraints and to choose freely, when necessary, personal self-limitation, suffering, or even death when circumstances demand it in order that justice might be done. It frees the convert from abject slavery to egocentric concerns and for selfless concern for others.

Experience teaches us that people can all too easily seek to divorce affective growth from serious moral considerations. Some therapists seem to assume that moral discussions have no place in the therapeutic process. When, however, emotional development abstracts from the moral consequences of affectively motivated behavior, it teaches people to acquiesce in an unhealthy infantilism. Similarly, scientists and scholars have disassociated the search for insight from the concerns of conscience. We live today in hostage to the destructive capacity of nuclear weapons in part because some physicists at Los Alamos did precisely that. When art ignores morality it degenerates into propaganda, pornography, and other forms of artistic or literary decadence. When religion divorces piety from morality, it becomes the tool of sinister social forces, schools believers to hypocrisy, and inculcates shallow pietism and moral apathy.

Moral conversion, by contrast, demands that affective health be measured at least in part by the moral soundness of emotionally motivated conduct. It demands that scientists and scholars judge the success or failure of experimentation and research by moral as well as speculative norms. It helps the religiously converted deal with moral dilemmas for which divine revelation offers no answer. It thus orients the other forms of conversion to realities and values that make strictly ethical claims.

Because affective, intellectual, and moral conversion can all occur in abstraction from the historical self-revelation of God, religious conversion, and in special ways Christian conversion, **transvalues** them. An experience undergoes transvaluation when it is viewed in a novel frame of reference that demands the re-evaluation in its light of what one has experienced heretofore. The eruption of God into human history and the novel evaluative frame of reference born of fiducial consent to the divine self-communication to humans demands the re-evaluation of all naturally experienced realities. They must be judged now in the light of their relationship to a self-revealing God and of the moral consequences which consent to that revelation entails.

Religious conversion transforms affective conversion into repentance before God of the disordered affections--the rage, fear, and guilt--that fester in the heart, blind human perceptions, and alienate people from one another and from God. It transforms the hopes engendered by natural conversion into religious aspirations. Religious conversion transforms intellectual conversion into reflective faith. Religious conversion transforms human moral striving into a religious love that includes and transcends every created good.

Christian conversion, moreover, demands a certain quality of hope, faith, and love. Christian converts open their hearts, their minds, their daily choices to the guidance and illumination of the Breath of Jesus who comes to transform them in His image by teaching them to live as God's children. As a consequence, biblical aspirations and images shape Christian hope in normative ways and demand an imagination schooled to discover God in concrete sensible realities. Christian faith advances in a community in which the sharing of the charisms of the Holy Breath creates an ambience of communal belief that engenders and sustains personal faith. Christian conversion demands that religious love express the mind of Christ.

Jesus demanded of his disciples consent to a specific set of moral values. Jesus preached, not a rational morality, but one born of faith. Authentic faith, he insisted, includes a childlike trust in the providential care of God that heals the heart's anxious tendency to cling to material possessions and frees it to share the material supports of life with others. Such sharing includes hospitality, because it seeks to bring into existence a community of faith and of mutual concern. Sharing also redefines the purpose of labor. One labors in order to avoid making needless demands on others and in order to have something to share with those less fortunate than oneself.

Jesus also demanded of his disciples unconditioned faith. Since faith expresses itself in one's willingness to share with others, unconditioned faith demands too that such sharing be in some sense unconditioned, at least in this sense that no person be excluded in principle from one's practical concern. Authentic Christian sharing advances on the basis of need and not of merit. In the Christian community, therefore, the sharing of the supports of life imitates the universality and gratuity of God's love revealed in Christ. It thus abolishes social distinctions based on class, race, gender, or tradition and creates a human community with universal outreach.

Christian faith also springs from the repentant acknowledgement of one's own sinfulness and of the sinfulness of the human race in general. The sharing born of repentant faith must also as a consequence express a mutual forgiveness that imitates the divine forgiveness revealed in Christ. Moreover, such forgiveness measures the authenticity of the Christian community's worship.

Christian conversion begins in repentance. As the hopeful heart expands to the divine and human beauty incarnate in Jesus, it inspires the desire to become like Him. Authentic commitment to Jesus, however, demands the willingness to submit to the ethics of discipleship He proclaimed. In this way Christian conversion **mediates** between affective and moral conversion for it begins in the converted heart and culminates in commitment to a divinely revealed moral vision of how humans ought to relate to one another in community.

Converted consent to Christ commits one then to live by His ethics of discipleship. That ethics helps give practical shape to Christian hope, faith, and love. It mediates the creation of therapeutic communities of hope whose fidelity to Jesus' moral vision expresses their ultimate hope in His second coming. It fosters the sharing of the charisms of the Breath of Christ that creates the shared faith consciousness of the Christian community that nurtures in turn the personal faith of its members. It defines the moral content of Christian love.

A Christian ethics of discipleship demands, then, far more than the decalogue with its negative proscriptions. It demands more than legal, commutative, or distributive justice. It commits the converted Christian to lifelong labor to bring into existence a certain kind of faith community of truly selfless love and concern whose members, like its founder, are willing to lay down their lives for one another and for those in need. By orienting human hope, belief, and moral striving toward a moral ideal that inculcates even greater selflessness than rational morality, Christian religious conversion enhances even further the freedom to transcend selfish, egocentric concerns engendered by natural moral conversion. In the process it further perfects personal moral liberty. It frees the imagination to perceive the reality of God in the concrete and sensible. It frees the mind to expand to a vision of divine truth. It frees the human heart to love with the atoning, forgiving love of Christ.

**g. The Characteristics of Authentic Personal Freedom.** Authentic personal freedom, as we have seen, roots itself in deeper soil than that which nourishes elementary human freedom. The latter grounds itself in the ability to distinguish realistically viable paths of action. The former grounds itself in a four-fold personal conversion. Conversion transforms elementary freedom into personally responsible freedom.

Because authentic personal freedom enhances elementary human freedom itself, it suffers from the same constraints. Environment, conceptual flexibility, the ability to think in different frames of reference, skills, personal decisions all cause authentic personal freedom to thrive or to languish.

Because authentic personal freedom resides in humans, it cannot, then, entirely escape the limitations of the human condition. It remains finite. In moments of irresponsible backsliding, it can flicker. Because each individual stands at a historically different stage in the conversion process, authentic personal freedom, like elementary human freedom, exhibits qualitative diversity. Finally, conversion frees from and frees for. It frees one from unrepentant, irresponsible behavior and frees one for personally responsible, selfless living.

Conversion, however, attenuates the constraints that condition human freedom. It enhances the human capacity to respond conceptually, opens up new and liberating perspectives on the human conduct of life, inculcates liberating virtues and the freedom to act selflessly, and engerders commitment to the creation of liberating environments of grace in which persons respond to one another with mutually nurturing concern.

Authentic personal freedom also enjoys traits absent from elementary human freedom. It acknowleges its accountabilty to other persons and to God. The fruit of self-discipline, it roots itself in cultivated virtue. It therefore submits freely to self-limitation, self-diminishment, and even to death when personal responsibility demands such suffering. In other words, personal conversion endows personal freedom with a moral self-transcendence that expresses personal care and concern for other people. Finally, because the cultivation of authentic personal freedom commits one to the cultivation of emotional, intellectual, moral, and religious authenticity, it demands idealism, realism, and patience: It demands idealism because the convert aspires to a self-ideal that measures the authenticity and inauthenticity of human personal relationships. It demands realism because every person falls somewhat short of the ideals to which authentic behavior submits. It demands patience with the spontaneous resistance to conversion that sin and ego inertia breed.

## (III)

Elementary human freedom roots itself in the human capacity to distinguish realistic alternatives of action. Authentic personal freedom roots itself in the dynamic interplay of affective, intellectual, moral, and religious conversion. These four forms of conversion define the scope of personal conversion. A truly liberating search for freedom from institutional oppression roots itself in a socio-political conversion authenticated by personal conversion.

**3. Socio-Political Conversion.** The distinction between personal and socio-political conversion results in part, but only in part, from the distinction between the human self and the environment which sustains or destroys its life. Every human person defines itself into a certain kind of self through dynamic interaction with its environment. Moreover, because the environment with which it interacts helps define the character of human personal experience, environmental forces stand within that experience and provide it with its "what," with the reality being experienced. The experiencing person provides the "who" (the experiencing self), and the "how" (the way experienced reality is experienced).

One's own personal decisions differ actually and concretely from the decisions that shape one's extracorporeal environment. As a consequence, the finite human mind can decide to take responsiblity for personal decisions, their motivations and consequences, without at the same time taking responsiblity for the decisions that shape its environment. That fact enables an individual to undergo a personal conversion without advancing to socio-political conversion.

An individual who has undergone personal conversion but not socio-political conversion lacks full authenticity. We shall examine the reasons why in greater detail shortly. For the moment it suffices to note that the personal convert who lacks socio-political conversion lives a somewhat privatized life. Such an individual may, however, function responsibly at an interpersonal level.

Interpersonal relationships exhibit the following traits. Those who stand in interpersonal relationships know one another's names and respond to one another with concrete immediacy. Interpersonal relationships give immediate satisfaction or cause immediate pain. They engage a relatively small number of individuals and can therefore be managed with greater ease than more complex, impersonal institutional relationships.

The personally converted may on occasion exhibit laudable concern to ensure the authenticity of the decisions of others with whom they enjoy an interpersonal relationship. Parents seek to educate their children to make responsible choices. Friends may call one another to accountability. As a consequence, the distinction between the self and its environment only partially grounds the distinction between personal and socio-political conversion. The personally converted need not prescind from the authenticity of every decision that shapes their environments. Rather, they tend to restrict such concern to interpersonal relationships. Those therefore who have yet to undergo socio-political conversion opt to ignore the authenticity of certain kinds of decisions taken by others, namely, those which shape the impersonal institutional structures that impinge on personal experience.

Personal relationships undergo inevitable institutionalization. Put technically, institutionalization results from the reciprocal typification of habitualized actions by identifiable groups of actors.[4] Put less technically, institutionalization occurs whenever people habitually assume recognized roles in their mutual dealings with one another. Roles prescribe a certain way of acting and endow social relationships with a specific habitual character. Such role playing occurs at an interpersonal level. For example, although different cultures define differently what is permitted to parents, children, grandparents, uncles, aunts, cousins, and in-laws, these profoundly interpersonal relationships all involve an element of role-playing.

As institutions grow in complexity, the quality of the relationships among the individuals that make them up takes on an increasingly impersonal character. The immediacy of interpersonal communication gives way to anonymous human dealings in which decisions are taken that shape the lives of nameless, faceless multitudes of individuals. In interpersonal dealings, responsibility can be assigned for specific acts with relative ease. A husband either remembers or forgets his wife's birthday. Children either obey or disobey their parents. The responsiblity for the decisions taken in large, corporate institutions is often shared and therefore less easy to pin down. Interpersonal relationships yield immediate satisfaction or pain. In large, corporate institutions both the reward of faithful service and the punishment for infidelity takes more time. That delay heightens the risk of injustice. Moreover, large, corporate institutions serve large constituencies. They can as a consequence accomplish more good or wreak greater evil than small, interpersonal institutions. The size, the anonymity, the diffuse responsibility, and the complexity of large, impersonal, corporate institutions makes them more difficult to control than institutionalized interpersonal relationships. Their massive power demoralizes individuals who would seek to change them and forces them into collaboration with others who also ambition institutional transformation.

An individual who lacks socio-political conversion prefers to leave in the hands of others the responsibility for those decisions that give shape to impersonal, institutional relationships. The politically converted, on the other hand, take responsibility (that is, they acknowledge their accountability) for the motives and consequences of the decisions that shape large, impersonal institutions to the extent that they can influence those decisions.

**a. The Moral Inevitability of Socio-Political Conversion..** When conversion occurs at a personal level but not at a socio-political level, the convert cannot claim full authenticity. Authentic people act with complete personal responsibility. The inauthentic act irresponsibly despite their commitment to do otherwise. Full authenticity comes with conversion at every level. Inevitably the personal convert who shirks socio-political conversion can never act with complete personal self-consistency. Let us reflect on why such inauthenticity follows with moral inevitability.

First of all, the personal convert seeks authentic self-understanding at an affective, intellectual, moral, and religious level. All personal self-understanding is, however, socially mediated and therefore conditioned by both interpersonal and impersonal institutional structures.

All institutions develop historically. Social roles are first evolved, then assigned, then legitimated as they are handed on from one generation to the next. The social roles we learn to play shape our self-understanding in both conscious and unconscious ways. One nurtured in a racist or sexist society can scarcely avoid socialization into racist or sexist attitudes. Moreover, every human belongs not only to small, interpersonal social groupings but also to larger, impersonal institutions like cities, nations, churches, businesses. The personal convert who refuses to deal consciously and responsibly with the inauthenticities implicit in the roles assigned by large, impersonal institutions will with moral inevitability succumb unconsciously to them and as a consequence fall short, even at a personal level, of complete converted authenticity.

Second, the moral inevitability of yielding to personal inauthenticity if one resists socio-political conversion also follows from the social processes by which institutions legitimate and maintain themselves. Institutions begin to acquire legitimation when the forces which gave rise to them are ignored, forgotten, or somehow obscured in the minds of their members. The very transmission of accepted social roles from one generation to the next forces institutions to legitimate themselves in the eyes of their members, for the new generation must be persuaded to act out the institutional roles assigned them. Within the histories of institutions we may distinguish three overlapping levels of legitimation. The active transmission of institutional roles provides the first level. It then engenders legends, myths, and rituals that re-enforce the traditional forms of social behavior. Finally, a society may construct rational explanations as well as ideologies that sanction the roles it assigns its members.

Legitimated societies need to maintain themselves against threats from within and from without. Heretics may arise within a social group who refuse to acquiesce in their assigned role or to accept the traditional explanations of why they should. Competing societies may propose, sometimes militantly, a world view that challenges and contradicts accepted forms of social behavior. Think, for example, of the challenges and contradictions rife in the contemporary confrontation among the first, second, and third worlds.

Threats to a traditional social order may be treated, eliminated, refuted, or assimilated. Elimination seeks the death of adversaries. Treatment uses therapy to reconcile dissidents to the **status quo.** Refutation seeks to discredit those who threaten social stability and thus to undermine or eliminate their acceptability and social effectiveness. Assimilation adjusts the traditional definition of social relationships and thus eliminates threatening individuals and groups by incorporating them into a new, mutually acceptable rearrangement of social roles and responsibilities. Recent theological developments in the Catholic church illustrate the processes of refutation and assimilation. At the second Vatican council many theological positions which prior to the council conservatives had attacked as heterodox came to be endorsed by the official pastoral magisterium. In other words the council elected to assimilate the new ideas rather than refute them. In the process the relationship of pope and bishops, of clergy, religious, and laity were radically redefined.

The maintenance of social order against threats from both within and without a given society inevitably engages vested social interests. Some injustice pervades every human society. The vested interests which perpetrate injustice rationalize them with propagandistic ideologies that seek to dull the consciences of both the dominant elites and the dominated. In every society, then, individuals will be socialized into roles that situate them with respect to exploiter or exploited, to power elites or to the powerless and marginalized. Inevitably, social roles shape personal self-understanding. No one can as a consequence attain full personal authenticity who refuses to deal with the institutionalized vested interests that willy nilly shape one's own personal attitudes, beliefs, and conduct to unjust and exploitative ends.

A third argument for the moral inevitability of socio-political conversion as a condition for complete personal authenticity can be derived from reflection on the dynamic interplay of the two levels of human socialization. Humans are socialized at a primary and at a secondary level. Primary socialization occurs within a family context.

Secondary socialization introduces the child into other subgroups within human society.

Children are linked to their parents with deep bonds of affection. Healthy children learn very early to trust their parents, and they tend to adopt with unhesitating spontaneity their parents' attitudes, beliefs, and vision of the world. The process of primary socialization tends to give lasting shape to the individual character.

Through secondary socialization the young are introduced into the interlocking subworlds that constitute the society that nurtures them: neighborhood, school, the workplace, politics. Some forms of secondary socialization can involve a high degree of emotional identification with one's mentors: for example, medical training, the religious indoctrination of converts, the study of music. In these instances, secondary socialization takes on many of the characteristics of a novitiate: isolation from disturbing influences, intense study under quasi-parental figures, sacrifice, commitment, reorientation of life style. More frequently, however, secondary socialization can be sloughed or unlearned with relative ease. The draftee returning to civilian life quickly unlearns the habits of boot camp.

Both primary and secondary socialization instill a host of attitudes, beliefs, and commitments that are accepted naively and uncritically. Converted authenticity, however, demands the critical revision of every habit tainted with inauthenticity. A child may imbibe from parents fundamentalistic religious attitudes, an ideological stance that masks serious social injustice, moral attitudes irreconcilable with responsible social behavior, habits irreconcilable with committed gospel living. Patriotism may motivate unthinking allegiance to chauvinism, militarism, economic exploitation of other nations. One may internalize the injustices inherent in a particular capitalistic or socialistic economy.

One cannot face adequately the inauthenticities bred into one's character through involvement in interpersonal and impersonal social structures without committing oneself to change those structures that breed injustice and inauthenticity. One cannot attend constantly to the pressures they exert upon one's attitudes, beliefs, and commitments. Unless changed, institutionalized injustice will continue to shape even the converted, however subtly and unconsciously, to its perverted ends.

A privatized response to the injustices inculcated by large, impersonal institutions will never engender complete personal authenticity. A privatized resonse to injustice abjures personally unjust activity but refuses to commit itself in an ongoing and systematic manner to eliminating institutionalized injustice. Those who advance to personal conversion without going on to socio-political conversion seek privatized, personal solutions to public, impersonal problems. Such solutions are doomed to sterility, for until unjust institutions are changed by social collaboration they continue to teach people, often in subtle, unconscious ways, to acquiesce in the role of oppressor or oppressed. Those who settle for privatized solutions to the injustices perpetrated by impersonal, public institutions also sin by omission, for they prefer not to act effectively against injustice even though their activity could make a difference. Finally, the Christian who acquiesces in privatized solutions to public problems of injustice disobeys the command of Christ to preach the good news to **every** creature, including the rich and the powerful.

Once one concedes not only the possibility but the moral inevitability of socio-political conversion as a condition for complete converted authenticity, one must also come to terms with the way in which such a conversion interacts with a fourfold personal conversion. We may identify two dynamics in the interface between personal and political conversion. First, socio-political conversion deprivatizes and thus authenticates all four forms of personal conversion. Second, a fourfold personal conversion authenticates socio-political conversion by providing the norms for responsible political behavior. Let us try to understand some of the complexities of these two dynamics.

    **b. Socio-Political Conversion Deprivatizes Personal.** Socio-political conversion **deprivatizes** personal conversion in two ways. First of all, it demands that the personally converted individual come to terms with The Others, with alien and often threatening persons, groups, and institutions in human society. Second, socio-political conversion culminates in personal dedication to one or more concrete political causes. It thereby commits the convert to collaboration with others in the reform of unjust social institutions. Let us reflect on how this occurs.

Every human personality is marked by biological, historical, and social limitations. A biologically based consciousness possesses only limited habits, limited skills. It views the world from a finite angle of vision. One's personal history determines the relative width of that angle. Moreover, individuals are socialized into specific social groups that lend a determined and therefore finite character to personal self-awareness. One is socialized into a specific family, economic class, city, region, nation, race, sexual identity. As a consequence one experiences members of other social groups as alien, unfamiliar, as THE OTHERS.

The Others may fascinate or tantalize, as in human sexual awakening. They can threaten as well. In situations of social conflict The Others can intimidate, terrify, enrage. We understand The Others initially in judgments of prejudice that can be tinged with bigotry. The human mind spontaneously categorizes the members of alien groups somewhat stereotypically. We look on certain forms of behavior as typically French, typically masculine or feminine, typically black, typically upper, middle, or lower class. Neurotic or psychotic hostility can suffuse such stereotypes with bigoted rigidity. Because of the superficiality of judgments of prejudice, confrontation with The Others can often demand the revision of attitudes, beliefs, values, or one's religious stance. Moreover, because one's own self-understanding is conditioned by the way one interacts with others in society, confrontation with The Others demands self-confrontation as well and the revision of one's own sense of personal identity. For this very reason interaction with The Others especially in situations of social conflict can challenge the finite human ego, saddled as it is with perennial inertia, to the depths of its being. The fact that such a challenge promises personal growth and an expanded horizon on reality does not make it any more initially appealing.

Inevitably socio-political conversion also plunges one into the maelstrom of socio-political conflict, where vested interests vie with one another for positions of power and privilege. It demands that one deal with individuals and groups that threaten one emotionally. It demands that one deal with ideologically contradictory opinions and with conflicting moral claims. It demands that one deal with those who profess unfamiliar and contradictory religious creeds.

Aggressive individuals welcome a good fight and thrive in the political fray. Other people (I suspect the majority of good folk) would just as soon avoid its unpleasantness. That reluctance keeps many an individual bound in a privatized and therefore only partially authentic form of personal conversion. Others refrain from confronting institutional injustice because the complexity and massivness of large institutions bewilder them. Others fear the moral contamination of political involvement.

Socio-political conversion not only forces confrontation with The Others, but it also culminates in personal dedication to one or more concrete political causes. We can within personal conversion distinguish stages of commitment. Even when personal conversion occurs suddenly and unexpectedly, it seems likely that the personality has been undergoing progressive transformation at an unconscious level. The sudden conversion raises that fact to consciousness and crystallizes it in a commitment. Socio-political conversion too ordinarily advances in stages that parallel the stages of personal conversion.

We can distinguish analytically eight possible stages within socio-political conversion. (1) **The Stage of Denial.** At this stage one closes one's eyes to the existence of impersonal, institutional evil and prefers to live in a familiar, privatized world to which The Others have no access or else access defined by the accepted injustices of the **status quo.** (2) **The Stage of Objectification.** At this stage one begins to acknowledge the injustices institutionalized in the **status quo** but disclaims any responsibility for them or any capacity to do anything about them. (3) **The Stage of Hesitant Openness.** At this stage one begins to acknowledge the possibility of a practical, socially and politically responsible, personal response to institutional injustice but remains loathe to take any concrete action to change the unjust situation or to revise one's social self-understanding. (4) **The Stage of Repentant Self-confrontation.** At this stage one begins to deal both theoretically and practically with the attitudes, beliefs, and religious and moral values that motivate one's apathy and inertia in the face of institutional injustice. (5) **The Stage of Convalescent Progress.** At this stage the converting individual begins to modify his or her social self-understanding by an initial critique and revision of oppressive attitudes, ideologies, social and religious codes but has yet to face all the demands which converted authenticity at a socio-political level demands. (6) **The Stage of Progressive Integration.** At this stage the converting individual begins to acknowledge the full scope of the institutional evils that infect human society and inspire personal inauthenticity. (7) **The Threshold of Conversion.** At this stage of socio-political conversion the potential convert stands personally and verbally committed to the cause of institutional justice but responds to institutional injustice only sporadically and haphazardly. (8) **The Stage of Full Socio-political Conversion.** At this stage the convert acknowledges that sporadic or haphazard opposition to institutional injustice fails to satisfy the demands of authentic, fully responsible living and espouses one or more major political cause.[5]

The socio-political convert must espouse concrete causes because none other exist and because failure to oppose institutional injustice helps perpetuate it. Inevitably, then, inactivity in the face of institutional injustice corrupts the apathetic by causing them to sin by omission.

Socio-political conversion also demands commitment to a cause because institutional inertia demands concerted, collaborative effort in order to right unjust social, economic, and political structures.

Active commitment to a major social and political cause alters personal self-understanding, for it completes the personalizing process we call conversion and transforms the personally converted individual into a fully responsible adult. By radically modifying one's social relationships, socio-political conversion reshapes the convert's self-understanding. It revises the convert's oppressive attitudes toward The Others and inspires dreams of a world freed of injustice. It forces the convert to discard ideologies that rationalize institutional wrongdoing, to denounce institutional evil, and to demand truth telling from the representatives of oppressive institutions. It expands one's awareness of moral responsibility to encompass concern for the common good; it inspires concern that the dignity of all persons, especially the marginal and oppressed, find respect at the hands of large institutions; and it motivates active defense of the right of every individual to a fair and human share in the good things of life. Socio-political conversion commits one to the cause of ensuring legal, distributive, and commutative justice for every member of society, especially those whose rights are most flouted. Finally, socio-political conversion leads the religious convert to judge institutions as well as individual persons in the light of the righteousness revealed by God. It forces the Christian convert to recognize that the ethics of discipleship proclaimed by Jesus defines not only the moral content of Christian charity but also the meaning of social justice. For the politically converted Christian no social order qualifies as completely just in the eyes of God unless its institutions ensure that every individual shares impartially in the blessings of this life on the basis of need rather than of merit only and unless institutions inculcate the willingness to forgive which Jesus demanded of his follwers. Clearly, as socio-political personal conversion deprivatizes personal conversion, it demands new kinds of responsibility from the personally converted. In this way socio-political conversion authenticates personal.

One may argue rationally that concern for the common good characterizes all responsible social behavior. That same concern flows inexorably from the moral demands of Christian discipleship. The common good consists in the totality of those conditions required to ensure that all individuals and groups in society contribute to and share in social benefits in an adequate and ready manner. Concern for the common good demands then that both personal and institutional behavior exhibit a preferential option for the poor. Such an option does not ally one narrowly to the lower class. Rather it seeks to incorporate the oppressed and the marginalized into the mainstream of social life by enabling them to participate fully in and to contribute actively to the shared life of a community.

Loyalty to a cause creates both groups and communities. Interpersonal relationships organize communities. Functional relationships organize groups. Since, however, members of groups also form interpersonal relationships, communitarian arrangements can also inform the shared life of groups. Loyalty to a cause offers both communities and groups a plan for social collaboration and binds together individuals dedicated to the same cause. Loyalty to the cause of justice also imbues human behavior with the spirit of self-sacrifice, discipline, and dedication that flows from moral conversion. It engages one personally but also transcends personal considerations by demanding that one be willing not only to live but, if necessary, to die for the cause of justice. Such loyalty creates solidarity with the oppressed. Dedication to the realization of a just social order even demands on occasion dedication to lost causes that make claims upon the conscience not because they will succeed but because God wills them. Loyalty to the cause of a just social order inspires visions of a world transformed, but it demands too that one deal realistically with the limitations and inertia of concrete social situations and rest content with partial victories when complete success eludes the servants of justice.[6]

Human finitude forces us to pick and choose among the concrete causes to which we actually devote our energies. Political activism needs to be balanced against other needs and responsibilities. I find it helpful to distinguish three levels of socio-political involvement: responsible citizenship, participatory activism, and full-time professional activism.

On most major issues of socio-political significance, most of us can act like responsible citizens. We can keep reasonably informed of the facts and arguments of the case; and when the time comes, we can vote conscientiously. The participatory activist collaborates with full-time activists to support some specific political cause. One might, for example join a political lobby like Bread for the World, Sane, or Sojourners and dedicate some time on a regular basis to actively pursuing the political goals of the organization one chooses to join. Such participatory activism demands more active commitment than responsible citizenship but falls short of the commitment of professional activists, who make the espousal of political causes a full-time personal career. In practice, the socio-political convert must decide which causes deserve different degrees of commitment. Every important cause deserves to be treated with responsible citizenship. Those who cannot engage in full-time political activism can and should, if they claim to have experienced political conversion, dedicate themselves whenever possible to one or other cause as a participatory activist.

**c. Personal Conversion Authenticates Socio-Political.** We have been reflecting on the way in which socio-political conversion transforms personal. It deprivatizes and authenticates the latter by demanding that affective, intellectual, moral, and religious growth transpire in social and political confrontation with The Others and by dedicating the convert in important and concrete ways to the cause of justice. Let us now begin to reflect on the ways in which personal conversion transforms socio-political conversion. As we shall see, personal conversion authenticates political by providing a normative insight into the meaning of political responsibility.

If the personally converted cannot achieve even full personal authenticity unless they advance to socio-political conversion, the politically converted cannot act in authentic ways to counteract injustice without undergoing an integral, fourfold personal conversion. Personal conversion yields a normative insight into the kinds of attitudes, beliefs, commitments, and religious hypocrisy that engender and perpetuate institutionalized injustice, and it inculcates the traits of character that foster responsible freedom in the service of justice.

**(1) Affective Conversion Authenticates Socio-Political.** All social structures root themselves in habits. Habitual patterns of acting are first typified, then legitimized and inculcated. Oppressive social structures can, then, express emotional attitudes; and those attitudes can engage the unconscious human mind.

Affective conversion facilitates the identification of disordered attitudes that engender unjust and oppressive social structures. Racism, sexism, and militarism, for example, all root themselves in deepseated emotions, many of them unconscious. Emotions perform two important cognitive functions. They disclose to us in relatively vague, initial perceptions the dynamic laws, or tendencies, present in the persons and things we encounter. Emotions also pass intuitive judgment on the best way to deal with those persons and things that we understand imaginatively. Images clarify our initial, vague, affective perceptions of the real. They lend meaningful shape to dreams, stories, lyrics, prophetic visions, and felt judgments of prudence and of discernment.

As we have seen, repressed negative emotions can engender varying degrees of personal bondage. They can also motivate social behavior. When they do, they cast people in stereotyped roles that entrap them and sow the seeds of social conflict. Among the images that shape human intuitive perceptions both consciously and unconsciously, archetypal images stand out for their capacity to organize and integrate for good or for ill imaginative perceptions and intuitive judgments of feeling. Racism, sexism, and some of the social expressions of militarism give evidence of engaging the dark, destructive energy of several archetypes.

Racism engages the archetype of the shadow. The shadow represents the dark side of the psyche: unconscious feelings of hostility, fear, and shame which an individual needs to face consciously but ordinarily fears to, at least initially. When the shadow surfaces in dreams it has the same sex as the dreamer. The emergence of the shadow normally chills the heart at first with terror. If, however, one learns to face and befriend the shadow by bringing to conscious healing the dark impulses it represents, the shadow takes on benign characteristics, as hitherto violent and potentially destructive emotions begin to be set to creative and constructive purposes. The refusal to face the shadow breeds shadow possession and the tendency to project onto other persons the shame, violence, terror, and guilt that fester in one's own heart. Because dark skinned persons symbolize to racists at an unconscious level aspects of themselves that they fear and loathe, they tend to project the very attitudes their own shadows symbolize onto innocent individuals whose only offense lies in the fact that they were born with a darker skin pigmentation. The refusal of racists to repent of their own neurotic and psychotic tendencies shapes the ways they speak and act toward blacks. They deride and insult blacks, stereotype them as racially inferior, avoid them socially, persecute them with economic, legal, and physical violence. In racist societies like our own, these destructive forms of behavior assume an habitual character and school both whites and blacks to acquiesce in stereotypical forms of behavior.[7]

An analogous process gives rise to the battle of the sexes. Hero myths abound in patriarchal, male-dominated cultures. The typical hero is born in obscurity, called to some momentous quest in which he must slay a dragon, rescue an imprisoned maiden, and return home triumphant to wed her and live happily ever after. Hero myths interpret through narrative masculine coming of age. In patriarchal myths only males dare heroic deeds of derring-do. Women are cast in passive roles. They must be rescued in their weakness and helplessness and gaze in admiration on the successful hero as he savors the fruits of his exploits. Institutionalized bigotry can and all too frequently does transform these archetypal images into stereotypes. Men and women are then schooled to acquiesce in rigid sex roles that either curtail or prohibit the freedom and opportunity that women enjoy in the social, economic, political, and educational arena.[8]

Militaristic societies are also characterized by macho strutting and bluster. The militarization of democratic societies occurs when the military exert decisive influence over political policies. Militarism feeds on a bellicose nationalism, chauvinism, ethnocentrism, and xenophobia. Militaristic societies expand aggressively, glorify military might, and idealize discipline, regimentation, and obedience to authority. Under the Reagan administration, we have witnessed a growing militarization of culture in this country that has escalated the arms race and moved the two great superpowers nearer to the undeclared hostility of the cold war and ultimately to nuclear holocaust.[9]

While machismo and its attendant neuroses and psychoses certainly feeds and is nurtured by militaristic social structures, the collective paranoia which motivates the arms race and is inspired by it engages another archetype besides that of the macho hero: namely, the archetype of the shadow. Militaristic rhetoric tends to project onto real or imagined adversaries the very aggressiveness on which it thrives. To the extreme peril of the rest of the human race the United States and Russia seem to be increasingly frozen in a shadow relationship in which each nation sees reflected in the other its own conscious and unconscious violent propensities.

Racism, sexism, and militarism, therefore, all illustrate large, impersonal, institutionalized tendencies that root themselves in and nurture disordered human attitudes charged with archetypal, symbolic power. Personal affective conversion authenticates political conversion in three ways: (1) It raises to consciousness the emotional disorders which impersonal, oppressive social structures engender and on which they feed. (2) It demands the repentant renunciation of all such disordered attitudes and the conduct they inspire. (3) By healing the human heart of bondage to unacknowledged rage, fear, and guilt, affective conversion also liberates the human imagination to envision a world unmarred by social oppression.

**(2) Intellectual Conversion Authenticates Socio-Political.** Intellectual conversion authenticates socio-political conversion by unmasking the ideologies that seek to rationalize situations of oppression. The term "ideology" has been used in a variety of senses. Here I define it as a popular pseudo-rationalization of some situation of injustice that postures as a self-evident truth. We may distinguish three common kinds of ideology: ideologies of isolation, ideologies of exploitation, and ideologies of forceful domination.

Ideologies of isolation fragment human society in oppressive ways. Individualism illustrates the process of which I speak. The founding fathers of this nation tended to acquiesce and popularize an aggressive, bourgeois individualism. The American romantics who created North American culture in the first part of the nineteenth century raised the cult of individual eccentricity to a fine art. Capitalism has transformed it into a way of life. Individualism breeds personal and public irresponsibility. It lulls the conscience into believing that any act taken in one's own self interest ultimately benefits the interests of others. In the process it clothes selfishness in the white robe of virtue. A generic ideology, individualism can assume a variety of forms and motivates other fragmenting ideologies.

Classism exemplifies a more specific kind of fragmenting ideology. Classist ideologies supply oppressive dominant groups with shallow rationalizations for continuing to exploit the weak and the marginal. Stereotypical conceptions of the poor common among members of the middle and upper classes illustrate the ways in which classist ideologies operate. The economically advantaged commonly assume that poor people possess little because they are lazy, shiftless, and irresponsible. In other words, they blame the poor for the degrading poverty in which they find themselves and thus absolve themselves and other financially advantaged individuals from the responsiblity of lifting a finger to alleviate the oppression born of poverty. Studies of poverty in this country reveal, however, that those poor who have no jobs ordinarily lack employment because they cannot work. Indeed, the aged, the physically disabled, female heads of households with large families comprise the bulk of the poor in this nation. Classist ideological rationalizations for ignoring poverty seek to preserve, with obfuscating rhetoric the social, economic, and political injustices that divide human society into advantaged and disadvantaged classes.[10]

Ideologies of segregation also exemplify socially fragmenting rationalizations of injustice. Racism, as Cornel West has shown, typifies the ease with which ideologies of segregation draw on a variety of cultural sources to isolate individuals and groups socially. During the renaissance and the enlightenment positive science defended its right to investigate every phenomenon, including the phenomenon of race. Linnaeus divided humanity somewhat facilely into four races: the european, asiatic, african, and american. He did not rank the races hierarchically. But the tendency to do so surfaced quickly in scientific treatises on race. Buffon believed that humans were naturally white and that dark skin, having resulted from life in a warmer climate, would fade in colder latitudes. Classical ideals of beauty derived from Greek art and philosophy endowed white anatomy with normative claims. As scientific thought advanced into the enlightenment, prejudice against the black race suffused speculation about race with overt bigotry. Montesquieu doubted that blacks belong to the human race. Voltaire believed that both blacks and Indians belong to a distinct species from whites. Both Hume and Jefferson believed in the black race's natural inferiority to the white. Kant questioned whether blacks could ever achieve anything culturally. Phrenology argued to the essential inferiority of blacks from the different shape and cranial capacity of black and white skulls. Religious fundamentalism stigmatized blacks as the descendants of Ham and cited the New Testament to justify enslaving blacks.[11] Sexist ideologies use similar rhetoric to stigmatize women as inferior, weak, untrustworthy, and fundamentally content with a subservient social standing.

Ideologies of exploitation rationalize the ways in which institutions abuse people unjustly for the purposes of reaping some economic or political gain. In this country capitalism has spawned a number of such ideologies. Capitalism began in England in the eighteenth and nineteenth centuries when the peasants were expelled from the land and forced to migrate to the big cities and sell their labor in order to survive. The same period of English history witnessed the decline of the aristocracy and the rise of the middle class.

Capitalism rests on the market system. The market system allows economic activity to respond to the windfalls and disasters of the marketplace. It allows individuals to seek work where they wish, at least in principle. It allows anyone (in principle) to buy and own land. Under the market system banks and financial corporations manage the flow of wealth into economic production. Money becomes capital when it is employed to make more money.

The factors of production which allow such accumulation of capital do not exist in a precapitalist societies. Those factors include the services of labor and of land and capital itself. In a capitalist economy aristocrats become poor, labor is divorced from the general fabric of day-to-day living, ancestral land is transformed into real estate, treasure becomes capital. The capitalistic market system empowers the members of the bourgeoisie to accumulate more and more wealth and allows the peasant class to rise or to perish within the system. Technology enables members of the middle class to gain advantage of their competitors in a free market economy. It also depersonalizes labor and leads to mass production.[12]

Capitalism has clothed itself in a variety of ideological garbs. It adopted **laissez faire** liberalism as its first pseudo-justification. **Laissez-faire** capitalism postulates that human society functions like an organism and follows its own laws of growth and decline, including economic laws. In its original formulation the doctrine of **laissez-faire** also adopted a Hobbesian pessimism toward human nature. It assumed that greed and self-interest motivate human economic acitivty but that the competition born of greed suffices to check its excesses. In other words, the competing greed of independent economic agents would allegedly prevent any one of them from achieving complete success.

**Laissez-faire** capitalism also assumed that the quantity of demand shapes the free market. It proposed the law of supply and demand as the driving principle of a capitalist economy. That law asserts that commodities in greater demand will draw higher prices, while commodities in less demand will draw lower. In the eighteenth and early nineteenth century, **laissez-faire** capitalists believed that the market regulates itself automatically, although the notion has fallen into economic ill repute in more recent times.

Adam Smith provided capitalism with this, its first ideology. He taught that the accumulation of capital by aggressive entrepreneurs benefits society as a whole. He anticipated that the number of available workers would increase and decrease with the increase and decrease of wages. He predicted that a free market would adjust itself automatically to the benefit of society as a whole. As wages rise, the number of workers increases. An expanded workforce produces more goods. The law of supply and demand lowers prices as the abundance of goods decreases the demand for them. Lowered income would then force the lowering of wages and a diminished work force. Fewer workers produce less commodities and thus force prices up. Smith predicted that with each cycle the economy would grow stronger to the benefit of the body politic. Therefore, he warned, let the economy alone. Government should not meddle in its organic workings but allow the market to take care of itself. For a time, this optimistic economic prognosis provided an important rationalization for the industrial revolution with all of its concomitant horrors: sweatshops, child labor, urban slums.

Since the days of Adam Smith the capitalist system has spawned other ideologies. It has clothed itself in the robes of democracy. It has depicted itself as the guardian of entrepreneurial creativity, as the best hope of the good life. It has claimed to stand guard over human freedom. None of these claims bear up under close scrutiny. Even though the emergence of democratic, parliamentary institutions parallelled the growth of capitalism, history offers no evidence that capitalism ensures the growth of political freedom. Rather, democracy reacts on the capitalistic system, either to attenuate some of its injustices or to become the tool of big business. Nor does capitalism guarantee the success of entrepreneurial aggressiveness. On the contrary, as Karl Marx correctly predicted, it tends to concentrate wealth and economic power in the hands of a few individuals and of a few large corporations. In the year 1984 alone approximately 500,000 small entrepreneurs fell victim to large corporations in the United States alone. We also have reason to question capitalism's ability when left to its own resources to guarantee the good life. A capitalist economy does not provision efficiently goods and services that do not wear a price tag: education, local government services, public health. In market societies tax breaks tend to favor the rich while the poor languish in misery. Capitalism commercializes culture and levels its quality to a marketable least common denominator. Moreover, contemporary capitalism, like contemporary socialism, suffers from a world-wide economic malaise, as unemployment, stagflation (economic stagnation combined with inflation), and financial instability suffuse the marketplace with disconcerting fickleness.

"Reaganomics" has provided North American capitalism with its most recent "ideology." Reaganomics proposes no coherent economic theory but dishes up to the public an eclectic mishmash of monetarism, supply-side economic rhetoric, militarism, deficit spending that drives the national budget through the stratosphere where Pentagon technocrats play at being Luke Skywalker, and a relentless assault on New Deal and Great Society programs. Under any capitalistic system, relief from the injustices inherent in a free market economy is effected by transfer payments on the part of the government from rich to poor. Reaganomics reverses the transfer. With its bailout of Chrysler Corporation and Citibank of Chicago and its massive tax breaks for the rich it practices a curious kind of socialism in its dealings with big business and the middle and upper classes but a ruthless capitalism in its dealings with the poor and marginal in our society.[13]

Capitalism also feeds traditionally on the foolish myth that its economic system can expand infinitely and that human technology can solve every problem, including those confronting a capitalist economy. History and science tell a different story. When technology solves one problem its solution often creates new ones. The water which technology pumped into the San Joaquin Valley in California in order to transform it into one of the great breadbaskets of the world now threatens to reduce that same valley to a desert because nature has provided no way to drain it off and the rising saline content of the accumulating pumped water is poisoning the fields. The successful industrialization of the east coast and midwest is killing whole forests with acid rain. We now try to convert nuclear power to peaceful uses but cannot dispose of its toxic waste. We know too that the planet earth contains only limited energy resources and that if we continue using them to fuel our factories at the present rate we will within a foreseeable future use them up. Similarly, if the rate of industrialization continues unabated, the temperature of the planet will rise, melt the polar icecaps, and inundate the industrialized coastal cities.[14]

The aggressive, exploitative character of capitalism also helps motivate colonialism. European colonialism of the nineteenth and early twentieth centuries has given way in the latter part of this century to neo-colonialism. Neo-colonialism uses economics rather than military conquest to keep third world countries in a permanent state of dependency on the industrialized nations of the north. Through organizations like the General Agreement on Trades and Tariffs (GATT), the World Bank, and similar institutions it ensures that the balance of trade favors the rich nations. Moreover, the emergence of multinational corporations in the international market has created economic organizations with more power than many nation states.[15]

Capitalism has long since proven its ability to generate ideologies of exploitation; but Marxism, which began as a revolutionary protest against the injustices of capitalism, has, through one of the many ironies that haunt its history, been transformed into an ideology of exploitation in its own right. Marxist communism has evolved into a system of bureaucratic collectivism in the Soviet Union. There the state owns the means of production, and the party bureaucracy owns the state through its totalitarian monopoly of political power. Communist collectivism exploits the workers and peasants in the precise sense that Marx himself gave to that term. Both groups are forced to surrender their surplus to the bureaucracy as a "free" gift to their rulers.[16]

The intellectually responsible political convert must in a contemporary context deal not only with ideologies of isolation and of exploitation but also with ideologies of forceful subjugation. In nineteenth century North America "manifest destiny" helped rationalize the conquest, subjugation, and doom of those native Americans who had not yet fallen victim to white wiles, guns, and diseases. It gave rhetorical justification to the annexation of Texas, to the proliferation of slave states, and to the war with Mexico in 1846. And as late as the 1890's it combined with chauvinism and racism to lend plausibility to the United States' annexation of Hawaii and other Spanish islands.

In the twentieth century expansionist politicians and militarists in the United States mouth a different rhetoric. They speak instead of "national security." The same kind of rhetoric emanates from militaristic regimes in Latin America. The doctrine of national security traces its lineage to that of **lebensraum,** which lent pseudo-respectability to the expansionist aggressiveness of Nazi Germany. Both doctrines portray the nation state as an organism with a life of its own. Territory, population, and national sovereignty are fused rhetorically into a single entity that allegedly needs expansion in order to survive. The doctrine of national security claims for the state the power to actualize the national will and organizes both domestic affairs and foreign relations into strategies that defend the "interests" of the nation. The energies of a powerful ruling elite are then channelled aggressively into the expansion of those interests through military, ideological, political, and economic means. The success or failure of this bellicose enterprise then measures the strength and growth of the state.[17] In this country the close alliance among big business, government, and the military commits this nation to a policy of neo-colonial exploitation of the third world, to peddling arms rather than humanitarian aid to other nations, and to macho posturing in our dealings with the Soviet Union.

Viewed as a revolutionary doctrine Marxism exemplifies a different kind of ideology of forceful domination. Dialectical materialism preaches the inevitability of class conflict and revolution as the only effective counter to the economic violence of capitalism. One may argue for the legitimacy of revolution in situations of extreme oppression. To insist on its universal inevitability smacks of ideology. Moreover, the exportation of the Russsian revolution to the nations of eastern Europe has in fact resulted in their forceful subjugation by Russian political and military might.

Intellectual conversion authenticates political conversion by freeing the political convert from mindless submission to ideologies of isolation, exploitation, and forceful domination. The intellectual convert declares personal independence from conventional patterns of thinking as soon as reason arises for calling the invalidity or inconsistency of popular beliefs into question. The love of truth which intellectual conversion inspires also motivates the ongoing criticism of the rhetorical defense of vested social, political, and economic interests. It motivates the acquisition of sound logical and methodological skills of reasoning that penetrate beyond ideological facades and demolish the weak rationalizations that buttress them. Intellectual conversion authenticates political conversion by freeing the mind to devise policies and strategies that serve the interests of justice rather than the vested interests of dominant elites. Finally, by alerting the political convert to the socially and historically conditioned character of beliefs and by underscoring both the strength and limitations of personal experince, intellectual conversion frees the political convert to tolerate positions that call his own into question and to seek the resolution of political conflict through critical dialogue.

**(3) Moral Conversion Authenticates Socio-Political.** Moral conversion authenticates political conversion by setting political converts individually and collectively in opposition to unjust social structures and by focusing the conscience on institutional injustice. Socio-political conversion, as we have seen, expands moral consciousness to include concern for the common good, for the rights and dignity of all persons, and for an institutional order that ensures that all individuals share impartially in the benefits of human society. Moral conversion integrates these insights into a coherent ethical vision. The individual who views contemporary society in the light of such a moral commitment develops a keen sensitivity to institutional violations of legal, distributive, and commutative justice. A capitalistic economy allows in principle for peasants and the proletariat to ascend the social ladder. But because capitalism gives unfair economic advantage to the upper and middle classes, the poor and marginal who swim in its turbulent waters often slip beneath the surface and drown. Moreover, as we have seen, the international economy has arranged tariffs and bank rates to the advantage of the rich industrial nations. Such policies conspire with corruption and irresponsibility in the third world to keep millions languishing in degrading poverty, while millions more starve slowly to death. The arms race diverts billions of dollars from the humanitarian purpose of ensuring the survival and enhancement of the lives of the destitute to the proliferation and deployment of weapons that threaten the very survival of human life on this planet. Behind the Iron Curtain and in dictatorships supported by the western democracies, prisoners of conscience languish in prison or writhe screaming beneath the hands of their torturers. Racism and sexism exacerbate the misery of the poor and deprive the more advantaged of opportunities due them as persons and members of society. Unbridled and irresponsible industrialization poisons the places where people live and spawns disease and death.

Moral conversion authenticates political conversion by teaching converts the meaning of political responsibility. It emboldens converts to denounce institutional injustice and commits them in concrete ways to achieve a just social order. It binds people together in prophetic opposition to tyranny and oppression, creates lobbies that call politicians and business bureaucrats to social accountability, exerts pressure for the passage and implementation of just legislation, and commits individuals and groups to labor for a social order in which the needs of all can be impartially met.

**(4)Religious Conversion Authenticates Socio-Political.** Even the devil quotes the Bible; and history testifies amply to the fact that religious rhetoric can be employed for unjust, exploitative, and manipulative ends. Only recently, at the beginning of his second term in office Ronald Reagan piously misquoted the gospel of Luke at some length in order to justify the further escalation of the nuclear arms race despite the fact that the immorality of such militaristic policies had been publicly condemned by the North American Catholic bishops and by other religious leaders in this country and around the world. But the churches are not always so outspoken. And when they fail to denounce injustice they collaborate with it tacitly. Religious individuals and groups can also offer pious rationalizations for perpetuating situations of gross injustice. Slave owners in Dixie quoted scripture in order to rationalize the degradation of blacks. When I was teaching high school in New Orleans in the late fifties a bigoted pamphlet entitled **God Gave the Law of Segregation to Moses on Mount Sinai** tried to persuade its readers that God blesses racial segregation. Its author was eventually excommunicated from the Catholic Church.

Religious conversion authenticates socio-political conversion by transvaluing in faith all unjust situations and purely natural political commitments and by orienting all political activity to the institutional realization of the justice decreed by God. Socio-political conversion, like affective, intellectual, and moral, can occur naturally, in abstraction from the historical self-communication and self-revelation of God. When that occurs, religious conversion demands that the aims and goals of socio-political conversion as well as the situations of injustice with which it deals be re-evaluated in the light of the moral consequences of religious faith in God. Christian conversion demands that those same realities and values be re-evaluated in the light of the definitive historical revelation of God accomplished in Jesus and in His Holy Breath.

Christian conversion demands therefore that oppressive attitudes, obfuscating ideologies, institutionalized injustice, and the hypocritical use of religious rhetoric for oppressive ends all be renounced not only as morally evil but as sinful. For we sin when we choose evil in deliberate violation of God's will. The Christian recognizes that the will of God for humanity found unique and normative historical embodiment in Jesus' perfect obedience and in the reign of God which He proclaimed. The Christian therefore measures the sinfulness of the human situation by the extent to which it contradicts the mind of Christ and the morality of discipleship which He inculcated. Christian theology calls situational sin original sin and concupiscence.

Christian conversion also relativizes every humanly conceived social and political cause by insisting that commitment to the cause of Christ, to the realization of God's reign on earth takes precedence over loyalty to any individual party, or social group. From the standpoint of faith social justice consists in the institutional actualization of the ethics of discipleship proclaimed by Jesus. For the mind of the incarnate Word reveals the mind of God. And His teaching about the way humans ought to relate socially ultimately discloses the kind of social order God wills for His children.

Finally, Christian faith demands that the convert look upon the conflict between the forces of evil and the reign of God as integral to the very historical process by which the triune God reveals and communicates himself to humankind. This truth is clearly enunciated in the gospels of Mark and of John. But it echoes in the preaching of Paul and in the other synoptic gospels as well. In Mark the Holy Breath sent to Jesus in His baptism impels Him into conflict not only with demons and with personal hypocrisy but also with the oppressive political and religious institutions of His time; and Mark's Jesus promises that She will teach to Jesus' disciples the same courage in that conflict as She taught their master. In John's gospel the battle between the forces of light and of darkness causes both to reveal their true identity, until the evil of Jesus' adversaries stands judged and condemned by the glory of the cross and resurrection. Jesus' disciples too, John warns, will be drawn into the same kind of revelatory struggle. Paul admonishes his converts that they have been consecrated by God to battle the principalities and powers of this world. And Matthew and Luke also in their own way discover the definitive, historical revelation of God in the conflict between Jesus and His disciples on the one hand and the evil forces that try to destroy them on the other.

These biblical insights take on enhanced significance when understood in the light of political conversion. The politically converted Christian feels compelled by God to confront unjust and oppressive social structures prophetically in the name of Christ and in the power of His Breath and to demand that they conform to the social order willed by God and required by submission to His reign. A democratic society like ours, which tolerates political pluralism, offers more opportunity than do dictatorial or totalitarian regimes for Christians to speak out on social issues and to bring political pressure to bear on the shaping of public policy. In societies where dissent is suppressed politically active and responsible Christians and those with whom they collaborate risk arrest, torture, and martyrdom. But whether the political climate of a nation favors free speech and political activism or not, a serious responsibility constrains the consciences of Christians not only to oppose and to denounce institutional injustice both personally and as a Church but also to banish any hint of institutionalized evil from the Christian community itself. For when we do battle with the force of sin, the light of grace shines on those who dwell in oppression and in the valley of death. In Breath-inspired conflict with evil the reality of God stands historically revealed.

**d. The Characteristics of Socio-Political Freedom.** We began these reflections in the hope of clarifying the meaning of the term "liberation." We have been led to distinguish three realms of freedom: elementary human freedom, authentic personal freedom, and the authentic search for socio-political freedom. We have already compared and contrasted the first two realms. We are now in a position to reflect on the ways in which the authentic search for socio-political freedom resembles and differs from the first two realms of freedom.

The same forces which condition elementary personal freedom also condition socio-political. Institutions can either oppress or enhance freedom. In either case they create an environment in which freedom must either thrive or languish. Illiteracy, propaganda, the presence or absence of educational opportunities, and other social forces can seriously lower the shared social, economic, and political awareness of masses of people and diminish their capacity to act freely. Not only individuals but groups can be socialized into a rigid mind-set that prevents them from seeing problems from a variety of perspectives. And when that happens, shared freedom sickens. Institutions express habits; oppressive institutions embody habitual injustice. Finally, policy and executive decisions create the social situations that either foster or inhibit the growth of responsible socio-political freedom.

Because it builds on and enhances elementary human freedom, the conquest of socio-political freedom shares with it many descriptive traits. Elementary freedom labors under the constraints of finitude. Similarly, no one ever experiences perfect socio-political freedom. Interpersonal as well as large, impersonal institutional structures condition the exercise of choice sometimes in creative, sometimes in destructive ways. Hence anarchists who imagine that they can abolish all institutional constraints, like individuals who long for total liberty, simply whistle in the wind.

Not only does socio-political freedom labor under the constraints of finitude, but, like elementary human freedom, it flickers. It varies from one social situation to another. A victorious stand for justice can be undermined or even nullified by an upsurge of political and economic oppression. Bigotry may retreat before therapy, reason, and faith only to flare out again unexpectedly. Electorates can yield to rhetorical manipulation by power elites or rally to the standard of justice.

Socio-political freedom also displays the qualitative diversity of elementary human freedom as different institutions channel human energy in different directions. As individuals are institutionalized into the subgroups and divergent universes of meaning that make up human society, they acquire different skills and learn how to interact with one another in a growing variety of ways. The children of Australian aborigines learn how to relate to parents and elders very differently from the children of suburban North Americans. Politicians learn different skills from engineers. Academicians acquire an intellectual freedom denied to most dockworkers. The institutional structure of society therefore shapes and specifies the qualitative diversity of elementary human freedom.

Unless personal conversion authenticates socio-political, the latter degenerates into the search for power, wealth, prestige, and egotistical pre-eminence. Inauthentic political activism breeds institutional oppression and imprisons oppressor and oppressed in emotional, intellectual, moral, and institutional dungeons. The authentic search for socio-political freedom frees individuals and institutions from such corrupting and debilitating bondage. Authentic socio-political conversion frees converts from servile acquiescence in unjust and oppressive institutions and frees them for collaboration with others in defending and advancing the common good locally, nationally, internationally. Like elementary human freedom, then, the authentic search for socio-political freedom has a janus face.

As we have seen, personal conversion makes elementary human freedom personally responsible. Socio-political conversion makes authentic personal freedom socially and politically responsible by deprivatizing it. The socio-political convert professes personal accountability for the institutional shape of society insofar as he or she can influence the decisions that structure it. And by deprivatizing the exercise of personal freedom, socio-political conversion engages converts in an ongoing dialogue with The Others and with those with whom they make common political cause.

Personal conversion endows the exercise of elementary human freedom with self-transcendence by freeing it from the constraints of a narrow egocentrism. Self-transcending freedom disciplines itself to respond to the legitimate claims of others. Socio-political conversin endows society with institutional and structural self-transcendence by demanding that the institutionalization of social intercourse display a flexibility that expresses and fosters an integral, five-fold conversion in all its members. The authentic exercise of socio-political freedom also acknowledges different spheres of institutional authority and competence and submits to their legitimate constraints. In other words it submits to justifiable institutional discipline at the same time that it opposes institutional injustice.

Growth in authentic personal freedom demands a blend of idealism, realism, and patience as one transcends the spontaneous inertia of the human ego and its resistance to growth and change. The growth and defense of socio-political conversion demands an even greater measure of idealism, realism, and patience as one grapples personally and collectively with the even more massive inertia of large, unmanageable, and intransigent institutions entrenched in their vested interests.

These reflections on the interplay between personal and socio-political conversion offer no specific strategy for institutional socio-political transformation. We need to tailor strategies to specific situations and their needs. Our reflections do, however, demand that Christians in this country oppose the multiple injustices inherent in a capitalistic economy such as ours. They do demand of us solidarity with the poor and the marginal. They do call us to promote the common good and to collaborate effectively in eradicating the causes of institutional injustice.

Whether these reflections have clarified the theological implications of the term "liberation" the reader may judge. They have, it seems to me, at the very least highlighted some of its complexity. They also call into question any attempt to privatize personal and Christian conversion. They challenge the converted to discover personal authenticity in active dedication to those concrete causes that foster the institutional realization of the reign of God on earth. They also call into question all political activism which fails to express the four forms of personal conversion.

Our attempt to probe the three levels of human freedom also suggests that a foundational theology of conversion and liberation theology have something to teach one another. We began this essay by tracing the development of black liberation theology in the United States. Our analysis of human freedom has forced us to address many of the issues which exercise both black and Latin liberationists. From liberation theology we have learned that a sound theology of conversion must build social analysis into its very method, for one cannot come to authentic self understanding without grappling with the economic, social, and political forces that condition human self-awareness for better or for worse. A foundational theology of conversion can, however, teach liberation theology something about the limitations of social analysis, for a comprehensive theology of liberation must deal not only wich the dynamics of personal conversion but also with the ways in which the dynamic interplay of personal and political conversion give normative direction to the human search for liberty in faith.

Some on completing these reflections may feel dismay at the complexity of conversion and of the human search for freedom. I have tried not to exagerate their complexity. I would, however, have betrayed my own responsibilities as a Christian teacher had I misled the reader through oversimplification. The complexity of the preceding analysis mirrors only dimly the complexity of human life itself. The following thoughts, however, may offer some comfort to the dismayed. The processes of conversion on which we have just reflected encompass a lifetime. Every human person stands at some point in the conversion process. Every human person can explore new realms of freedom. Conversion challenges us, but it also humanizes us. It offers us possibilities of new life. We experience its sacrifices as growing pains. Moreover, God invites us to conversion; He does not impose it as an insupportable burden. Rather he offers it as a precious opportunity. Religious conversion launches us on the enterprise of exploration into God Himself. Christian conversion teaches us to discover that God in the compassionate face of Jesus. He knows our human condition because He chose freely to experience it. He understands our limitations and invites us lovingly to transcend them. When we fail to respond, he reminds us that we need only acknowledge our need for God's forgiveness in order to experience it. Nor do we walk the paths of conversion alone. We advance along them as God's people called and strengthened by His Breath to dare and accomplish what we could never dream to do by human strength alone.

### Endnotes

[1]The following titles will introduce interested readers to North American black liberation theology: James H. Cone, **Black Theology and Black Power** (New York: Seabury, 1969), **A Black Theology of Liberation** (Philadelphia and New York: Lippincott, 1970), **The Spirituals and the Blues** (New York: Seabury, 1972), **God of the Oppressed** (New York: Crossroad, 1975), **For My People: Black Theology and the Black Church** (New York: Maryknoll, 1984); James Deotis Roberts, **A Black Political Theology** (Philadelphia: Westminster, 1980), **Liberation and Reconciliation: A Black Theology** (Philadelphia: Westminster, 1980), **Black Theology Today: Liberation and Contextualization** (New York and Toronto: Mellen, 1983); Cornel West, **Prophesy Deliverance** (Philadelphia: Westminster, 1982); Major J. Jones, **Black Awareness: A Theology of Hope** (New York: and Nashville: Abingdon, 1971), **Christian Ethics for Black Theology** (New York and Nashville: Abingdon, 1974); Cecil Wayne

Cone, **The Identity Crisis in Black Theology** (Nashville: AMEC, 1975); Michelle Wallace, **Black Macho and the Myth of the Superwoman** (New York: Dial, 1978); Lawrence Lucas, **Black Priest/White Church** (New York: Random House, 1970); Albert Cleage, **The Black Messiah** (New York: Sheed and Ward, 1968); Gayraud S. Wilmore, **Black Religion and Black Radicalism: An Interpretation of the Religious History of the Afro-American People** (New York: Maryknoll, 1983); Joseph R. Washington, **Black Religion: The Negro and Christianity in the United States** (Boston: Beacon, 1964).

[2]In **Faith and Ideologies** Juan Luis Segundo develops a brief and finally inadequate phenomenology of freedom in the course of enunciating "five decisive facts." (1) Every human seeks satisfaction. (2) Freedom is gradually and steadily lost as we use it. (3) No human can explore the limits of human satisfaction. (4) The social structure of experience is necessary for the use of freedom. (5) Reality has an objective structure which we know by using it. (6) Meaning and efficacy are two distinct but complementary dimensions. Fact (2) and fact (4) deal with the human exercise of freedom. Segundo fails, in my opinion, to distinguish adequately the three levels of freedom developed in this essay, nor does he distinguish adequately different kinds of freedom. Had he done so he might have recognized the inadequacy of his suggestion that freedom is gradually lost the more we use it. While one may cheerfully concede that every human life span contains only a finite number of choices and that old age limits the realistic possibilities of choice with increasing severity, those who grow in selflessness as they advance toward death in an ever deepening union with God experience greater and greater freedom from the things of this world and greater and greater freedom for those of the next. In the case of such faith filled people freedom (or at least a certain kind of it) increases as they move on to death. Moreover, while Segundo correctly notes the social context for the human exercise of freedom he fails to develop this insight in any detail. Cf. Juan Luis Segundo, **Faith and Ideologies,** translated by John Drury (Maryknoll, NY: Orbis, 1984) 21-25.

[3]Cf. Karl Menninger, Margin Mayman, and Paul Preuser, **The Vital Balance: The Life Process in Mental Health and Illness** (New York: Viking, 1963) 162-270.

[4]The theory of socio-political conversion developed here draws on the insights of George Herbert Mead, Peter L. Berger, and Thomas Luckmann; cf. George Herbert Mead, **Mind, Self, and Society From the Standpoint of a Social Behaviorist,** edited with an introduction by Charles W. Morris (Chicago: University of Chicago Press, 1962); Peter L. Berger and Thomas Luckmann, **The Social Construction of Reality: A Treatise in the Sociology of Knowledge** (New York: Doubleday, 1967).

[5]For a parallel schematization of the stages of personal conversion, see: Donald L. Gelpi, S.J., **Experiencing God: A Theology of**

**Human Emergence** (New York: Paulist, 1978) 179-185.

[6]Josiah Royce's philosophy of loyalty casts significant light on this dimension of the conversion process; cf. Josiah Royce, **The Philosophy of Loyalty** (New York: Macmillan, 1908).

[7]Cf. Gordon W. Allport, **The Nature of Prejudice** (New York: Doubleday Anchor, 1958); Cornel West, **Prophesy Deliverance** (Philadelphia: Westminster, 1982).

[8]Cf. Donald L. Gelpi, S.J., **The Divine Mother: A Trinitarian Theology of the Holy Spirit** (Washington: University Press of America, 1984) 215-238.

[9]Asbjørn Eide and Marek Thee, eds., **Problems of Contemporary Militarism** (London: Croon Helm, 1980).

[10]John A. Shiller, ed. **The American Poor** (Minneapolis: Augsburg, 1982).

[11]Cornel West, **op. cit.**

[12]For a beginner's introduction to the mysteries and myths of capitalism, see: Robert L. Heilbroner and Lester Thurow, **Economics Explained** (Englewood Cliffs, NJ: Prentice Hall, 1982); Robert L. Heilbroner, **The Worldly Philosophers** (New York: Simon and Schuster, 1980).

[13]Robert Lekachman, **Greed Is Not Enough: Reaganomics** (New York: Pantheon, 1980).

[14]For a sobering assessment of the future of capitalism, see: Robert L. Heilbroner, **An Inquiry into the Human Prospect** (New York: Norton, 1974); Michael Harrington, **The Twilight of Capitalism** (New York: Simon and Schuster, 1976).

[15]For a popular introduction to these issues, see: Susanne C. Toton, **World Hunger: The Responsibility of Christian Education** (Maryknoll, NY: Orbis, 1982); for an insightful reflection on the moral dilemmas of developing the third world, see: Dennis Goulet, **The Cruel Choice: A New Concept in the Theory of Development** (New York: Atheneum, 1971).

[16]Cf. Harrington, **The Twilight of Capitalism**, 50.

[17]Cf. Jose Miguez Bonino, **Toward a Christian Political Ethics** (Philadelphia: Fortress, 1983) 69-71.

# The Liturgical Reforms of Vatican II: The Unfinished Revolution

Other councils of the church have attempted to regulate sacramental discipline, but only the second Vatican council undertook the herculean task of revolutionizing the way Catholics pray. The liturgical revolutionaries who shaped the council's sacramental theology thought of themselves as traditionalists. The reforms they promoted sought to effect a return to earlier and more adequate modes of praying sacramentally. Nevertheless, measured against the standard of popular liturgical piety in the first part of this century, the ordinary Catholic in the pew on Sunday felt the impact of the council's decrees as more a revolution in worship than a reform of it.

In the present essay I will attempt to reflect on some of the forces that motivated that attempted liturgical coup, on the changes it inspired and on the challenge the council's teachings continue to pose to contemporary Catholics. The revolution in worship which Vatican II began has not ended. Issues in sacramental theology which the council either ignored or sidestepped still cry out for resolution. Indeed, some of the unintended fallout of the council's reforms pose a grave threat to the very survival of sacramental piety in this country.

My remarks divide into five headings. First, I would like to contrast the approach to sacramental reform undertaken in Vatican II with that taken in the other two great sacramental councils: the council of Florence and the council of Trent. Second, I would like to examine three forces that shaped Vatican II's sacramentalism decisively: the liturgical movement, existential sacramentalism, and the struggle between liberals and conservatives within the council itself. Third, I would like to summarize the council's sacramental teachings, both those contained in the decree on the sacred liturgy, **Sacrosanctum Concilium,** as well as other teachings about sacramental worship formulated in other conciliar documents. Fourth, I would like to review the attempts to date to implement the council's sacramental teaching and assess both its successes and failures. Finally, I would like to take a look toward the future by dealing briefly with three post-conciliar issues in sacramental theology: ecumenical dialogue about the sacraments, women's ordination, and the dwindling number of sacramental and eucharistic ministers in the North American church.

How then does Vatican II's approach to the sacraments differ from that taken by other councils? Only three councils have tried to deal systematically with all the Christian sacraments: the council of Florence in the fifteenth century, the council of Trent in the sixteenth, and Vatican II in the twentieth.

The bishops at Florence turned to sacramental theology pretty much as an afterthought. A council that sought unsuccessfully to reconcile Rome and Constantinople, Florence wrestled primarily with the issues raised by the Photian schism: namely, does the Holy Spirit proceed from the Father alone or from both the Father and the Son? Photius, the patriarch of Constantinople (820-891), who had excommunicated the pope for meddling in the internal affairs of his see (thus provoking his own retaliatory excommunication by the pope), had held that the Spirit proceeds from the Father alone. The Latin tradition and the Latin creed by contrast taught that the Spirit proceeds from both the Father "and the Son." As the conciliar debates dragged on at Ferrara and then at Florence, it became clear that some eastern fathers of the church had taught that the Spirit proceeds from the Father "through the Son." On the dubious principle that saints (that is, fathers and doctors of the church) cannot disagree, the bishops finally voted that "through the Son" means for all practical purposes the same thing as "and the Son." Only after consensus had been reached on this sensitive point did the council deal with the sacraments.

As Rome contemplated reunion with the eastern orthodox churches, fidelity to canonical instincts demanded the regularization of relationships between the papacy and the eastern communions from which it had been separated for centuries. In that context the bishops at Florence drew up the Decree for the Armenians: a document that sought to regularize sacramental discipline in the Armenian church. It canonized seven rituals as sacramental and defined the legal essence (matter, form, and minister) of each rite. The document envisaged regularization, not revolution.[1]

Pre-Vatican-II Catholics imbibed Tridentine sacramental piety. Tridentine sacramentalism reflected two interrelated concerns: the concern of the bishops and theologians at Trent to correct the abuses in late medieval ritual practice and a desire to clarify the differences between Catholic and Protestant sacramental theology. The opening debates at Trent expressed the futile hopes of some that the council might reconcile these two warring theological camps. The Decree on Justification, perhaps the most creative document approved at Trent, tried to reformulate Catholic doctrine in sympathetic response to issues raised by the Protestant reformers; but by the time the council came to debate the sacraments, all hope of conciliation had died. In its later sessions the council contented itself with underscoring the differences between the two positions and with correcting abuses. A return to sound ritual discipline and a defence of late medieval sacramental piety and practice set the tone for Tridentine sacramental teaching. As a consequence, Tridentine sacramentalism expressed ritual conservatism rather than revolution.[2]

Of the three great sacramental councils only Vatican II dreamed of revolutionizing worship. Three forces endowed the council's sacramental teaching with a creative zeal to transform. Two antedated the council itself: the liturgical movement and the development of existential sacramentalism on the European continent.  A third and decisive force emerged during the council debates:  namely, the council's clear domination by liberal bishops who had been chafing for decades under the constraints of a centralizing curial conservatism and who responded enthusiastically to Pope John XXIII's visionary call for **aggiornamento.** Let us reflect on each of these three forces in turn; for each helps contextualize the council's sacramental teaching.

Some scholars trace the roots of the liturgical movement all the way back to eighteenth century France where an attempt was made to organize lay piety around both the eucharist and praying the breviary. But the movement roots itself more proximately in the work of Prosper Gueranger (1805-1875) who restored the Benedictine Abbey at Solesmes and transformed it into an important liturgical center.   The work of Gueranger heightened Catholic liturgical consciousness especially in Europe.  But the liturgical reforms of Pius X (pontificate: 1903-1914) and the pioneering work of the Belgian Benedictine Lambert Beauduin launched the liturgical movement as a movement.  Pius X encouraged active lay participation in the eucharist, frequent communion, and regular Sunday worship.   He promoted communion for children and partially reformed the liturgical calendar.  These early reforms paved the way for other changes.  Beauduin's work helped transform the Benedictine abbey of Mont Cesar in Louvain, Belgium into a major liturgical center before the second World War.  Other such centers began to mushroom in Europe and the United States: Maria Laach in Germany, Klosternberg in Austria, Collegeville in the United States.   Scholarly studies of the history of Christian ritual alerted theologians to the privatized character of sacramental piety in the first part of this century.  Instead of being the communal celebration it had been in the early church, the eucharist had degenerated popularly into a ritual backdrop for individual communion. The awkwardness of encouraging lay participation in rituals celebrated in the dead Latin language led pastors and theologians both to push for sacraments in the vernacular.   The more liturgical theologians learned about the history of Christian ritual the more it convinced them that most people participated in the sacraments with little understanding of their true significance.  In the wake of the second World War liturgical ferment centered in France.[3]

Post-war sacramental theology added fat to the fire.  In the period between the two World Wars Martin Heidegger launched existentialism as a philosophical movement.   And by the end of the second World War, existential ideas had begun to color the way continental European theologians thought about the sacraments. Existential philosophy concerns itself with the problem of meaning.  In **Being and Time** Heidegger had argued that history provides the human mind with its total pattern of meaning.   Existential philosophy also mounts a telling critique of impersonal, objective patterns of thinking.  It dismisses the search for pure objectivity as illusory.   And it celebrates the importance of meaningful, interpersonal encounters.

As such ideas began to permeate sacramental thinking, they encouraged the historical retrieval of the evolution of Christian worship as an important key to the meaning of the sacraments. Measured by the norm of history, however, the popular practice of sacramental piety seemed hopelessly privatized and individualistic, insensitive to the communal, ecclesial dimensions of worship, unaware of its eschatological dimensions. Scholars began to realize that ritual inertia had perpetuated sacramental practices that had lost their original meaning for most people.[4]

That realization plus dissatisfaction with the detached objectivity with which scholastic manuals of sacramental theology described the workings of sacramental grace led existential European theologians to describe sacramental worship as a meaningful interpersonal encounter with Christ. They began calling for the sacramentalization of the whole of Christian life as the event that gives full meaning to ritual worship. In the process they began to reassimilate something close to the sacramentalism of many of the Fathers of the church whose Platonism caused them to see revelations of God everywhere. Existential theologians began to speak of Jesus and of the Church as primordial sacraments, as revelatory events of grace celebrated in the seven ritual sacraments. These theological advances were destined to color Vatican II's approach to sacramental worship. The council would speak of the sacramentality of the church. It would insist that the rituals of the church should not only be meaningful to those who celebrate them but even self-explanatory. It would try to recover the communal dimensions of Christian sacramental piety and in the process to deprivatize it.

The liturgists and liberal sacramental theologians who shaped the teachings of Vatican II came to the council, therefore, with a program for liturgical reform. But their dreams of transforming Christian worship would have gotten nowhere had they not enjoyed the support of a liberal majority of bishops at the council. Moreover, the conciliar debates about the liturgy make it quite clear that the power struggle between the liberal bishops and curial conservatives which gave Vatican II its drama also helped revolutionize its approach to sacramental reform
The issues which divided liberal from conservative in the debate on the schema on the liturgy illustrate the pont I am trying to make. Curial conservatives resisted any change in ritual worship as ill-conceived and disturbingly radical. They sought to reserve the decision whether or not to translate the liturgy into the vernacular to the pope (acting, of course, through his curial representatives). They opposed communion in the hand, communion under both species, and concelebration. They warned that liturgical changes would scandalize the faithful, that the revisionists were only aping the Protestants, and that too much active participation of the laity in sacramental worship would distract them from their prayers. The liberals supported vernacular worship, citing the example of Jesus who spoke the language of his contemporaries and of Paul the apostle who demanded that Christian worship be intelligible. They insisted that the

bishops acting through regional councils should regulate sacramental worship. They called for cultural pluralism, not Roman uniformity, in the official worship of the church. They insisted that the sacraments should communicate the gospel to contemporary people, especially to the young, and that unless translated into the vernacular and updated they would fail to do so. They pushed for all the concrete changes in the liturgy which the conservatives feared. The liberal bishops' pastoral concern to reserve to the episcopacy the right to adapt liturgical worship to the needs of the local church struck terror into the hearts of the curial conservatives because it symbolized the very things they feared most: decentralization of authority, pluralism, and diminished papal and curial control of the affairs of the church. Paradoxically, however, the very intransigence of the conservative minority fed the reforming zeal of the liberal majority and enhanced the revolutionary tone of the documents they wrote and endorsed.⁵

What did Vatican II teach about the sacraments? The council's most systematic treatment of sacramental worship is found in the Constitution on the Sacred Liturgy (**Sacrosanctum Concilium**; hereafter abbreviated SC). It attempts to provide guidelines for "the renewal and fostering of the liturgy" in an updated, contemporary church (SC, 1). The document makes very strong claims about the importance of liturgical worship. It looks upon liturgical worship, especially the eucharist, as effecting the work of redemption and as a concrete revelation of "the real nature of the true Church" (SC, 2). The council situates its sacramental teaching, like its teaching on most other subjects, in a trinitarian context: The Father has revealed Himself to us in the historical mission of His Son; Father and Son send the Spirit into the world. The mission of the Spirit coincides with the mission of the Church into the world to proclaim the risen Christ and to incorporate people through Christian baptism into the paschal mystery (SC, 6). The liturgy, then, manifests the presence of the risen Christ; through it He exercises His priestly ministry in the world today. That fact makes Christian sacramental worship "a sacred action surpassing all others" (SC, 7). The council underscores the eschatological character of Christian worship, describing it as a foretaste of the heavenly liturgy in our celestial Jerusalem (SC, 8). While Vatican II acknowledges that liturgy does not exhaust either the activity of the Church or the prayer of Christians, it nevertheless speaks in the most exalted terms of the importance and efficacy of sacramental worship. It asserts unambiguously that "the liturgy is the summit toward which the activity of the Church is directed; at the same time it is the fountain from which all her power flows" (SC, 10). As we shall soon see, events in the post-Vatican-II church are moving sacramental worship in this country toward a crisis that challenges Catholics individually and collectively to decide whether they truly believe these exalted claims about the importance of liturgical and sacramental worship.

The bishops at Vatican II ambitioned much more than a structural reform of the rites of the church. They called for the transformation of liturgical attitudes and for an ongoing updating of liturgical consciousness through scholarly investigations into the history of the sacraments. They insisted on the communal, ecclesial character of Christian worship, decreeing that "the full and active participation by all the people" in the public worship of the church defined the supreme goal of liturgical reform. Ordained leaders were to become "masters" of the liturgy and exercise a ministry "permeated with the spirit and power of the liturgy" (SC, 14). The study of liturgy they elevated to the status of a major theological discipline, calling for the training and installation of professors of liturgy in seminaries, religious houses of study, and theological faculties (SC, 15). All seminarians were required to study the liturgy. Professors of theology were instructed to show the relationship of the more traditional theological disciplines to Christian worship (SC, 16). Religious and clerics were exhorted to develop a liturgical spirituality (SC, 17). Pastors were instructed both to promote the ongoing instruction of the faithful in liturgical theology and to ensure their active participation "both internally and externally" in sacramental worship (SC, 19).

The bishops who set out to revolutionize the worship of the church at Vatican II envisaged an orderly revolution. Regulation of the official worship of the church was reserved to bishops conferences. "Therefore," **Sacrosanctum Concilium** warns, "absolutely no other person, not even a priest may add, remove, or change anything in the liturgy on his own authority" (SC, 22). The reform of Catholic sacramental and liturgical worship was also to conform to the norms approved by the council. Correct order was to be preserved in worship and a clear definition of the functions to be performed by different participants: priest, servers, lectors, commentators, the community (SC, 28-32). "Noble simplicity" should characterize the revised rites, as well as pastoral effectiveness. The bishops called for rituals that are "short, clear, and unencumbered by useless repetitions" (SC, 34). The revised lectionary should introduce the laity more systematically to Sacred Scripture. In eucharistic worship the homily received new prominence in order to increase the pastoral benefits of the sacrament to worshiping participants (SC, 15).

In a clear repudiation of bureaucratic overcentralization, **Sacrosanctum Concilium** called for the adaptation of rituals to different groups, regions, and cultures "provided that the substantial unity of the Roman rite is maintained." Liturgical flexibility was especially urged upon mission countries. Once again, however, change was to advance in an orderly fashion under the control of the local bishops conference and in consultation with the Holy See (SC, 40). And care was taken to establish at a diocesan level the administrative structures needed to ensure a carefully controlled reform of worship (SC, 41-46).

All the rites of the church were to be overhauled, including the eucharist "in such a way that the intrinsic nature and purpose of its several parts, as also the connection between them, can be more clearly manifested." They could be celebrated in the vernacular. Concelebration and communion under both species were sanctioned (SC, 50, 54, 63). A catechumenate similar to that practiced in patristic times was restored as a prelude to adult baptism (SC, 64). A new ritual was to be devised for accepting baptised Protestants into full eucharistic communion with the Roman Catholic church (SC, 65). The rite of anointing was transformed from a sacrament of the dying to the sacrament of the sick and its healing purpose clearly vindicated (SC, 73). The celebration of marriage, confirmation, and religious profession within the eucharist was encouraged (SC, 71, 78, 80). Both the divine office and the liturgical calendar were slated for overhaul (SC, 83-111). And norms for sacred music and the regulation of liturgical art were approved (SC, 112-129).

One cannot help but be struck by the concrete, practical nature of the decree on the liturgy. In effect, the bishops set the seal of official approval on the liturgical movement and on the reforms in worship for which it called. And they established the bishops conferences as the authority competent to implement those reforms.

Debate over liturgical reform opened the acts of the council. But the theology of the council evolved in the course of its four sessions. And in other documents the bishops returned to the sacraments and gradually expanded the council's sacramental doctrine.

One should not, of course, expect the thought of a council to advance with the consistency and symmetry of a personal systematic theological statement. The teaching of Vatican II coheres roughly and organically, even though the documents reflect all the political tensions that shaped the conciliar debates. Liberal and conservative views are sometimes juxtaposed with no hint of how they can ultimately be reconciled. Some documents, like the Decree on the Church's Missionary Activity (**Ad Gentes**), attempt to build consciously on earlier documents approved by the bishops. Other doctrinal advances seem to have happened almost accidentally. Indeed, a contemporary student of the council's proceedings may well wonder if the voting bishops always grasped the full implications of their decisions.

Conciliar teaching on the relationship between the charismatic and the sacramental dimensions of Christian worship offers an intersting case in point. The original schema on the church prepared by conservative Vatican theologians placed great emphasis on its hierarchical structure and on the necessity for obedience to authority. The liberal bishops rejected the document and called for a more pastoral statement about the church. The document they finally approved spoke of the church as a mystery that transcends its institutional structures. Instead of equating church with hierarchy, it described the church as the people of God and the hierarchy as servants of God's people. Moreover, instead of reducing the laity to passive submission to hierarchical decreees, the Dogmatic Constitution on the Church speaks of lay Christians as charismatically anointed to apostolic service to the church and to the world.

The groundwork of the theology of the laity which the council canonized had been laid by Yves Congar, Karl Rahner, and others who had invoked a Pauline theology of the gifts, or charisms, of the Holy Spirit as a useful theological rubric for elaborating a lay spirituality. Cardinal Ruffini, one of the leaders of the curial conservatives, objected to talk of charismatic laity and urged a return to the hierarchical vision of the church proposed by the Vatican architects of the original schema on the church. Cardinal Seunens, supported by the oriental bishops, rallied the liberals to endorse the idea of a charismatically anointed laity.

In conciliar teaching on the gifts of the Spirit, the Holy Spirit enjoys sovereign freedom in dispensing the gifts; they impose on those who receive them the right and responsibility to respond; and while the hierarchy must discern and sanction the movement of the Spirit, they must never quench that movement (**Lumen Gentium, 4, 7; Apostolicam Actuositatem, 3, 30; Ad Gentes, 23, 28; Presbyterorum Ordinis, 9).**

As we shall see, these conciliar teachings throw light on a problem in sacramental theology that has surfaced since the council: namely, the ordination of women. At this point, however, we are primarily concerned with the development of conciliar theology itself.

Having lost the battle over the charismatic character of lay spirituality, the conservatives pushed to have the hierarchy too declared charismatic. As a consequence one finds in the theology of Vatican II a curious distinction between hierarchical and charismatic charisms. Granted the tone and stance habitually adopted by the conservatives at the council, one cannot help but suspect that their insistence on the charismatic character of hierarchical ministry was not untouched by a certain clerical elitism and by authoritarianism. If the laity were to be characterized as charismatic, the hierarchy could be no less charismatic and must be portrayed as having the gifts that judge and rule the other charisms. Paradoxically, however, the council's teaching on the "hierarchical" gifts had other more revolutionary implications. It made it clear that in judging the authenticity of charismatic impulses in the church ordained leaders must respond with sensitivity to the action of the Spirit throughout the Christian community. Moreover, Vatican II made a clearer link between the charismatic and the sacramental dimensions of Christian worship than any other council of the church. In effect, the council's teachings implied that the sacrament of orders both confers and confirms charisms of community leadership and service (**Lumen Gentium, 4).**

These theological advances made at the council prepared the way for an important post-conciliar development in lay spirituality: the Catholic charismatic renewal. In evaluating this movement the American bishops quite correctly cited the teachings of the council in order to justify the initial provisional approval they gave the movement. A prolonged reflection on the significance of this movement lies outside the scope of this essay, suffice it to say that despite the many positive benefits the movement has brought to the church, popular designation of a particular charismatic impulse as "the charismatic renewal of the Church" has obscured an important facet of conciliar teaching: namely, that all Christians are charismatically anointed by the Spirit to serve the church and the human community, not just those who attend prayer meetings.

Other ironies attend the political jockeying in the council that shaped its sacramental teaching. Liberals and conservatives split most profoundly over the question of episcopal collegiality. The collegial character of church government was first proclaimed in the Dogmatic Constitution on the Church. The same document resolved a disputed point among sacramental theologians: it asserted the sacramental character of episcopal consecration. **Lumen Gentium** asserts:

> This sacred Synod teaches that by episcopal consecration is conferred the fullness of the sacrament of orders, that fullness which in the Church's liturgical practice and in the language of the holy Fathers of the Church is undoubtedly called the high priesthood, the apex of sacred ministry (**Lumen Gentium** 21).

Post-conciliar sacramental theology faces the problem of reconciling sacramental teachings like this one with the council's clear and unambiguous affirmation of the priesthood of all believers. Some theologians have suggested that if we are to take really seriously New Testament teaching about the priesthood of the Christian community, we would be well advised to conform our language for describing ordained ministry to New Testament norms as well. The Letter to the Hebrews offers the only **ex professo** New Testament treatment of the meaning of priesthood. It speaks of Jesus, rather than of bishops, as possessing the fullness of the priesthood. Indeed, for the author of Hebrews, as supreme high priest Jesus has put an end to the need for anything resembling the Levitical priesthood of the Jewish people (Hb 3:1-5:10).

In the wake of the council we may discern two different kinds of language for speaking of the priesthood of the ordained. The more traditional Catholic language traces its roots roughly back to the fourth century of the Christian era when the Christian clergy through imperial patronage became bureaucrats in the Roman empire. In order to stave off too much imperial meddling in the internal affairs of the church, bishops began to contrast their own sacred, priestly authority with the secular authority of the emperor and to depict themselves as the quasi-levitical priests of the new covenant. This movement in theology, known as sacerdotalism, marked a major departure from New Testament patterns of thinking. And eventually it combined with the hierarchicalism of a sixth-century Syrian who wrote under the pseudonym of Dionysius the Aeropagite and who shaped in influential ways medieval perceptions of ordained ministry. Dionysius portrayed the structures of the Church as an imitation of the angelic hierarchies and imagined grace as descending from God down through the nine angelic hierarchies, then through the clerical hierarchy of bishop, priest, and deacon and finally down to the people. A hierarchical, sacerdotalist account of the priesthood portrays it as essentially different from the priesthood of the faithful. Ordination is said to elevate the Christian priest and cleric above the people and to give him authority over the people. As we have just seen, in defining the sacramentality of episcopal consecration, **Lumen gentium** speaks from just such a medieval perception of the role and function of the ordained leader. Bishops possess the fullness of ordained priesthood and stand at the "apex of sacred ministry."

Since the council, however, a second way of perceiving Christian priesthood has been developed largely in response both to the council's encouragement of biblical studies and to its strong insistence on the priesthood of the faithful. This alternative perception of priesthood avoids the language of sacerdotalism and hierarchicalism. It recognizes the public responsibilities and therefore the authority of ordained leadership. It defines those responsibilities in ways that echo the teachings of Vatican II, but it speaks of Jesus only rather than of any mere creature as possessing the fullness of the priesthood. It portrays both clergy and laity as participating in the priesthood of Jesus through their membership in the priestly community that is the new Israel. Finally, it differentiates between the priesthood of the faithful and the priesthood of the ordained on the basis of the different kinds of responsibilities and functions each exercises in the church. In other words, instead of speaking of the bishop as having the fullness of the priesthood and everyone else as having a smaller share in a priesthood which only the bishop enjoys fully, such a theology would locate the fullness of the priesthood in the risen Christ and see each member of the church as enjoying a different functional participation in that priesthood.[6]

I spoke earlier of an irony that attends Vatican II's teaching on the sacramental character of episcopal consecration. As we have seen, this doctrine was put forth in the same dogmatic constitution that endorsed the collegial character of church government. Throughout the second, third, and fourth sessions of the council Pope Paul VI showed a pastoral concern to conciliate the disgruntled conservative minority, probably in order to avert a schism in the church in the wake of the council. When **Lumen Gentium** was promulgated officially, the liberal bishops were miffed to find an announcement attached to it signed by the conservative Cardinal Felice, the Secretary General of the council. The announcement gave norms for interpreting the document. It stated among other things:

> In view of conciliar practice and the
> pastoral purpose of the present Council, this

sacred synod defines matters of faith or morals as binding on the Church only when the Synod openly declares so.

Other matters which the sacred Synod proposes as doctrine of the supreme teaching authority of the Church each and every member of the faithful is obliged to accept and embrace according to the mind of the sacred Synod itself, which becomes known either from the subject matter or from the language employed, according to the norms of theological interpretation. (Announcement made by the most Excellent Secretary General of the **Most Holy Council** at the 123rd General Congregation, November 16, 1964.)

In effect, the announcement recognized **Lumen Gentium** as authoritative but denied that the interpretation laid claims to being an infallible pronouncement. This assertion of its fallibility, and therefore of its ultimate revisability, would make it easier for the conservative minority to go along with it. Ironically, however, the announcement also applied to those passages which reflected the mind of the conservatives. Since the teaching on the sacramentality of episcopal consecration is contained in **Lumen Gentium** the announcement left the door open theologically to a more biblical interpretation of episcopal priesthood than the one proposed by the council itself.

The council advanced official pastoral catechesis on the sacraments in other ways as well. It insisted that sacramental worship not only unites believers to Christ and sanctifies them, but it also nurtures the entire apostolate of the Church including the lay apostolate (**Apostolicam Actuositatem**, 3; **Lumen Gentium**, 7, 11, 26, 33, 37; SC, 6,7,9). The council recognized a triple purpose to sacramental worship: to sanctify, to build up the body of Christ, and to give worship to God. As signs the sacraments also instruct. They both presuppose faith and nourish, strengthen, and express faith (SC, 59).

The council also tried to find a closer rapprochement between a Catholic and a Protestant understanding of ordained ministry than had been possible at the Council of Trent. Both Luther and Calvin had placed the proclamation of the word at the heart of ordained ministry. Calvinist theology especially had downplayed both the importance and the efficacy of sacramental worship. Trent by contrast portrayed the ordained priest primarily as a cult leader. Vatican II broadened a Tridentine interpretation of the understanding of ordained ministry by locating the proclamation of the word at the heart of sacramental ministry. In the process the council combined a Protestant with a Tridentine theology of ordained ministry. This transformation of the Tridentine mass priest into a Protestant proclaimer of the word was intended as an ecumenical olive branch to Protestant Christians; but in effect it changed the rules on many of the already ordained clergy who had been trained to function in large measure as Tridentine Mass priests (**Presbyterorum Ordinis,** 4).

The council transformed ordained ministry in other ways as well. During the sixth century the order of deacon had degenerated for all practical purposes into a steppingstone to the priesthood. The subdiaconate together with a host of minor orders like lector, porter, acolyte had added even more rungs to the hierarchical ladder. Prior to the council, investigation into the history of the sacrament of orders had alerted theologians and liturgists to the fact that in the early church deacons had exercised a stable ministry in the commuity along with bishops and priests. The proponents of ritual reform began calling for the reestablishment of a permanent diaconate in order to augment the number of available sacramental ministers, especially in countries suffering from a shortage of priests. This impulse within pre-conciliar theology bore fruit in the council's restoration of the permanent diaconate. Moreover, while the bishops chose to sidestep the issue of abolishing obligatory priestly celibacy, they opened the door to married people joining the clergy as deacons. The council also left to the local bishops' conferences to decide the fate of the sub-diaconate and of the other minor orders which had proliferated in the medieval church (**Lumen Gentium,** 29, **Orientalium ecclesiarum,** 17, **Optatem totius,** 12). The bishops of this country chose to streamline the hierarchy by abolishing both the sub-diaconate and minor orders. And they approved the permanent, married diaconate.

The council elected to sidestep another issue touching the theology of sacred orders: namely, what relationship in principle obtains between the presbyterate and the episcopacy. In point of fact in the first and second centuries we find in the Christian community two styles of church government: government by a single bishop and government by a group of elders similar to synagogue elders. The latter were called presbyters or priests. Over the centuries the episcopacy eclipsed the presbyterate and evolved into the chief governing authority of the church. Theologians, however, continue to debate how these two authority structures within the community ought in principle to relate to one another. In the absence of a clear theological consensus, the bishops at Vatican II were content to describe priests as assistants to the bishop and to discuss at length the pastoral responsibilities of bishops and priests to one another and to the laity. In effect, they settled for the practical, disciplinary regulation of the pastoral relationship between priests and bishops and left to some future council the resolution of the much thornier question of what the relationship between these two forms of leadership ought in principle to be. Moreover, in the wake of the council the enhanced activity of priests' senates has restored to the presbyterate some of its earlier character of a governing board of elders. Similarly, the establishment of parish councils has pushed the principle of subsidiarity one step further and has opened the door to lay participation in the governmental structures of the church

(**Lumen Gentium,** 28).

As the council debates advanced, they cast light on other sacraments as well. But in dealing with the sacraments of initiation, the council documents offer a much more detailed catechesis on baptism than on confirmation. The council's failure to deal with this sacrament in any extended way reflects the degree of theological confusion that surrounds this ritual. We shall return to this point in another context. At present, however, we are attempting to summarize the salient points of the council's own sacramental teaching.

Through baptism, the bishops taught, Christians are formed in the image and likeness of Christ and united to Him (**Lumen Gentium,** 7). Baptism makes believers children of God (**Ibid.,** 11). Both faith and baptism are necessary for salvation (**Ibid.,** 14). Baptism plunges us into the paschal mystery (**SC,** 6), effects regeneration, incorporates into the body of Christ (**Ad Gentes,** 21) and into the People of God (**Presbyterorum Ordinis** 5, **Unitatis Redintegratio,** 3). The only advance in conciliar catechesis on baptism present in such pronouncements lies in the biblical flavor of these teachings. The council, however, took a revolutionary step when it recognized that every baptised Christian, whether Catholic or not, belongs to the Church and is destined by baptism for full eucharistic communion (**Unitatis Redintegratio,** 3, 22, 23). That pronouncement called for a major transformation of Catholic-Protestant relationships. In effect it taught that from the standpoint of the Catholic community Protestants should no longer be regarded as heretics and excommunicates but as Chrisians and members of the church separated by historical circumstances from full eucharistic communion.

As for confirmation, the bishops remained content to speak of it in vague terms as a rite which empowers the baptised to witness publicly to Christ in the power of the Spirit. Nevertheless, how this spiritual strengthening and commissioning differs from the grace of baptism remains obscure in the council's teachings (**Lumen Gentium,** 11, **Ad Gentes,** 11, **Presbyterorum Ordinis,** 2). At one point the council states that confirmation joins the baptised more fully to the Body of Christ, but it leaves unexplained how one can be more fully joined to the church than by baptism (**Presbyterorum Ordinis,** 5).

The council documents themselves deal only cursorily with the rites of reconciliation and anointing. They encourage the pastoral use of the rite of reconciliation and call for its revision (**Christus Dominus,** 29, **Presbyterorum Ordinis,** 13, 18; **SC,** 7). They urge that the rite express true repentance and contrition (**Presbyterorum Ordinis,** 5). Though the council dealt only briefly with the rite of anointing, there its teachings make genuine innovations. In effect, the bishops rejected the popular misinterpretation of the sacrament as the sacrament of the dying and reasserted its original purpose: faith healing. The rite is to be administered to the sick and the aged in the expectation that it will bring them relief (**Lumen Gentium**, 11, 28, 73; **Presbyterorum Ordinis**, 5).

Although Vatican II offers fairly extended reflections on Christian family life, it discusses the sacrament of marriage only briefly. Moreover, in dealing with this sacrament the bishops were on the whole content to repeat traditional doctrine. They remind married Christians that in virtue of the sacrament of matrimony they "signify and partake of the mystery of that unity and fruitful love which exists between Christ and His Church" (**Lumen Gentium**, 11). They depict the marriage covenant as a sacramental symbol of the new covenant (**Gaudium et Spes**, 48). They speak of the sacrament of marriage as a seal and sanctification of the mutual fidelity of the spouses (**Gaudium et Spes**, 49). The council did, however, advance conciliar teaching on marriage in two important respect. Vatican II raised questions about the link between the marital love and the indissolubility of marriage and it asserted more clearly than any other council a Pauline understanding of the charismatic character of Christian marriage. The sacrament confers the gifts or charisms which married Christians need in order to fulfill their obligations as parents and spouses (**Lumen Gentium**, 11).

Such, then, are the principal doctrinal and pastoral assertions of the Second Vatican Council concerning Christian sacramental worship. The bishops promulgated the constitutions and decrees of the council over twenty years ago. How has the Council's liturgical revolution fared in the interim? In order to answer that question we must reflect on two distinct but interrelated developments: first, we must examine the official implementation of the council's decrees. Second, we need to examine the unofficial fallout which accompanied that implementation. Finally, we need to face and if possible to resolve questions and issues in contemporary sacramental theology which the Council sidestepped as well as problems that have arisen since Vatican II.

The official revision of the rites of the church for which Vatican II called is roughly complete. The new lectionary unfolds the riches of the Bible so successfully that it has been adopted not only in the Catholic church but in many main line Protestant churches. All the sacraments have been streamlined in their structure and embellished with special rituals for special occasions. They are now celebrated in the vernacular. Among the more revolutionary changes the new rites bring to the experience of Christian worship we should name the rehabilitation of the catechumenate and the transformation of the rites of reconciliation and of anointing.

The council had called for the restoration of the catechumenate but had left the terms of the restoration vague. The restored catechumenate advances in three stages. During the precatechumenate potential candidates make inquiries about membership in the church and advance through prayer and instruction to an initial christian conversion. The second stage lasts for several years. During this period the catechumens with the help and support of other members of the community not only study Catholic doctrine but are also expected to advance in Christian moral practice and prayer. The third stage usually occupies the Lenten preparation for Easter, the preferred feast for the baptism of adult catechumens. During the Sundays of Lent, the scrutinies are celebrated during which the community prays for and exorcises the catechumens in preparation for baptism. This period of intensive preparation culminates in baptism, confirmation and first communion ordinarily during the Holy Saturday vigil ceremony. After baptism the neophytes enter into a more advanced "mystagogic" catechesis that seeks to facilitate their full and effective incorporation into the Christian community.

The new rite of reconciliation provides for both individual and communal celebrations of the sacrament. The little black box has been replaced by confessional rooms which provide the option of either anonymous or face-to-face confession and absolution. Tridentine teaching on this sacrament assimilated it to medieval, ecclesiastical courts with the confessor functioning as judge and the confessee as the self accused. The new ritual stresses forgiveness and reconciliation more than judgment and guilt. It invites penitents to deal not only with wrongs they have done but with the healing in faith of the disordered attitudes that motivate sinful behavior.

The new rite of anointing not only simplifies the traditional ritual but also situates this sacrament clearly within the total healing ministry of the Christian community. While the administration of the sacrament is reserved to the priest, other members of the community are urged to exercise a charismatic ministry of healing by visiting and praying with the sick.

Besides transforming the rites of the church, the council has changed Catholic worship in other ways. We now have married deacons functioning as pastors and sacramental ministers, lay eucharistic ministers, liturgical planners, guitars in church, communion under both species and in the hand, the gradual development of an indigenous North American hymnody, official lectors, in general more active participation by the worshipping community in eucharistic worship, homilies at most eucharists. And yet ...

And yet all is not well with Catholic sacramental worship. One still hears complaints of boredom and tedium in church. Confessions have dropped dramatically in numbers. As a consequence the revised rite of reconcililation is (ironically) celebrated with far less frequency than the older Tridentine ritual. One still hears complaints from liturgists that even the revised rites need further revision. One has the impression at liturgical conventions that despite the fact that the liturgical movement through the council achieved all of the initial goals it set itself, sacramental worship is still plagued by apathy and misunderstanding. The new rituals presuppose a living worshipping community to contextualize them and give them meaning. And as a consequence of the council Catholics have come to expect ritual worship to celebrate the presence of God in the worshipping community. Nevertheless, one hears complaints commonly enough that the living, day-to-day experience of membership in a Christian community is hard to come by and that more often than we would like to admit, our revised eucharists do not yield a living sense of the presence of God. A member of my own family recently told me that he had stopped attending Sunday liturgy because the rite just did not mean anything to him. He goes to church often but finds solitary prayer more meaningful. How many of us know relatives and friends with similar problems?

What went wrong? Why has the liturgical revolution inaugurated by the council to date met with only partial success? **Sacrosanctum Concilium,** the Constitution on Sacred Liturgy, warns that the transformation of Christian worship ambitioned by the council requires more than the revision of rituals. It demands conversion of heart. The council's decree states the matter quite plainly:

> The sacred liturgy does not exhaust the entire activity of the Church. Before men can come to the liturgy they must be called to faith and to conversion: "How then are they to call upon him in whom they have not believed? But how are they to believe him whom they have not heard? And how are they to hear, if no one preaches? And how are men to preach unless they be sent?" (SC, 9)

Since the council Catholic theology has experienced a renewal of interest in the dynamics of conversion. Bernard Lonergan has suggested that conversion means much more than changing churches or even than changing faiths. In **Method in Theology** Lonergan argues for distinguishable moments in the conversion process: intellectual, moral, and religious. He has since conceded the need to add a fourth moment: affective conversion. And we still need to add a fifth: political conversion.

Through conversion people take responsibility for themselves and for their lives in some identifiable segment of their experience. Through intellectual conversion I take responsibility for the truth and the consequences of my beliefs about myself, my world. Through moral conversion I take responsibility for ensuring that my decisions conform to sound ethical norms and ideals. Through affective conversion I take responsibility for my own emotional health and integration. Through political conversion I take responsibility for seeing to it that the social structures of the world in which I live express and foster integrally converted behavior. These four forms of conversion can all occur naturally: i.e., in abstraction from the gracious, historical self-revelation

-156-

of God in Jesus and the Holy Spirit. But religious conversion, which is always an event of grace, allows for no such abstraction. For the religious convert takes responsibility for responding in an appropriate way to the free self-revelation of God in human history.

The five moments in the conversion process all occur independently from one another. In other words, one may be converted at one level and unconverted at another. Moreover, we need to distinguish initial from ongoing conversion. I am converted initially when I first make the decision to live responsibly in some area of my experience. Ongoing conversion demands of me that I live out the consequences of initial conversion.

In any given Christian community, one can take it as morally certain that the individuals who comprise it will be living their lives at different levels of conversion or the lack of it. Moreover, given the fragmented and sinful character of human life and social structures, even individuals naturally converted at a moral, intellectual, affective, or political level may not have yet learned how to let the message of the gospel inform and transform their behavior.

In the theology of Vatican II, Christian worship will be experienced in its full sacramentality when it is celebrated in communities of integrally converted people. When read in the light of theological reflection since the council, this fundamental demand of the council continues to pose to the church a challenge of staggering pastoral proportions. It means that liturgical reform will never be complete until Christians gather to worship in communities in which all its members are facing and dealing with personal emotional hangups, are engaged in ongoing and responsible dialogue about the meaning of life and of Christian revelation, are making morally responsible choices not only in their private lives but in establishing and reforming human social structure, and are growing through union with God in personal and shared prayer. In point of fact, we live in a sinful world and in a sinful church that falls all too often far short of that lofty ideal. We live in a country more committed to creating weapons of destruction capable of annihilating all human life on this planet than to feeding the hungry and clothing the naked. We live in a church and in a society marred by sexism, individualism, secularism, materialism, and every nameable sin and foible. Human ego inertia and the persistent human preference for security over the dangerous enterprise of exploration into God imprisons many in fear and apathy.

The liturgical reforms prescribed at Vatican II have only succeeded partially because they demand much more than the streamlining of rituals. They demand the graced and practical transformation of the entire church in hope, faith, love, and active Christian witness. The sacraments of the Church always effect something. But as Paul the apostle pointed out to the Christians at Corinth during the first century of the Christian era, when those who celebrate them live unconverted lives the sacraments effect not divine grace but divine judgment. The reverse is also true. We experience the Christian community as a primordial sacrament, as an event of salvation that gives meaning to ritual prayer to the extent that both individually and collectively we live integrally converted lives. The worship we actually experience in the post-Vatican-II church lies somewhere between these two extremes.

A notable failure in the sacramental theology of the council has moreover contributed, in my opinion, to the partial failure of its liturgical revolution. The theological failure to which I refer should not, however, be laid solely at the feet of the bishops and theologians who wrote the council documents. Their failure reflects a deeper flaw in Catholic belief and practice. I am speaking of the failure of Vatican II to provide an adequate explanation of the meaning of the sacrament of confirmation.

Nor has the situation improved much since the council. Theologians still scratch their heads over this ritual and confess that they are not quite sure what it means. Scholarly research into the history of confirmation provides some help but not very much. We know that in the first centuries of the Christian era, the rite of initiation of adults advanced in stages, baptism through immersion, then the anointing of the neophyte, the laying on of hands and invocation of the Holy Spirit, and finally full participation in a communal, eucharistic celebration. The fathers of the church debated back and forth when the Holy Spirit was actually given in the course of the ritual but they could reach no consensus.

By the middle of the third century water baptism and the ritual invocation of the Spirit were beginning to become unglued. In northern Africa priests were allowed to baptise people in danger of death but could not invoke the Spirit. That part of the rite was reserved to the bishop. And if the person baptised recovered, he or she was to be brought to the bishop who would then supply the second part of the rite of initiation. By the high middle ages, the reservation of the second moment of the initiation rite to the bishop had transformed it into a ritual completely distinct from baptism. But theologians then and now could not agree on what the ritual accomplished. They agreed that it gave the Holy Spirit. But they also believed that the distinct rite of baptism also did that. How could confirmation give something that had already been received? Like **Sacrosanctum Concilium** theologians spoke of a strengthening of the baptismal gift of the Spirit; and like **Sacrosanctum Concilium** they remained extremely vague when pressed to explain the nature of that strengthening.

But even though Vatican II failed to clear up this debated point in sacramental theology, it pointed the way to its resolution. It did so by summoning all the baptised to openness to the charismatic anointing of the Spirit, by insisting that the graces of the rites of initiation span a lifetime, and by asserting in an initial, if partial, manner a relationship between the charismatic and sacramental dimensions of Christian living. The council made the link between charism and sacrament most clearly in dealing with the vocational sacraments of orders and matrimony. But if these sacraments confer the charisms needed to perform specific ministerial services in the church, might not the relationship between charism and sacrament be broadened?

In **Charism and Sacrament** I have tried to show that if we are willing to accept the traditional medieval distinction between the seven gifts (**dona**) of the Holy Spirit and the Pauline charisms, or service gifts, then we can explain quite simply how the Holy Spirit can be given in baptism and in confirmation in two distinct ways.[9] By the seven gifts of the Holy Spirit, I do not, however, mean as medieval theologians did, seven distinct habits infused into the soul at the instant of baptism. The graces of both baptism and of confirmation, as Vatican II insists, span a lifetime. The rites of initiation express lifelong commitments. Baptism begins a process of life-long transformation in the Spirit, Who teaches us to live in Jesus' image. Lifelong docility to the Spirit in putting on the mind of Jesus is what I mean by the **dona Spiritus Sancti,** what has traditionally been called the "seven gifts" of the Holy Spirit. Such docility constitutes one of the most fundamental graces of baptism, though not the only grace. All Christians in virtue of their baptism receive exactly the same call: to let the Spirit teach them to live Christlike lives. Every Christian therefore who responds to the graces of baptism in the course of his or her life grows in hope, faith, and love as religious conversion graciously transforms the heart, the mind, and moral practice. In virtue of baptism every Christian receives the same call to docility to the Spirit in putting on the mind of Jesus.

Nevertheless, while every Christian is called to receive one or other of the Pauline service gifts, not every Christian is called to receive the same gift. The graces of baptism are common to all believers. The service gifts are particularized, adapted to individuals and to specific situations, for we are called to serve in different ways and in different situations. The graces of baptism and the Pauline service gifts, the charisms, differ therefore as graces and can be conferred by different rituals. The council of Florence speaks of confirmation as the Pentecost of each believer. On Pentecost the Spirit began the visible graced transformation of the church through an outpouring of the charisms of service. In confirmation, then, baptised Christians commit themselves to live in lifelong openness to whatever charisms of service the Spirit chooses to give them. In virtue of the rites of initiation, therefore, all Christians are called to live not only holy but charismatic lives of service.

The liturgical revolution ambitioned at Vatican II will remain incomplete until we can bring Christians to live both these commitments not only as individuals but as communities. The Christian community achieves full faith consciousness as a community only when all of its members live lives conformed by the Spirit to the mind of Jesus and only when all the Pauline gifts of service give dynamic shape to its shared living and praying. Christian communities come to shared consciousness in faith only when gifts of prayer, including the gift of tongues, suffuse it with the same sense of the presence of God as suffused the community on the first Pentecost, only when prophetic voices summon the believing community individually and collectively to ongoing repentance and hope, only when teachers recall God's saving deeds in history and point believers to a common future in Christ. Christian communities will come to full consciousness as communities only when the word of God is proclaimed with such power and expectant faith that it is accompanied by signs of healing, only when discerners help believers to distinguish the impulses of grace from the deceptions of the evil one, and only when community leaders, both official and unofficial, facilitate in effective ways the community's many ministries and prophetic witness to the world.

Shared openness to all the Pauline service gifts is not, then, as Vatican II has correctly insisted, a Christian extra curricular. If we are to live integrally converted Christian lives we must as individuals and as communities cultivate all the charisms of the Spirit. For the sharing of the service gifts is not an optional appendage to Christian faith. It is living faith itself.

The liturgical revolution inaugurated by Vatican II will never succeed fully until we can bring all Christians to acknowledge their call in the sacrament of confirmation to live lives open to whatever gifts of service the Spirit chooses to give them and until church leaders allow all Christians full scope to exercise all their gifts in ministry to the church and to the world. For the sharing of the charisms of the Spirit endows the church with the primordial sacramentality that gives meaning to its ritual worship. Communities which stifle or ignore the illumination and empowering of the Spirit will as a consequence continue to know boredom, apathy, and divine judgment in their shared sacramental worship.

The theology of confirmation which I have just sketched provides, moreover, an important key to understanding why the sacraments do in fact form a system. Theologians have traditionally spoken of the sacramental system, but no really satisfying explanation of the principle that unifies the system has been universally accepted. It has for example been suggested that the sacraments form a system because they address different moments in the human life cycle. A sounder explanation of the unity of the sacramental system, however, discovers in the dynamics of conversion the principle that draws the rites of the church into a dynamic unity. The sacraments of initiation ritualize an experience of conversion. Adult initiation ritualizes and seals a conversion that has already occurred. Infant baptism introduces a child into the community of faith that will nurture it to adult conversion. Through baptism a Christian stands committed to living in lifelong openness to the Spirit who conforms us to Jesus by teaching us to put on His mind in hope, faith, and love. Through confirmation the convert stands committed to living in lifelong readiness to receive whatever gifts or charisms the Spirit may choose to give. Among the charisms the Spirit bestows, two demand ritual confirmation: the call to official, public, apostolic ministry in the community, which is sealed by the sacrament of orders, and the call to the ministry of marriage, which is sealed by the sacrament of matrimony. As we have just seen, Vatican II speaks clearly and explicitly about the charismatic character of both of these forms of ministry in the church. The council, as we have also seen, recognizes that the ordained are bound to proclaim the word in season and out of season. Every authentic ministry of proclamation is confirmed by signs of healing: the healing which initial and ongoing conversion itself effects, physical healing, and even on occasion miraculous healing. The sacraments of reconciliation and of anointing ritualize the healing which results from ongoing repentance in faith by transforming the prayer for healing into a public, official, ritual reaffirmation of one's baptismal commitment. Both rites therefore sanction officially a charismatic ministry of healing. The eucharist, the greatest of the sacraments, celebrates the paschal mystery, the victory of Christ over the powers of darkness, a victory which becomes visibly manifest in a community of integrally converted people whose lives are in process of visible transformation through the charismatically inspired deeds of service they perform. In other words, the dynamics of initial and ongoing conversion which the Spirit effects through supernatural faith, hope, love, and the charisms of service unifies the rituals of the church and transforms them into what we call the sacramental system.

What issues promise to shape the future of sacramental worship? As we have seen, with the second Vatican council the Catholic church officially joined the ecumenical movement. Protestant observers were invited to the council on Rome's initiative, and subsequent to the council significant advances have been made in official dialogues toward theological agreement. Nevertheless, despite the agreement between Anglicans and Catholics concerning the meaning of eucharistic worship, substantial consensus in sacramental theology continues to elude the churches. Not only are we faced with a bewildering diversity in sacramental practice, but the churches have yet to reach any solid agreement concerning what a sacrament does and how many sacraments there are.

We will not see the end of ecumenical dialogue about the sacraments soon. But I would like to suggest a possible theological strategy for moving toward consensus. The time has come for the different churches to stop comparing lists of sacraments. We have done that for centuries and we know that they do not match. We also need, as Lutherans and Catholics recently did in what concerns the theology of justification, to put aside traditional red-flag words that trigger the most irrational prejudices of the Reformation and Counter-reformation. All Christians, Catholic or Protestant, agree that baptism and the eucharist are sacraments. I see no reason in principle why Catholic and Protestants cannot reflect more seriously on their experience of converted worship in those sacraments they acknowledge. Out of such reflection we ought to be able to derive a common understanding of what a sacrament is. If we can agree to that definition in principle we can then move to an examination of the experience of converted worship in the other rituals of the church in order to see whether or not they qualify as sacraments. But we must leave the pursuit of such dialogue to the theologians.[8]

Before, however, we bring these reflections to a close two other problems in sacramental theology which have arisen in the wake of the council deserve our attention. I refer of course to the ordination of women and to the shrinking number of official sacramental ministers in the North American church. Does the council's own sacramental theology cast any light on these vexing issues?

The council condemned discrimination on the basis of sex in the most forceful terms. It demanded that all such discrimination be "overcome and eradicated as contrary to God's intent" (**Gaudium et Spes,** 29). It deplored social practices which deny women the right and freedom "to choose a husband, to embrace a state of life, or to acquire an education or cultural benefits equal to those recognized for men" (**Ibid.**). It demanded that the personal dignity of both wife and husband be respected within marriage (**Gaudium et Spes,** 30). It called for a greater participation by women in the Church's apostolate (**Apostolicam Actuositatem,** 9). It acknowledged that mothers have domestic responsibilities, but warned that the fulfillment of those responsibilities should not betray people into underrating the social progress of women (**Gaudium et Spes,** 52). It called for fuller participation of women in cultural activities (**Gaudium et Spes,** 60). Nevertheless, while all of these pronouncements point in a direction that suggests the possibility of ordaining women, Vatican II failed finally to address the question directly.

Since the council conflicting signals have been emerging from the Vatican. One gathers from statements made by Pope John Paul II that he does not at this time favor the ordination of women. The Roman curia has issued two conflicting pronouncements on the matter. A report of the Biblical Commission examined the pros and cons of New Testament teaching on the subject and concluded finally that nothing in the New Testament forbids the ordination of women. On the other hand, the Sacred Congregation for Doctrine has issued a declaration signed by the head of the congregation (not by the pope) which takes a very different stand. It attempts to argue from scripture, from tradition, and from reason against the ordination of women. The arguments of the latter document have not been well received in the theological community as a whole. Biblical scholarship since Vatican II suggests that women did in fact exercise official, public leadership in the original Christian community.[9]

Do the teachings of Vatican II cast any light on this hotly debated question? I myself believe that they do. The council makes four pronouncements which taken together equivalently assert that a competent woman charismatically anointed by the Spirit with gifts of leadership has in fact a right to be ordained. Vatican II asserts clearly and unambiguously that the Holy Spirit moves freely in the Christian community and dispenses the charisms without constraint (**Ad Gentes,** 23). At the same time the council recognizes that official church leaders have the responsibility to discern  but never to suppress the Spirit's charismatic anointing (**Lumen Gentium,** 12). Among the charisms the Spirit gives, the council numbers the charism of apostolic leadership, which the sacrament of orders confirms (**Gaudium et Spes,** 7). Finally, the council clearly asserts that anyone charismatically anointed by the Spirit has the right and duty to exercise that gift for the benefit of the community (**Apostolicam Actuositatem,** 3). Vatican II makes these four pronouncements in different documents, but it does assert all four. Taken together they lead to the conclusion that any competent woman gifted by the Spirit with the call to apostolic leadership has the right and duty to exercise that gift in the community without impediment from the hierarchy. Moreover, since one cannot exercise the gift of apostolic leadership without ordination, it would follow that women so gifted have the right to be ordained.

The dwindling number of priests in the North American church raises another set of challenges. The four sessions of the council spanned the years 1963 to 1965. John F. Kennedy was assassinated during the second session of the council. And the task of implementing the council's decrees began in the Age of Aquarius with its hippies, anti-war protests, and Selma marches. Events such as these plus disillusionment with public leaders and horror at the brutal murders of Robert Kennedy and Martin Luther King plunged the nation into a season of alienation and turmoil in which accepted values and institutions seemed to fall apart at the seams.

Inevitably, the Church too was drawn into the turmoil. Sacraments began to be used as instruments of political protest. I can remember when I was studying at Fordham University an anti-war eucharist celebrated on the sidewalks of New York. Priests and nuns marched arm in arm with hippies, blacks, and alienated young people to defy the dogs and cattle prods of the Selma police. Inevitably church institutions too became the target of disgruntled protest. Priests and nuns changed their traditional garb for ordinary secular dress. Vocations to both the diocesan priesthood and to religious life dropped alarmingly. The ranks of the priesthood were further decimated by the departure and subsequent marriage of many. I remember a cartoon of the period showing a group of priests at a class reunion singing together "Wedding Bells Are Breaking Up That Old Gang of Mine."

The cumulative impact of reduced vocations and departures from the priesthood is beginning in the eighties to hit the parishes and to hit them hard. There are fewer and fewer priests to go around. The situation promises to get worse not better.

How can we deal pastorally and intelligently with this crisis? We certainly need to do something. And we might well begin by surveying the choices that face us.

We could of course choose to do nothing, and we can easily predict the consequences of such an option. Sacramental ministry in this country would begin to resemble sacramental ministry in South America. That is to say, we would have fewer and fewer priests to go around. The eucharist would be celebrated with increasing rarity. The harried priests who would survive would be transformed into Tridentine mass priests and their ministry would become increasingly limited to cultic functions. I find no way to reconcile such a do-nothing solution to the problem of dwindling numbers of priests with Vatican II's insistence of the sublime importance and centrality of sacramental and especially of eucharistic worship to the life of the church.

If we cannot do nothing, what can we do? Four alternatives suggest themselves. We could begin to ordain married men. We could begin to ordain women. We could increase the number of lay sacramental ministers. Or we could do all three. Let us reflect breifly on each of these alternatives.

Priestly celibacy was not imposed effectively in a legal manner until the first Lateran council in 1123. Recent scholarly research into the motives behind this legislation suggest that whatever its justification in the twelfth century, that justification no longer exists. Questionable ascetical ideals helped motivate the legislation of celibacy. But apparently the bishops at Lateran I imposed it on the clergy partly as a way of ensuring that benifices would not be lost to the church through inheritance.[10] From a theological standpoint, we know that the charism of celibacy and the charism of apostolic ministry differ. As a consequence, there is no reason in principle why the Spirit of Christ cannot call married people to ordained ministry. Moreover, the experience of the Protestant churches testifies that when the possibility of ordaining married people exists that that is precisely what the Spirit of Christ does. The revocation of obligatory celibacy as a condition to priestly ordination would also remove a major obstacle to union among the churches.

We have already reflected on the ways in which Vatican II's teachings cast light on the question of women's ordination. The most common objections to the ordination of women are the following: Jesus did not ordain women and, since ordination confers a character on the ordinand which conforms the individual to Jesus, it cannot be conferred on women who differ in gender from Jesus. I myself find both objections inconclusive and specious. Jesus' call of the twelve is nowhere in the New

-164-

Testament portrayed as their ordination to the priesthood. The historical Jesus promised the twelve not that they would be priests but that they would function as judges in the new Israel (Mt 19:27-29, Mk 10:23-27, Lk 18:28-30). Moreover, the New Testament gives some evidence that the house churches in the early church were sometimes presided over by a husband-wife team, presumably the owners of the house in which the community met for worship.

As for the character conferred by ordination, it would seem to consist in nothing more than the way in which the rite of ordination transforms one decisively into an ordained leader of the community. The rite seals one as servant of the community and as some one publicly responsible for its well being. It also conforms one to Christ. Similarity to Christ in the New Testament, however, is never predicated on the basis of gender but on the basis of a faithful obedience to His teaching and example which imitates His own faithful obedience to the Father. The rite of ordination commits one to live out such obedience as a public leader of the community. There is no reason in principle why ordination could not conform women as well as men to Christ in the obedience of faith.

Besides, ordaining the married and women, we could also increase the number of lay sacramental ministers. There is for example no reason in principle why lay people already engaged in a ministry of healing could not be prepared and authorized to administer the sacraments of healing. Catechists and those who prepare young Christians for marriage could be authorized to administer the rites of initiation. We could also increase the number of lay deacons. But more deacons would not supply us with more eucharistic presiders. Could we have lay presiders at the eucharist? Here the research into the history of the sacraments which Vatican II mandated is beginning to turn up a few surprising facts. It seems that in segments of the early church prophets rather than the ordained were looked upon as what we would today call ordinary ministers of the eucharist. It also seems to have been a common practice in the African church for some member of the community to preside at the eucharist in the absence of the regular ordained leader.[11]

Ordination to the priesthood will, of course, always have a necessary relationship to the eucharist. One cannot be officially appointed to lead a eucharistic community without being officially appointed to lead its eucharists, but divergence of eucharistic discipline in the early church from our present practice suggests that the ordained leader's right to lead eucharistic worship need not be interpreted as an exclusive right and that, when it is pastorally advisable, it could conceivably be shared with others. For in the last analysis the history of sacramental worship suggests that in order to function as a sacramental minister one needs only public authorization within a particular ritual tradition.

It seems unlikely that we will reach a theological consensus on the possibility of lay eucharistic presiders soon. The question, however, has been raised and raised in consequence of the research into the history of sacramental worship mandated by Vatican II. Were we to move collectively and with due process to ordaining the married and women and to extending the role of lay sacramental ministers we would have effected a revolution in sacramental worship that goes beyhond anything sanctioned by the council. On the other hand, we have no reason to suppose that the revolution in worship which Vatican II began is fundamentally over; nor have we any good reason to hope that it will ever end. To tell the truth Vatican II only advanced a revolution begun two thousand years ago when the Son of God lived, died, and rose and breathed His transforming Breath into the hearts of His disciples.

### Endnotes

[1] Joseph Gill, S.J. **The Council of Florence** (Cambridge: Cambridge University Press, 1959).

[2] Hubert Jedin, **A History of the Council of Trent,** translated by Ernest Graf (2 vols.; New York: Nelson, 1949-1961).

[3] F. McManus, **The Revival of the Liturgy** (New York: Herder and Herder, 1963).

[4] Edward Schillebeeckx, O.P., **Christ the Sacrament of the Encounter with God** (New York: Sheed and Ward, 1963); Karl Rahner, S.J., **The Church and the Sacraments,** translated by W.J. O'Hara (Freiburg, Herder, 1963).

[5] Xavier Rynne, **Letters from Vatican City: Vatican Council II, the First Session** (New York: Farrar, Straus, 1962).

[6] Albert Vanhoye, S.J., "Sacerdoce commun et sacerdoce ministerile," **Nouvelle Revue ministerielle Theologique,** 97 (1975) 193-207; Donald L. Gelpi, S.J., **Charism and Sacrament: A Theology of Christian Conversion** (New York: Paulist, 1976) 187-258.

[7] Bernard Lonergan, S.,J., **Method in Theology** (New York: Seabury, 1972).

[8] For a lucid summary of the state of the question in ecumenical dialogue about three of the sacraments see: **Baptism, Eucharist, and Ministry** (Faith and Order Paper No. 111) (Geneva: World Council of Churches, 1982).

[9] Leonard Swidler and Arlene Swidler, eds. **Women Priests: A Catholic Commentary on the Vatican Declaration** (New York: Paulist, 1977); Elizabeth Meier Tetlow, **Women and Ministry in the New**

**Testament: Called to Serve** (New York: University Press of America, 1980); Elizabeth Schussler Fiorenza **In Memory of Her** (New York: Crossroad, 1984).

[10]Samuel Leuchli, **Power and Sexuality** (Philadelphia: Temple, 1972); Charles A. Frazee, "The Origins of Clerical Celibacy in the Western Church," **Church History** 41 (1972) 149-167.

[11]Bernard Cooke, **Ministry to Word and Sacrament** (Philadelphia: Fortress, 1976) 532; Edward Schillebeeckx, O.P., **Ministry: Leadership in the Community of Jesus Christ** (New York: Crossroad, 1981) 50-52; John A. Coleman, S.J., "The Future of Ministry," **America** (March 28, 1981) 243-249.

## RELIGIOUS AND LAY SPIRITUALITY:
## REFLECTIONS AFTER VATICAN II

In the early days of the second Vatican council one of the Protestant observers, a Classical Pentacostal, was approached by one of the episcopal delegates.

"How does it feel," the bishop asked, "to be a Protestant observer in Rome at a council of the Catholic church?"

"I feel," the Protestant retorted, "like Ezechiel in the valley of the bones." When the bishop's face fell at this reply, the Protestant added with a twinkle in his eye, "But that's all right. The bones are beginning to move."

And move they did. They took on flesh and sinew, stood up and breathed with the Breath of the living God. The vast majority of the bishops responded enthusiastically to Pope John XXIII's call for **aggiornamento,** for an updating of the church that would allow it to relate with greater pastoral effectiveness to people living in the second half of the twentieth century.

The ordinary Catholic in the pew felt the impact of the council most immediately in its liturgical reforms; but Vatican II ambitioned much more than the reform of church ritual. It called upon Catholics everywhere to revise their perceptions of the church, of themselves, and of the world in which they live.

Over twenty years after the closing of the council, many Catholics in this country still look back to it with confusion and some misgiving. Many still do not understand what the documents of the council ambitioned, how they challenged traditional Catholicism, and the new kind of church they projectd. Right-wing groups within the church still agitate for an abrogation of the council's decrees and for a nostalgic return to an idyllic form of Tridetine Catholicism that probably never existed.

This confused state of affairs should come as no surprise. The full implementation of the reforms of Vatican II will probalbly take several generations. We need to continue training both ordained and lay leaders who understand the vision of the council and who embody that vision in their ministry. At the time the council was called, American lay Catholics tended to look on priests and bishops as the church's real apostolic ministers. No one spoke popularly about the apostolate of the laity, or if they did so, they probably imagined something carefully controlled and supervised by the hierarchy. The clergy for their part had by and large been trained to function as Tridentine mass priests. They tended to conceive their ministry as largely administrative and cultic. I remember good priests who used to take mechanical counters devoutly

-169-

into the confessional in order to total the number of times they had administered the sacrament in the course of their ministry. As priests they understandably cherished celebrating the eucharist. By and large, then, ordained ministry meant caring for church institutions and sacramental ministry.

Then with apparent abruptness Vatican II changed the rules that governed church ministry. The council placed chief responsibility for Christianizing secular society, the lion's share of the church's total apostolic endeavor, squarely on the shoulders of the laity. Almost overnight, it seemed, priests were expected to preach with the eloquence of Protestant evangelicals, to display in their homilies a mastery of sacred scripture for which their education had not adequately prepared them, to collaborate with lay ministerial teams, and to conduct the revised rites of the church like liturgical experts. Nor did these changes exhaust the council's list of new pastoral expectations.

In point of fact despite their apparent abruptness, the changes the council legislated resulted from generations of scholarly work and grassroots movements in the church. To the ordinary North American parish priest and his flock, however, the changes came like a thunderclap. Moreover, in the twenty years since the council, lay catholics have frequently enough received mixed signals about the council from their ordained leaders. Some of those already ordained at the time of Vatican II have made the transition to a new understanding of pastoral ministry and the church with considerable grace. Others, however, still chafe under the reforms. Moreover, as the number of clergy in this country diminishes with predictable rapidity, the burden of pastoral leadership even within the church will pass more rapidly than many would like to acknowledge to the laity, laity who in many instances still have to absorb the message of Vatican II.

How did this council try to change the church? Catholics by and large now take the council's liturgical reforms for granted; but what other changes in church order did the council ambition?

Catholics before Vatican II lived in a highly centralized church. A creeping curialism inspired by the first Vatican council's lopsided focus on the papacy had encouraged an extreme centralization of church authority in Rome and with the growth of modern communications had concentrated historically unprecedented amounts of power in the hands of the papal curia. Vatican II attempted to change this excessively monarchical, centralized vision of the church's government into a more decentralized, collegial one. It established national conferences of bishops as a check to the newly acquired power of the Roman curia. In portraying church government as collegial rather than monarchical, the council also opened the door to a modest democratization of Catholic church life. Priests' senates were transformed into bishop's advisory councils on diocesan policy. In a furhter application of the principle of subsidiarity parish councils extended "collegiality" of a sort down to a grass-roots parish level.

Vatican II also attempted to transform a church marked by legalism and canonical uniformity into a church that respects cultural diversity and proclaims an incultruated gospel. It challenged theologians, pastors, and lay apostles to use local customs and patterns of thought in order to help people understand the gospel in images and categories already familiar to them. At the same time the council ambitioned a prophetic evangelization of all peoples that informs local cultures with gospel values.

Vatican II sought as well to terminate the Catholic counter-reformation which the council of Trent had begun. Vatican II summoned a triumphalistic church that regarded itself as the sole guardian of religious truth to repentant participation in ecumenical dialogue not only with Protestant and Eastern Orthodox Christians but with other world religions as well. Instead of imagining the living church as the spotless bride of Christ which it one day hopes to become, the council spoke of the church instead as a pilgrim people on the way to the fulness of light and holiness but still blinded by sin and limitation and always in need of deeper conversion to Christ and to the gospel. Instead of depicting validly baptised Protestants as heretics and the Eastern Orthodox as outsiders, the council spoke of them as church members not yet in full eucharistic communion with the church of Rome.

Vatican II also revised the way in which Catholics ought to think about their ordained leaders. Before the council, Catholics by and large meant the hierarchy when they used the term "the Church." Vatican II, by contrast, described the church first of all as a mystery of divine grace that transcends its visible structures of government. The council also explicity refused to equate the church with the heirarchy. Instead it spoke of the church as the entire people of God and located the hierarchy within the body of the church. Instead of speaking of the ordained as the exclusive sacramental channel of grace to the unordained, the council spoke also of the extrasacramental, charismatic activity of the Holy Breath in the lives of God's people. Instead of depicting the hierarchy as standing over the church, it situated ordained ministry within the church and portrayed it as the evocation through both preaching and the administration of the sacraments of the Breath's charismatic anointing. Having evoked the gifts, the ordained also bear the responsibility and therefore have the authority for discerning and coordinating the charismatic ministry of the unordained. Nevertheless, the council limited the pastoral use of authority in the church. Ordained leaders must distinguish between authentic and inauthentic manifestations of the Breath of God, but they can never suppress Her authentic inspirations. Indeed, the council linked the rights and duties of the unordained within the church to their charismatic inspiration by the Breath of Jesus: those whom She calls charismatically to ministry have the duty to respond.

They therefore also have the right to expect the rest of the church to acknowlege and encourage their ministry. Instead of casting the laity in a role of passive obedience to the hierarchy, Vatican II entrusted to them most of the church's apostolic responsibilities: as apostles the laity bear chief responsibility for christianizing secular society. In that mission they function as ministerial co-workers with the hierarchy.

The council also transformed Catholic perceptions of religious life. Instead of elevating vowed living above the vocation of all baptised Christians, Vatican II described it as one way among others of living out either a Christian baptismal commitment or a vocation to ordained ministry. Vatican II summoned religious to recover their diversity by retrieving both the biblical basis of vowed living and the specific vision of their founders. The council also instructed religious to adapt their institutes to the changed demands of twentieth-century living. Finally, Vatican II explicitly rejected a medieval, hierarchical understanding of religious life which situates religious below the clergy but above the ordinary lay Christian in the scale of perfection and closeness to God. Instead the council acknowledged that vowed living offers a legitimate vocational option to clergy and laity alike.

Finally, Vatican II ceased speaking of the church as a perfect society in relationship to that other perfect society, the state. The council spoke rather of the church's mission in service to the modern world. That mission commits the church as a whole to a dialogic relationship with human secular society in which each has important lessons to learn from the other.

One could detail other Catholic perceptions of the church which Vatican II attempted to revise; but these suffice to give a feeling of the council's vision of what **aggiornamento** demands. This essay focuses on one of those changed perceptions: namely, on the council's depiction of lay religious as lay Christians with vows. I select this facet of the council's ecclesiology for examination because I believe that it has important implications for understanding both lay spirituality and the spirituality of the three vows of religion. It also casts light on the council's overall apostolic thrust.

My argument divides into two major parts. First, I will attempt to detail the council's understanding of the contribution which the laity in general, married Christians, and religious are each expected to make to the shared life of the church. I will try to highlight the council's position by contrasting it with a medieval perception of the place and mission of religious and laity within the church. Second, I will draw on a theology of Christian conversion in order to ground these conciliar teachings. More specifically, I will attempt to show that when interpreted in the light of the dynamics of Christian conversion, a New Testament ethics of discipleship grounds simultaneously not only the sprituality of lay Christians, both married and single, but also the vows and ministry of lay religious. In the process of so doing I will also explore the ways in which the apostolate of the laity casts light on the secular character of vowed living.

(I)

Before Vatican II Catholics in this country tended to perceive the role and function of religious and laity in the church with medieval eyes. Paradoxically, these contemporary perceptions echoed in significant ways the theology of a sixth-century Syrian who wrote under the pseudonym of Dionysius the Areopagite. I say paradoxically, but the popular persistence of at least a modified version of Pseudo-Dionysius's quaint vision of the church well into the twentieth century illustrates how slowly religious ideologies die when they are buttressed by institutional sanctions.

**The Acts of the Apostles** names the real Dionysius among the handful of converts which the apostle Paul made in Athens (Acts 17:34). Mistaken by medieval theologians for a first-century writer, his pseudonymous, sixth-century counterpart was accepted during the middle ages as speaking with almost as much authority as the apostle Paul himself. As a consequence, during the middle ages the writings of Pseudo-Dionysius enjoyed far more theological authority than they actually deserved. Theologians imagined quite incorrectly that this sixth-century writer described a first-century church order. They therefore fallaciously accepted his vision of the church as making normative claims which history belies.

Pseudo-Dionysius viewed the church as a hierarchical monolith. His thought fuses Neo-Platonic mysticism and biblical angelology. The visible church on earth, he believed, participates in the order and beauty of the angelic hierarchies. He divided the nine choirs of angels into three hierarchies, three choirs in each hierarchy to honor the trinity; and he imagined grace and religious enlightenment descending from God through the angelic hierarchies down into the visible church.

He divided the church on earth into two hierarchies. Bishops, priests, and deacons comprise the upper, clerical hierarchy; religious, lay Christains, and catechumens comprise the lower. In such an ecclesiology grace and light flows from the angelic hierarchies into the clerical hierarchy and from the clerical into the lay. Moreover, within the lay hierarchy lay religious who bind themselves by vow to live the evangelical councils, rank above the rest of the laity in holiness and spiritual influence. Clearly, in such a hierarchical vision of the church, the ordianry lay person functions almost exclusively as the passive recipient of grace and religious understanding, which flow from the clerical hierarchy into religious and from religious into the laity.

Vatican II restored both the catechumenate and the permanent diaconate. Prior to the council, however, catechumens functioned less visibly within the church. In the popular Catholicism that nurtured me,

-173-

lay people stood on the bottom rung of the hierarchical ladder for all practical purposes. Lay folk were supposed to keep the ten commandments and the laws of the church. Religious stood a rung above them, for religious actively pursued holiness by vowing to live the "evangelical councils." The clergy stood over the laity, priests over deacons, bishops over priests, and the pope over all. The clergy functioned as the sacramental channels of grace and as dispensers of divine truth. Had I read Pseudo-Dionysius's **The Ecclesiastical Hierarchy** as a youth, I would have found his vision of the church congenial.

The integralists at Vatican II viewed the church not only in hierarchical but in starkly monarchical terms. They opposed the collegial vision of church government which the council eventually endorsed and held that the pope alone rules the church, that he alone enjoys the power to bind and loose, and that bisiops have no other teaching function than to hand down papal doctrine to the faithful. They denied that the laity could be commissioned to apostolic ministry directly by Christ or charasmatically inspired by His Breath. They held instead that any commissioning of the laity for ministry must proceed from the hierarchy. In their vision of the lay apostolate the laity merely perform obediently tasks set them by the clergy. The integralists feared that the liberal attempt to portray the laity as charismatically inspired would undermine clerical control of lay activities in the church.

The decrees of Vatican II paint a very different portrait of the lay apostolate. We may group the council's major teachings about the laity under five headings. (1) Vatican II offers a definition of the term "laity." (2) It explains the origin of the lay apostolte in the church. (3) It describes the scope and exerise of the lay apostolate. (4) It underscores the call of lay Christians to holiness and sketches the rudiments of a lay spirituality. (5) It describes diverse forms of the lay apostolate and suggests strategies for pursuing them. Let us reflect on each of these topics in turn.

(1) **Vatican II offers a definition of the term "laity."** In one sense, **Lumen Gentium,** the Dogmtic Constitution on the Chruch, endorses the traditional distinction between laity, religious, and clergy. By the term "laity" it means unordained Christians who have not pronounced the vows of religion. In virtue of their baptism the laity participate in the priestly, prophetic, and regal ministry of Jesus Christ (**Lumen Gentium,** 32; hereafter this document will be abbreviated as LG). Later, however, the same document clarifies the connotations of these distinctions. **Lumen Gentium** specifically repudiates the medieval notion that religious life occupies an intermediate place between the clergy and the laity in the hierarchical structure of the church. Rather, religious constitute a category distinct from both clergy and laity because both can elect to pronounce the vows of religion. The document states:

From the point of view of the divine and

hierarchical structure of the Church, the religious state of life is not an intermediate one between the clerical and lay states. Rather, the faithful of Christ are called by God from both these latter states of life so that they may enjoy this particular gift in the life of the Church and thus each in his own way can forward the saving mission of the Church (LG, 43).

In other words, the vows of religion provide both clerics and laity with a specific way of exercising their apostolate within the church.

(2) **Vatican II explains the origin of the lay apostolate in the church.** In the debates of Vatican II liberals and conservatives split on their interpretation of the origin of the apostolate of the laity. Conservatives, as we have seen , wanted to ground the apostolate of the laity in a formal commissioning by the hierarchy. The liberals at the council rejected this notion and wrote a very different version of the origins of the lay apostolate into the documents of Vatican II. The council teaches that the lay apostolate expresses the mission of the church as a whole (LG, 33). It flows from the vocation of every Christian (**Apostolicam Actuositatem**, 1; hereafter this document will be abbreviated AA). Christ calls all lay Christians to the apostolate and sends them the Holy Breath to equip them with the charisms they need to serve effectively (AA, 3). The apostolic activity of the laity flows from their sacramental incorporation into the body of Christ and is nourished by the eucharist (AA, 3). The baptised need not, however, wait for the heirarchy to tell them how to minister to others. Rather they should follow the lead of the breath of Christ and claim the authority and initiative which Her inspirations sanction (AA, 34).

(3) **Vatican II describes the scope and exercise of the lay apostolate.** Vatican II describes the apostolate of the laity as universal in its scope, like the mission of the Church which it expresses (LG, 32-33; AA, 1-33). The council stresses the predominantly secular character of lay apostolic activity; but nowhere do the council documents characterize the lay apostolate as narrowly or exclusively secular. Living in the midst of secular transactions, lay Christians are, however, especially charged to labor for the humanization and spiritual renewal of the temporal order of society (AA 2, 5, 7). This Christian witness engages the entire life of the laity, who follow a poor, humble suffering messiah (AA, 5,16). The laity should strive to renew the temporal order by laboring for justice, by defending violated human rights, by opposing the illegitimate restriction of human liberty, by promoting international collaboration and world peace (LG, 36-37; AA3, 7-8).

Nevertheless, while the council entrusts the renewal of secular society especially to the laity, it does not confine the lay apostolate to the sphere of the secular. The scope of the lay apostolate includes the church (AA,9). The council speaks of a close, reciprocal relationship between the apostolic mission of the clergy and the laity. Both share in the priestly, prophetic, and royal office of Christ (LG, 34; AA 2). A common apostolic mission unites pastors and their flocks (AA,2). Clergy and laity need to minister mutually to one another (LG, 32; **Presbyterorum Ordinis**, 9). Moreover, the apostolic labor of the ordained bears practical fruit in a laity consecrated to the task of bringing Christ to a sinful and secularized world (AA, 10).

The collboarative relationship between the clerical and lay apostolates has other consequences. The council speaks of three fundamental rights of lay Christians within the church: a right to instruction, a right to the sacraments of the church, and the apsotolic right and duty to exercise their charismatic gifts (LG, 36; AA 3). The Laity should have access to every missionary undertaking in the church, including parish ministry (AA,10). The right of Christians in good standing to receive the sacraments may also demand more active participation of the laity in the actual administration of the sacraments (LG, 33). In places where Christians suffer persecution, the very sacramental survival of the church may demand that lay ministers of the rites of the church supplement the sacramental ministry of the ordained (AA, 1,7). Similarly, the ordained need to foster and promote the divinely inspired apostolic work of lay Christians (AA, 10)

(4) **Vatican II underscores the call of lay Christians to holiness and sketches the rudiments of a lay spirituality.** The right and duty of all baptised Christians to function apostolically by an appropriate exercise of their personal charisms implies another right: the right to adequate preparation for the lay apostolate (AA, 28). The Training for the lay apostolate should respect the predominantly secular character of their mission. It should insert lay Christians into their social milieu by providing them with practical, technical, and general cultural training. It should inculcate an authentic Christian humanism and a sensitivity to humane values (AA, 31).

Adequate training for the lay apostolate must, however, advance beyond a purely theoretical or merely secular form of instruction. It should provide the laity with a spirituality, with a practical way of approaching God by deepening faith and sound religious judgment. It should prepare lay Christians to live and proclaim the gospel. It should foster their growth in holiness. It should prepare them to witness against the materialism of secular society by proclaiming and promoting Christian social teaching. Preparation for the lay apostolate must also teach Christians to love others in the name and image of Jesus; for only by ministering lovingly can Christians prolong the mission of the Word incarnate. Charity binds Christians to one another in the work of the apostolate and teaches them to reach out to the marginal and the oppressed. It motivates the Christian search for social justice among persons and nations (AA, 8). In a world threatened by nuclear holocaust and torn by dissension and violence, lay apostles must seek the ways of peace. In poverty and meekness they must walk in the footsteps of a suffering messiah, who died for our freedom (LG, 36). The lay apostolate must express the faith, hope, and love that binds Christians in mutual friendship. It must also breathe with the spirit of the beatitudes (LG, 4).

(5) **Vatican II describes diverse forms of the lay apostolate and suggests strategies for pursuing them.** The lay apostolate includes any legitimate kind of apostolic work. The fields of the lay apostolate embrace, then, both the church and the world. Vatican II, however, noted five lay apostolic fields of special contemporary urgency: (a) lay collaboration in the ministry of the ordained (b) Christian marriage, (c) ministry to youth, (d) social justice ministries of all sorts, (e) the promotion of international justice and solidarity among all people (AA, 9-14). Of the five, the council documents speak in most detail about Christian marriage, social ministry, and ministry to the international community.

The teachings of the council on Christian marriage echo traditional Catholic doctrine, but they also highlight the apostolic opportunities which Christian marriage offers. Christian spouses collaborate in a work of grace that consecrates them to witness in faith to one another, to their children, and to their households. The council insists on the sacred and inviolate character of the marriage bond. Vatican II also calls upon civil governments to protect and support the family as the first vital cell in the body politic. Governments should ensure families adequate housing and education, humane working conditions, social security, and a just tax system. Families, for their part, function as apostiolic teams in a variety of ways: by adopting orphans and abandoned infants, by showing Christian hospitality to strangers, by aiding adolescents, by helping young couples prepare for matrimony, by teaching Christian doctrine in the home, by supporting other families in times of crisis, by caring for the aged (AA, 11).

The council also expressed a deep concern to defend marriage and the family from many of the threats to its stability in contemporary society. Vatican II reminds Christians that the institution of marriage was established by God the creator and then sanctified by Christ, who transformed it into a sacramental symbol of His union with the church (**Gaudium et Spes,** 48; hereafter this document will be abbreviated as GS). The council proposes a lofty ideal of conjugal love: thoroughly human, pure and undefiled, rooted in a solid virtue and not just in erotic attraction (LG,49). In defending the fruitfulness of marriage, the council documents allow that, while procreation binds Christians as a duty, it does not exhaust the purpose of marriage. The council, moreover, sanctions responsible family planning in the light of the gospel (GS, 50).

The documents of Vatican II portray Christian marriage as a school for holiness. All the members of the Christian family, parents and children, mutually sanctify one another in love (LG, 48). The family schools its members to a deeper humanity. The responsibility for such schooling rests primarily on parents, who must model for their children the meaning of Christian holiness (LG, 48, 51). By their loving presence in the home and by their teaching and example, parents must also educate children to a sound undrstanding of Christian married life as a special vocation in the church (GS, 51).

In addition to fostering marriage as an important form of the lay apostolate, Vatican II provides the church as a whole and lay apostles in particular with important guidelines for engaging in social ministry and for promoting both international jutice and the solidarity of all peoples. Lay apostles need to confront the issues raised by contemporary culture, to promote justice in society, in the economy, and in politics, and to foster international harmony and peace.

In its treatment of contemporary culture, the council cites three areas of special apostolic concern. (a) Christians must labor to free others from the shackles of ignorance by ensuring the universal availability of basic cultural education. The council condemned specifically the feminization of ignorance and defended the rights of women to full participation in the cultural benefits of contemporary society. (b) Christians must face the complex challenges posed by the human need for a balanced cultural education: the integration of scientific and humanistic studies with one another, the need to ensure that the family continues to function as the primary communicator of culture, the need to vindicate the role of the church in fostering and animating culture, the need to promote sound methods of education, the need to find means for using the leisure created by technology for the ends of cultural development. (c) Christians need to mobilize the resources of the Christian community and to face and resolve the problems and challenges posed by a culture increasingly dominated by technology (GS, 53-62).

More specifically, lay Christians need to recognize the impact today of science on human values. Technology has created a network of communications that empowers cultural dialogue at an international level. International cultural dialogue among peoples of vastly different cultural heritages and traditions promises in turn to foster a new universal humanism that transcends narrow regionalism and nationalism. Lay apostles also need to labor for a just and humanizing use of technology that conforms to gospel values. Finally, the laity must collaborate with their ordained leaders in promoting an inculturated evangelism that challenges cultural injustices and oversights even as it demonstrates the gospel's capacity to renew every human culture.

In confronting contemporary economic life, the council reintegrated a number of fundamental principles of Catholic social doctrine that regulate economic conduct. It insisted on the dignity of the human person and of human labor. It vindicated the human duty and consequently the human right to work. While acknowledging a diversity of economic roles and responsibilities, the council, nevertheless, defended the right of workers to found and belong to labor unions. Vatican II, however, subordinated the right to private property to the more fundamental principle that God intends the goods of the earth for all. In other words **all**, not just the rich and propertied, have a right to own property sufficient to ensure not only survival but a humane life. Accordingly, the council documents call upon governments to correct abuses of private ownership and upon investors to provide employment and sufficient income for workers.

In assessing human politics Vatican II lays down the fundamental principle that governments exist in order to secure the common good. The common good:

> . . .embraces the sum of those conditions of social
> life by which individuals, families, and groups can
> achieve their own fulfillment in a relatively
> thorough and ready way (GS, 74).

Citizens have a right to vote, but they too must exercise it in ways that advance the common good. When human rights are temporarily and legitimately curtailed for the sake of the common good, governments have the responsibility to restore them as soon as possible. The laws of a land and its system of social services should also promote the common good. Everyone should oppose political injustices (GS, 75).

In confronting the international community, the council urges Christians to labor for a just peace. It exhorts the world leaders to move effectively to outlaw war as a means of securing political and national aims. Vatican II condemns total war, calls for an end to the arms race, and challenges the superpowers to move beyond a policy of nuclear deterrence toward the destruction of their nuclear arsenals. It condemns vast outlays of money for armaments as an intolerable injury to the poor (GS, 80-82).

In a more positive tone, the council documents invite the community of nations to transcend narrow nationalistic aims for international economic collaboration in creating a world market in which developing nations can use their resources for the benefit of their own citizens, in which more advanced nations foster the economic growth of less advanced, and in which the international community effects the economic and social reforms needed to stimulate and coordinate the development of all the nations. Vatican II endorses informed and morally acceptable solutions to excessive population growth. It also urges all Christians to universal collaboration with one another and with all people of good will to establish a just social order (GS, 83-90).

We have been reviewing the principle teachings of Vatican II that cast light on lay spirituality. We have examined the council's definition of the relationship between lay Christians and lay religious, its account of the origins, scope, and exercise of the lay apostolate, its description of the kind of spirituality required of lay Christians, and its vision of the forms and strategies of the lay apostolate. What has the council to say about lay religious and their contribution to the church?

The documents of the council speak much more laconically of the role and function of lay religious within the church. **Perfectae Caritatis,** the Decree of the Appropriate Renewal of Religious Life, sought primarily to counteract the legalistic uniformity into which vowed living had lapsed in the nineteenth and early twentieth centuries. It invited the orders and congregations to return to the sources of Christian life and to reappropriate the original inspiration of their respective founders in order to rediscover their specific identity as a religious community. It also challenged religious to adapt their way of life to the changed conditions of contemporary culture. All such adaptation should, however, ensure a close following of Christ in the gospel as well as preserve the specific character and purpose of each religious institute (**Perfectae Caritatis, 2;** hereafter this decree will be abbreviated as PC).

The council also offered five criteria for adapting religious life to changed contemporary conditons: (a) sensitivity to the physical and psychological constraints of modern living; (b) the fostering of genuine community; (c) the needs of the apostolate; (d) the requirements of a given culture; (e) the specific social and economic conditions in which religious live and function (PC, 3)

Predictably, the council placed the vows of chastity, poverty, and obedience at the heart of all religious spirituality. The vow of chastity consecrates religious to a life of celibate love of Christ and His church. Its practice demands mortification, prudent concern to observe the safeguards of chastity, and custody of the senses. Poverty consecrates religious to living poorly in fact as well as in spirit, though religious may possess and use what they need for temporal life and for their apostolic work. Poverty also binds religious to common life. Through the vow of obedience, religious attempt to imitate a messiah who obeyed even unto crucifixion and death. In practice the relgious institute of each order or congregation regulates the relation between superiors and subjects. Superiors, however, should exercise a parental, interpersonal government which reverences the maturity and freedom of subjects and which empowers the religious communities they govern to serve the rest of the church in the spirit of their proper institute (PC, 12-15).

For the most part Vatican II described the spirituality of religious in somewhat traditional language. Religious must die to sin and to the world, grow in virtue, serve the church, renounce themselves to follow Christ, live lives of contemplation and of active service, cultivate love of the Scriptures and devotion to the eucharist (PC, 5-6). At several points, however, the council offers clarifying insights into the scope of religious spirituality. It insists that the vows of religious root themselves in Christian baptismal consecration. That fact would seem to suggest that the vows of religion offer one a concrete way of living out the responsibilities binding upon all baptised Christians but without exhausting the ways in which that might be done (LG, 44; PC, 5). Each religious institute highlights one or more facet of Jesus' own ministry: contemplation, proclamation of the good news, healing, conversion, deeds of charity, obedience, the blessing and care of children, missionary work (LG, 46; **Ad Gentes,** 18, 40-41). The council insists too that even though vowed living demands reunuciation, it also allows and should foster balanced personal development as well as involvement with secular society (LG, 46). That involvement would seem to imply that lay religious share in the secular character of the lay apostolate as a whole. They actively collaborate with their bishops in fostering the work of the diocese (**Christus Dominus,** 35), and they participate in the apostolate of the rest of the laity (AA, 25-26).

(II)

We have just examined some of the chief doctrinal affirmations enunciated by Vatican II concerning the apostolate exercised by baptised Christians and by lay religious. In the present section of this essay we will begin to explore those facets of Christian converstion which help to ground conciliar teaching on this subject. First, however, we need to define a few basic terms.

I define conversion as the decision both to renounce irresponsible behavior and to take responsibility for the development of some distinguishable area of human experience. I distinguish personal from socio-political conversion. By personal conversion I mean the decision to take responsibility for some facet of one's own experiential development. In other words, personal conversion focuses on the motives and consequences of one's own individual decisions. On the other hand, by socio-political conversion, I mean the decision to take responsibility for trying insofar as one reasonably can to influence the decisions of others, especially of those who mold the policies and corporate acts of large, impersonal institutions. More specifically, the politically converted seek to ensure that social structures express and foster integral human conversion before God.

Personal conversion divides into affective, intellectual, moral, and religious conversion. The affective convert takes responsibility for cultivating personal emotional health and balanced esthetic sensibilities. Intellectual converts take responsibility for the truth or falsity of personal beliefs and for the adequacy or inadequacy of the frames of reference in which they fix those beliefs. The morally converted take responsibility for the ethical motives and consequences of their own personal decisions. The religiously converted take personal responsibility for responding to some historical self-revelation and self-communication of God on the terms that that revelation demands. In other words, religious converts consent to God in faith. Christian converts consent in faith to the one God historically revealed in the incarnate Word and in the Holy Breath.

I also distinguish between natural and graced conversion. Natural conversion occurs in complete abstraction from the historical self-revelation and self-communication of God. Severe depression or other forms of emotional anguish may, for example, lead one to decide to face one's emotional hang-ups with the help of others and to cultivate healthier emotional sensibilities. The experience of deceit, venality, or institutional injustice may also motivate an intellectual, moral, or socio-political conversion untouched by supernatural faith. Religious conversion, however, always results from the action of divine grace, since it expresses consent in faith to some gratuitous intervention of God in history.

In the reflections which follow, we will concentrate on two important dynamics that structure Christian conversion. By the dynamics of conversion I mean the ways in which the different forms of conversion mutually condition one another. The two dynamics of conversion on which we will concentrate hold an important key, as we shall see, to understanding the relationship between lay and religious spirituality expounded in the documents of Vatican II. Let me first describe briefly the two dynamics in question. Then we shall examine in greater detail how they structure the experience of conversion and how they illumine the scope of both lay and religious spirituality.

I formulate the first dynamic in the following fashion: (1) **Christian conversion mediates between affective and moral conversion.** We perceive realities other than ourselves in two ways: nonrationally and intuitively, on the one hand, and rationally and logically, on the other. The first Vatican council teaches correctly that the act of faith does not result from rational argumentation (DS 3041). Yet people do consent to God in faith. If converts do not consent to God rationally and logically, then they do so nonrationally and intuitively.

Some converts seem, however, to think their way into Christianity. A careful examination of such conversion will, however, reveal that while the thought processes which culminate in Christian commitment may clear away rational objections to religious belief, nevertheless, when the consent of faith itself occurs, it does not result from some purely rational argument but from a felt encounter with the mystery of sensibly visible divine beauty. Theologians have traditionally and correctly described Christian faith as a leap. We take that leap when we abandon controlled processes of rational thinking and respond intuitively with our hearts to some event of divine grace.

Christians convert initially to God by responding affectively and intuitively to the divine beauty incarnate in Jesus and in believing people who resemble Him. Christian conversion begins, then, in the heart; but the consent of faith commits the convert to discipleship. Disciples imitate Jesus by putting on His mind: His attitudes, His beliefs, His moral and social vision. Paul the apostle imagines converts putting on Christ like a garment. The image suggests the complete transformation of personal and social relationships which Christian conversion effects. The committed disciple consents, then, to Jesus' vision of what it means to live as a child of God in His image. Since that consent entails important moral consequences, it changes the way Christians form their consciences. After conversion they must judge the morality or immorality of specific choices not only in the light of a reasonable perception of the way responsible people ought to act but also in the light of the moral demands of discipleship. In this way, then, Christian conversion mediates between affective and moral conversion.

I formulate thus the second dynamic of conversion which we will examine: (2) **Christian conversion seeks to transvalue affective, intellectual, moral, and socio-political conversion when these transpire naturally.** I use the term "transvalue" in a technical sense. We transvalue sensations, feelings, images, or concepts when we transpose them from one frame of reference to another. When that occurs, the new frame of reference demands that we re-evaluate our former perceptions in its light. When, for example, children pass from adolescence to adulthood, they need to transvalue parental relationship in the light of their changed social status.

Affective, intellectual, moral, and socio-political conversion can, as we have seen, occur naturally: i.e., in abstraction from the historical self-revelation of God accomplished in Jesus and in the Holy Breath. Christian conversion, therefore, creates a novel context for understanding natural affective, intellectual, moral, and socio-political development: namely, the context of faith. Moreover, Christian conversion, engages one totally: heart, head, conscience, and institutionally mediated realtionships. Christian converts who have learned to act responsibly in each of these four realms of experience in abstraction from the demands of discipleship must on converting to Christ reach a new insight into how those demands change affective, intellectual, moral, and socio-political behavior. As the commitment of faith transvalues affective conversion, it changes it into repentence and supernatural hope. As it transvalues intellectual conversion, it transforms it into supernatural faith. As it transvalues moral conversion, it transforms it into Christian love. As it transvalues socio-political conversion, it transforms it into the Christian search for a just social order.

We shall presently examine each of these transformations in greater detail. We may, however, conclude on the basis of what has already been said that a fuller understanding of both dynamics demands a more detailed insight into the moral exigencies of Christian discipleship. An ethics of discipleship gives concrete meaning to the way Christian converts form their consciences. It therefore illumines the first dynamic, which justifies the invocation of specifically Christian values in moral decision making. An ethics of discipleship also supplies important criteria for transvaluing the processes of natural conversion. It therefore also illumines the second dynamic, which governs every form of graced human development.

In the course of the rest of this article, I will attempt to explore further these two dynamics of conversion by developing the following theses: (a) Jesus inculcated an ethics of discipleship that binds the consciences of all those who profess to follow Him in faith. (b) Moral transformation in the image of Jesus also demands that His disciples use their charismatic gifts to build up the body of Christ. (c) Moral transformation in the image of Jesus commits His disciples both individually and collectively to confront institutional injustice and to demand that human policy decisions as well as personal morality submit to the ethical demands of discipleship. (d) Christian discipleship transforms Christian families into apostolic communities of hope, faith, love and service. (e) The vows of religion seek to express one legitimate way of living out the moral consequences of Christian discipleship. In the process of arguing these theses, I will attempt not only to demonstrate the soundness of Vatican II's depiction of lay and religious spirituality but also to show how both forms of Christian living embody profoundly analogous ways of responding to the gospel.

(a) **Jesus inculcated an ethics of discipleship that binds the consciences of all who profess to follow Him in faith.** Jesus of Nazareth most certainly resonated in some measure with the apocalyptic aspirations of His people. He may well have imbibed His apocalypticism in part from John the Baptiser, who proclaimed an immanent divine judgment and the coming of one greater than himself through whom that judgment would be pronounced (Mt 3:1-12; Lk 3:1-18; Mk 1:1-8). Though scripture scholars debate the extent to which Jesus Himself identified with the figure of the Son of Man, the vision of the Son of Man in the apocalyptic book of Daniel seems to have colored His preaching (Mt 24:29-31; Mk 13:24-27; Lk 21:25-27).

Jesus, then, absorbed ideas and influences from the Jewish apocalyptic of His day, but He also transformed them creatively by using them to interpret His own sense both of relating to God in a privileged way as Son and of having been sent by **Abba** in the power of the Holy breath to proclaim the divine reign's immanent arrival (Mt 4:17; Mk 1:1-14). Moreover, He seems to have regarded the miracles He performed as evidence that the kingdom was already being established in His own ministry, even though its full establishment lay somewhere in the future (Mt 1:1-15, 11:2-15; 24:26-46).

Jesus' **Abba** experience also colored His understanding of the moral conditions for entering into the kingdom. He summoned His disciples to a filial morality, to enter into His own human experience of living as God's obedient Son. In Mark, the oldest of the gospels, we find Him enunciating a coherent vision of the way His disciples must live. He repudiates the hair-splitting legalism of some of His pharisaical contemporaries and insists that righteousness flows from purity of intention (Mk 2:23-3:6,7:1-23, 12:38-40). He summons His disciples to a faith in **Abba's** providential care and concern for them that binds them to Him in the practice of petitionary prayer (Mk 11:24). Jesus reveals **Abba's** will. He teaches that entry into the kingdom demands the willingness to obey God's commandments. Discipleship, however, demands more than torah piety. Jesus' followers must freely sell their possessions and give them to the poor (Mk 10:21-22). This self-divesting of worldly possessions does not bind an elite group among the disciples. Rather, it defines the practical meaning of discipleship itself . Jesus' followers must despise hoarded wealth as the greatest obstacle to entry into the kingdom (Mk 12:38-40). They must eschew the behavior of rich hypocrites who pray piously while exploiting the poor (Mk 12:38-40). They by contrast must practice an open hospitality to the poor and dispossessed that imitates Jesus's own table fellowship with sinners, even as it simultaneously gives practical meaning to the great commandment (Mk 2:15-17, 12:29-30, 9:37, 10:15-16). This willingness to share one's possessions with sinners and outcasts expresses in Jesus' eyes belief in **Abba's** forgiveness (Mk 2:5-12, 15-17). It must therefore incarnate mutual love and mutual forgiveness (Mk 9:41). Mutual forgiveness, moreover, measures the authenticity of the disciple's prayer (Mk 11:25). Discipleship also demands the reunuciation of the pride and power of the great ones of this world. Among Jesus's followers the least must be treated as the greatest (Mk 9:34-35). Not only must the disciples avoid scandalizing one another in any way, they must even imitate their master in His willingness to forgive in advance those who would murder Him (Mk 8:3-9, 9:42-50).

Matthew's Jesus makes similar moral demands of His followers. They must live in an expectant faith and trust in **Abba's** providential care that both heals any tendency to cling in anxiety to worldy goods and frees one instead to respond to the moral constraints of submitting to God's reign (Mt 6:24-36). Such faith finds expression in a willingness to share one's possessions with the needy and the outcast. It also defines a basic condition for entering and possessing the kingdom (Mt 25:31-36). There can be no a priori conditions set on one's willingness to share with others, for sharing must imitate the perfect love of **Abba,** who reaches out to saint and sinner alike (Mt 5:43-48). Sharing must include not only the marginal and the outcast but also one's enemies (Mt 5:43-45, 9:10-13). It expresses a mutual forgiveness that allows one to claim God's forgiveness (Mt 6:12). Among Jesus's disciples the haughty conduct of the princes of this world must yield to a mutual service that imitates the simplicity of children. Finally, mutual forgiveness authenticates prayer (Mt 20:24-28, 18:1-4,19:13-15).

Luke, who wrote his gospel for a church that had begun to relinquish its hope for an immanent parousia, seems to have feared that familiarity with this world could lead Christians into worldliness. He not only endorses the same moral vision as Matthew and Mark; he radicalizes it. The disciples of Jesus must renounce personal possessions and distribute them to the poor. This sharing expresses faith in the Father's providential care and introduces one into the kingdom of God. Moreover, sharing with those who cannot repay the favor nourishes the eschatological hope of Christians who look for their reward in the life to come (Lk 12:22-34, 16:9-13, 18:28-30). Luke's Jesus also cautions against seeking to derive one's life from riches (Lk 12:15, 16:10-12). Attachment to riches enslaves the wealthy and prevents them from entering the kingdom. It prevents the service of God (Lk 16:13, 18:18-27). Moreover, gross avarice and indifference to the suffering of the poor plunges one with the rich man of the parable into hell (Lk 16:19-31). Luke even hints that cynical love of wealth so contradicts obedient trust in God that it prevents belief in the resurrection (Lk 16:31). The true disciples of Jesus live poorly in imitation of their teacher and exemplar, Jesus Himself (Lk 14:33, 10:57-58). Sharing must go beyond handouts. It should include a hospitality toward the poor and outcast that finds special reward in the resurrection of the just (Lk 14:12-13, 21).

Luke's Jesus, like Matthew's and Mark's, demands not only faith in God but unconditioned faith. Unconditioned faith expresses itself in a sharing of possessions and practical concern for the poor that excludes no one in principle and imitates the perfection of the Father's love, Who sends blessings to the good and evil impartially (Lk 6:32-36, 14:12-14).

Finally, in Luke as in Matthew and Mark, Jesus founds the kingdom, not on power politics, but on a worship of **Abba** whose sincerity is measured by personal repentance and by the willingness to forgive others (Lk 5:32, 6:36-37, 11:3, 17:4).

We find, then, in the synoptic gospels a consistent account of the moral consequences of discipleship. The Jesus they portray teaches that entry into the kingdom demands a faith in God's providential care that frees one to share one's physical possessions with others. The disciples must share on the basis of need and not of merit. Such sharing expresses a mutual forgiveness that imitates God's own forgiving love; and mutual forgiveness authenticates the disciples' worship. Christian sharing excludes no one in principle but welcomes the sinner, the marginal, the outcast. It expresses hope in a God who rewards the compassionate in this life and in the next.

All three synoptic evangelists promise that those who follow Jesus can also expect to be drawn into His passion. The same forces that crucified Him will persecute and murder them (MK 13:11-13; Lk 12:11-12; Mt 28:18-20). In Acts, Luke dramatizes the fulfillment of this promise by describing the persecutions that afflicted the first disciples, persecutions typified in the ordeals of Peter and especially of Paul.

In several other documents of the New Testament, we find significant echoes of the moral vision which the synoptics ascribe to Jesus. In the exhortation which closes the letter to the Romans, for example, the apostle Paul sketches for the Roman community his own moral teaching. The exhortation alternates between the proclamation of general principles and their application to specific moral problems. For example, after exhorting the Romans to universal love, Paul launches into a more concrete discussion of the way believers should regard pagan authorities (Rm 13:1-7). Similarly, after exhorting the Romans to mutual love in community, Paul ends with an extended reflection on how Christians should deal lovingly with the scrupulous members of the church (Rm 14:1-15). If, however, the reader brackets those sections of Paul's exhortation which deal with practical applications and focuses instead on the ideals of Christian moral conduct he inculcates, one will discover that those ideals echo in striking ways the moral vision of Jesus proclaimed in the synoptics. Christians moved by the Breath of Jesus must share both Her charisms and the physical supports of life with one another in community. Sharing must proceed on the basis of need not of merit. Paul particularly commends the practice of hospitality. Christian sharing should express mutual forgiveness and reconciliation in Christ's name. It should include even one's enemies, for sharing in faith seeks to unite those whom sin formerly divided. The Christian community should reach out to the poor with special care, concern, true friendship and service, and not with condescention born of class and privilege. Finally, Christian sharing must express a mutual love that goes beyond what the law requires (Rm 12:9-21, 13:8-10).

One also hears echoes of Jesus' moral vision in the letter of James. A spokesman for Palestinian Christianity, James excoriates classist attitudes among the disciples of Jesus. Christian assemblies should tolerate no distinction between rich and poor (Jm 2:1-4). True faith expresses itself in the willingness to share one's physical possessions with others (Jm 2:14-16). Christians should banish all slander and dissension from their midst and live instead in mutual love (Jm 2:8-9). They must recognize that heaped up wealth breeds sinful arrogance and unbelief even as it calls down the wrath of God (Jm 4:13-5:6). All should hope in the second coming (Jm 5:7-11).

The New Testament gives us reason to assert, then, that the ethics of discipleship which the synoptics put upon the lips of Jesus did in fact inform the shared lives of both Palestinian and Pauline Christians. We catch real but more fragmentary echoes of Jesus' moral teaching in the Johannine tradition, where the doctrinal concerns of the fourth evangelist take precedence over concern for describing in detail the ethical consequences of discipleship.

Like the synoptic writers, John places the obedience of faith at the heart of Christian practice. He summons Jesus' disciples to good deeds and to authentic worship in spirit and in truth. John inculcates mutual love and mutual service. He warns that Jesus' disciples can expect to be drawn into his passion. He teaches trust in **Abba's** providential care (Jn 3:18, 21, 4:23, 6:29, 10:27-28, 15:26-27, 16:7-10, 23-24).

John, however, explicates the moral consequences of Christian faith in terms that also contrast with the synoptics. All three synoptic evangelists affirm the divinity of Jesus; but the fourth gospel make the confession of Jesus' divinity the most basic test of Christian faith in God (Jn 6:29, 8:24, 56, 11:25, 14:1, 6). Moreover, instead of insisting in the manner of the synoptics on the need to share one's bread with others gratuitously as an expression of faith in **Abba's** providential care and as a sign of a mutual forgiveness that authenticates worship, the fourth gospel largely reduces the moral consequences of discipleship to two fundamental commands: believe in Jesus as God incarnate and love one another in His image. Moreover, the fourth evangelist sees the ultimate exemplification of the love commandment in Jesus' redemptive death on the cross (Jn 13:15-16, 34-35, 15:9-17). John the evangelist also makes faith in Jesus' real eucharistic presence the test of true Christian worship (Jn 6:48). For the synoptics, as we have seen, mutual forgiveness authenticates worship.

The Johannine epistles echo the moral themes of the gospel, but they also give evidence that some of the kinds of behavior which the synoptics require of the followers of Jesus were also prized in the Johannine community. The first letter of John warns against the worldly pomp and pride to which the rich succumb (1 Jn 2:15-17); and it insists that Christian love must bear fruit in caring for the needy (1 Jn 4:20-21). The Johannine community also prized hospitality and deplored breaches of it that divided the community (Jn 13:20, 1 Jn 1:5, 10).

The shifts which the fourth evangelist makes in his presentation of the moral consequences of discipleship correspond to specific pastoral needs in his community. John wrote his gospel for a community not only in conflict with the synagogue but also plagued from within with an early form of gnosticism. John's adversaries in the community seem to have denied that God could take on flesh, that Jesus' physical death had any redemptive value, and that Christians really ate His body and drank His blood in the eucharist. For John, then, faith in these doctrines guarantees in a fundamental manner the authenticity of faith. For the rest, the fourth evangelist reduced the moral demands of discipleship primarily to the love commandment and to the willingness to bear up under persecution. Even in his explanation of the love commandment, John links it explicitly to doctrinal concerns, namely, to faith in the redemptive efficacy of Jesus' death.

A comparison of the Johannine and the synotic traditions reveals, therefore, that the latter provides us with a more detailed account of

Jesus' moral teaching than does the fourth gospel. Moreover, the New Testament gives us solid reason for asserting that the moral vision which the synoptic evangelists ascribe to Jesus shaped the moral practice of not only the Pauline and Palestinian churches but even, as the letters of John suggest, that of the Johannine community as well. That fact gives us solid reason for tracing the synoptic understanding of the demands of discipleship back to the historical Jesus.

The first quest for the historical Jesus contrasted sharply the Jesus of history and the Christ of faith. In **The Quest for the Historical Jesus,** Albert Schweitzer dissected its failure. Discouraged scholars abandoned the quest temporarily but resumed it in the latter part of this century. At first the new questers tended to contrast the Jesus of history and the Christian community's proclamation of the risen Christ. As first the new quest advanced, however, those who pursued it have emphasized the continuities that link Jesus to the Christian kerygma. The have also distinguished between "the real Jesus" and the "the historical Jesus." The real Jesus lived two thousand years ago and walked the streets of Galilee and Judea. From the New Testament witness scholars reconstruct the historical Jesus in the light of principles that attempt to distinguish "authentic" Jesus from embellishments added to His portrait by the Christian community.

Scholarly reconstruction of the historical Jesus has yielded a cumulative insight into the man, His vision, and His career. Among the principles invoked to authenticate different facets of the portrait which the evangelists draw of Jesus, the principle of dual irreducibility argues that teachings attributed to Jesus in the New Testament which find no parallel in either the Jewish or gentile traditions of the early first century should be considered historically authentic. New questers invoke this principle, for example, in order to authenticate both Jesus' **Abba** experience and His proclamation of the reign of God. The same principle authenticates Jesus' moral vision which the synoptic evangelists depict in loving detail. Nowhere else in the literature of the period do we find the unique ethics of faith which Mark, Matthew, and Luke place on the lips of Jesus. That ethics makes faith in **Abba** practical. It binds all the disciples of Jesus and teaches them how to live as children of God in his image. It spells out the conditions for discipleship and membership in the kingdom. And it gave practical orientation to Pauline, Palestinian, and even Johannine Christianity, even though, as we have seen, for doctrinal reasons the fourth gospel fails to describe Jesus' moral doctrine in the same detail as the synoptics.

(b) **Moral transformation in the image of Jesus demands that His disciples use their charismatic gifts to build up the body of Christ.** As we have seen, Christian conversion contributes two important dynamics to the total process of conversion. It mediates between affective and moral conversion and it transvalues affective, intellectual, and moral conversion. The first dynamic echoes the Christian convert's commitment to live according to Jesus' moral vision. The second ensures that the same moral vision informs Christian hope, faith and love.

We can legitimately characterize the morality of discipleship which Jesus proclaimed as filial, in the sense that it commits Jesus' followers to serving as God's instruments in bringing into existence a specific kind of faith community: namely, a community in which trust in God's providential care frees its members to share the physical supports of life with one another, a community in which sharing proceeds on the basis of need and not of merit, a community in which mutual sharing embodies mutual forgiveness and authenticates worship.

Active participation in the life of such a community presupposes admission into its company. Inevitably, then conversion to Jesus culminates in the rites of Christian initiation. In submitting to the sacraments of initiation, converts profess their willingness not only to subscribe to the Christian community's religious beliefs and ideals but also to contribute actively to its shared life in a way that expresses the mind of Christ.

Conversion claims the convert's entire person: heart, mind, and conscience As Jesus' religious vision transforms the heart, it gives rise to Christian hope. As it transforms the convert's mind it gives rise to Christian faith. As it transforms the convert's moral choices, it gives rise to Christian love. Moreover, the ethics of discipleship which Jesus proclaimed helps endow Christian hope, faith, and love with its distinctively Christian character. Converted Christians dream in hope of the day when God's will will be done on earth as in heaven. Through faith they discover God's will definitively revealed in the moral teachings of His only begotten Son. That faith teaches them, moreover, that Christian love derives its specific moral content from filial morality of faith which Jesus embodied and inculcated. In other words a New Testament ethics of discipleship provides Christian hope with a specific communal ideal. That same ethic helps give Christian faith its content. It also endows Christian love with specific moral content.

A morality of discipleship also binds individual disciples and the Christian community to one another in mutually lifegiving ways. The shared hope, faith, and love of the community nurtures and forms the hope, faith, and love of individual believers. They, however, contribute to the hope, faith and love of the community by sharing with the other members of the church the physical supports of life, by their concern for the neediest, by living a life of forgiving, atoning love, and by actively participating in shared worship.

Moreover, a filial ethics of discipleship implicitly motivates a Pauline theology of the gifts, or charisms, of the Holy Breath. Paul, as we have seen, expected his churches to live in fidelity to Jesus' moral vision, but he also realized two other important facts. He knew that the

Breath of the risen Christ creates the church by inspiring its hope, faith, and love. He also knew that the Holy Breath had been given in eschatological abundance not to individual Christians but to the community as a whole. From these two facts he correctly concluded that in the postresurrectional church, the disciples of Jesus had more than material possessions to share in faith. They could share the Breath of Jesus Herself. By the charisms of the Holy Breath Paul meant particular manifestations of Her saving activity in the lives of believing Christians. The Breath of Jesus transforms the church into the living body of Christ when She inspires its members to share Her inspirations with one another. Deeds of faith must, then, if they claim to proceed from the Breath of Jesus, incarnate His mind. They must, in other words, embody and inculcate the filial morality of faith He lived and inculcated.

Church leaders too must exercise their charismatic ministry in the community in ways that embody the mind of Jesus. Their ministry must emobdy and nurture the hope, faith and love of the community as a whole by proclaiming Christ in season and out and by providing the Christian community with effective pastoral leadership. One cannot, of course, lead a worshipping community effectively unless one also leads it in worship, even though ordination need not in principle confer the exculsive right to lead community worship.

When viewed as a social process the gracing of human affectivity demands the creation of therpeutic Christian communities of hope. Such communities result in part from the sharing of the material supports of life , as Jesus demanded of His disciples, in part from the mutual love and support of the members of such communities, in part from the healing that prayer produces. The sharing of the material supports of life in mutual forgiveness creates an atmosphere of support in which individuals can both face in repentant trust those wounded places in the heart still in need of healing and renounce sinful attitudes that still separate one from God and from the other members of the community. Active concern to reach out to the marginal and alienated creates a safe place in which they too can hope to come to repentence. As repentance heals the heart, the latter expands in hope to the vision of a world transformed according to the mind of Christ. Zest for realizing that vision inserts individual believers into the shared life of the Christian community, which seeks to emobdy Jesus' religious vision.

When viewed as a social process faith consists in sharing the charisms of the Holy Breath in community; for that sharing creates the shared faith consciousness of the church. Shared consciousness differs from individual consciousness. Individual consciousness results from discriminating different realities and from understanding their relationship to one another. Shared consciousness results from a complex dialogic process. Communities reach shared consciousness by coming to understand their historical origin and development, for those events define the nature of the community. A community comes to further shared awareness when on the basis of a common insight into its identity it aspires to a common future and then orchestrates the gifts of its members to realize that future.

In the Chistian community the complex process that produces shared faith awareness results from the sharing of the charisms of the Holy Breath. Gifts of prayer and of healing endow the community with a sense of God's presence. The gift of tongues reminds it of the first Pentecost and teaches the community to regard Pentecost as an ongoing event in the life of the church. Gifts of prophecy and of teaching enable the community to retrieve its history and to project its shared future in repentant faith and hope. Gifts of discernment allow the community to distinguish between true and false doctrine, between healthy and unhealthy aspirations, and between loving and destructive courses of action. Finally, the action gifts, like administration, pastoral leadership, and helping endable the community to orchestrate the gifts of its members in order to achieve shared self-understanding and a future rooted in God. As individual believers share their charisms with the community, their Breath-inspired service enhances the shared faith consciousness of the community even as the shared faith of the community tutors the believer's personal faith.

Viewed as social process, Christian love consists in the collective effort of Christians to embody the mind of Jesus in deeds of faith. It consists, therefore, in the actual sharing of the material supports of life and of faith itself in a mutual love and forgiveness that imitates the forgiving love of God revealed to us in Jesus. Mutual forgiveness measures the sincerity of the community's shared worship. The practical love of the Christian community teaches its members how to live in loving imitation of the Lord. It forgives those who fall short of the ideal to which we are called in Christ and encourages them to practical recommitment to a life informed by gospel values.

These insights into the dynamics of conversion ground several facets of Vatican II's depiction of lay spirituality. The council insists that God calls all Christians to a life of holiness, but it leaves the term "holiness" vague and undefined. A New Testament ethics of discipleship gives the term "holiness" specific moral content. While the council insists that lay Christians especially should labor for the Christianization of secular society, it nevertheless teaches as well that the lay apostolate includes ministry within and to the Christian community as such. It correctly characterizes that ministry as charismatically inspired. It correctly portrays the ministry of church leaders as the evocation through proclamation and shared whorship of the Breath's charismatic inspirations and as the discernment and coordination of the charismatic ministry of lay Christians. A theology of Christian conversion grounds these teachings by showing that openess to the Breath's charismatic inspirations flows, as the apostle Paul saw, inevitably from the experience of sanctification. Moreover, by thematizing the moral consequences of conversion to Christ, that same theology explicates important criteria for judging whether or not allegedly charismatic deeds of service truly flow from the Holy Breath of Jesus. They can make that claim only if they embody His mind. Finally, by showing that all authentic ministry within the church must seek to bring into existence a community of hope, faith, and love which embodies the mind of Christ, a theology of Christian conversion endorses the collaborative character of lay and clerical ministry on which Vatican II insisted.

(c) **Moral transformation in the image of Jesus also commits His disciples both individually and collectively to confront institutional injustice and to demand that human policy decisions as well as personal morality submit to the ethical demands of discipleship.** Confronted with the complexity of twentieth century living, contemporary Christians cannot help but feel the false allure of privatized religion. Two forces in contemporary North America conspire to enhance the attractiveness of privatized piety: the all-pervaisive individualism that infects our culture and the spontaneous self-preoccupation of the finite human ego. Socialization attenuates the egocentrism which human consciousness shares with all other forms of biologically based, conscious life; but socialization rarely overcomes completely the powerful instincts for growth and survival that motivate ego-based activity. Individualism panders to human self-preoccupation by offering pseudo-rationalizations for ignoring the needs and sufferings of others and for concerning oneself narrowly and irresponsibly with one's own self-satisfaction. When selfish individualism dons the vestments of privatized religion, it breeds a hypocrisy that spells the death of authentic Christian faith. The search for security replaces the search for God. Practical concern for others in God's name gives way to the self-indulgent amassing of "personally meaningful" acts of piety.

Privatized piety subverts Christian faith by suffusing it with inauthenticity. We succumb to inauthenticity when we choose to act irresponsibly despite our professed intention to do otherwise. Those who acquiesce in privatized piety have presumably experienced at least some kind of initial religious conversion, but they fallaciously imagine that they can cultivate a faith-filled, interpersonal relationship with God while simultaneously ignoring the massive suffering caused by unjust social, economic, and political institutions. Authentic new covenant religion demands otherwise. It measures the sincerity of personal commitment to God by practical concern for others, especially for the marginal and the needy. Practical concern for those in greatest need seeks to eliminate the personal and institutional causes of their neediness.

Privatized faith also underestimates the extent to which impersonal, secular institutions shape personal faith awareness. In our own nation captialism, consumerism, and commercialistic materialism have successfully transformed every capital sin save sloth into a pseudo-virtue. The attitudes and the ideologies which rationalize such all pervasive attitudes cannot but infect the hearts and minds of self-professed Christians who ignore them systematically by retiring into the deceptive comfort of privatized devotion.

The missionary thrust of Christianity combines too with the moral demands of convenant faith in order to exclude privatized piety. The Breath of Christ constrains believers to proclaim the gospel to all creatures, including those who make the executive and policy decisions that for good or ill direct the actions of large, impersonal, corporate institutions.

As we have seen, Christian conversion lacks full integrity unless it includes a socio-political moment. The socio-politically converted commit themselves to doing what lies within their power in order to ensure that the human decisions which shape the policies and corporate acts of large, impersonal instituional structures express and foster integral conversion. Even the socio-politically converted can on occasion through ignorance, oversight, or human limitation serve as the pawns and dupes of massive institutional injustice. How much more vulnerable to such manipulation are those who resist conversion at a socio-political level!

The integrally converted need, however, to balance political activism with personal growth. In all likelihood, only a relatively small proportion of the intergrally converted will either experience the opportunity or possess the skill to engage in full time, professional political activism. Almost everyone can, however, find some time to lend support to full-time activists dedicated to the pursuit of justice and to do so in ways that go beyond the minimal requirements of responsible citizenship.

The complexity and intrasigence of large institutions inoculates them against the efforts of isolated individuals who seek to change them in the interests of justice. Even moderately effective attempts at institutional reform result then, from corporate effort. Those who oppose institutionalized injustice need, then, to make common cause with like-minded individuals who also long for a just social order. Socio-political conversion commits one, therefore, to some concrete cause, as inevitably human finitude forces socio-political converts to opt among the specific issues to which they intend as individuals consecrate their energies.

The human search for justice takes on a Christian character when it derives its definition of social justice from the moral teachings of Jesus. As we have already seen, when a filial, New Testament ethics of discipleship transvalues affective, intellectual, and moral conversion it transmutes them into Christian hope, faith, and love respectively. That transformation inserts the convert into the graced social process we call the church. As Christian conversion transmutes and transvalues socio-political conversion, it replaces human conceptions of a just social order with God's own. In Jesus' filial ethics of discipleship we discover a vision of the way humans are called by God to relate to one another not only individually and personally but also socially and institutionally.

Some theologians have decried the moral vision of Jesus as utopian. They have warned that human institutions will never perfectly embody that vision and should not, as a consequence, be expected to do so. In effect these theologians privatize Christian morality by confining it to the sphere of the individual and interpersonal and by relegating any attempt to deal with human institutions to the tender mercies of **Realpolitik.** Those who espouse such a position fail to understand the way the Christian conscience functions creatively. They concede that gospel morality challenges us individually and personally. The fact, however, that we fall personally short of living the gospel does not excuse us from trying to live it better in the future. As Christians we adhere to the moral demands of discipleship not because we know in advance that we shall walk the path of the gospel perfectly, but because God wills it. We seek to shape human institutions to the moral vision of Jesus for the same reason.

In confronting situations of institutionalized injustice and oppression, we should, then, never lie to ourselves about the ideal social order to which God calls us in Christ. Rather we should judge the sinfulness of our institutions by the extent to which they violate Jesus' moral vision. Then we should allow the Breath of Christ to teach us to use our imaginations creatively in faith to advance the next possible step toward a more perfect realization of the kingdom not only in our private, personal dealings with one another but also in our institutional transactions.

Although the documents of Vatican II do not invoke explicitly the filial ethics of discipleship which I sketched above, one can nevertheless use Jesus' moral teaching in order to ground the council's social doctrine. Catholic social doctrine has traditionally invoked a certain number of general principles in dealing with human institutions and social interaction. The principle of nonmalfeasance states that people should not inflict harm on one another. The principle of beneficence asserts that people ought to minister to one another's needs. From these fundamental principles three others follow: namely, that the exigencies of the common good restrict individual autonomy and self-determination, that every human person possesses an inalienable dignity in the sight of God which human moral choices must respect, and that God intends the goods of creation for use and benefit of all and not just the privileged few.

These principles govern the social teachings of Vatican II which propose strategies for dealing apostolically with contemporary culture and with the economic and political structure of modern society. In seeking to make the benefits of human culture available to everyone, to avoid humanly destructive methods of education, to curb the destructive uses of modern technology, and to foster a universal humanism that transcends narrow regionalism and nationalism, the council invokes all of these principles simultaneously. Vatican II's defence of the dignity of human labor expresses a more fundamental belief in the dignity of each person. In its defence of labor unions and in its condemnation of abuses of private ownership, the council explicitly cites the principle that God intends the goods of creation for the enjoyment of all. Vatican II insists that governments exist in order to secure that common good. Concern for the common good also motivates its call for a new international economic order. Its condemnation of total war, of the use of nuclear weapons, and of the impovrishment effected by the nuclear arms race implicitly invokes the principles of nonmalfeasance and beneficence.

The traditional moral principles which Vatican II invokes in order to devise strategies for dealing with modern secular society can, however, themselves find grounding in Jesus' moral doctrine as we find it preserved in the gospels, especially in the synoptics. His filial ethics of discipleship gives specific moral content to the principle of beneficence, for it requires His disciples to reach out in active concern for others on the basis of their need rather than their merits only . The principle of nonmalfeasance forbids all acts that contradict the principle of beneficence. For the follower of Jesus, then, it condemns all actions which contradict a New Testament ethics of. discipleship. Catholic insistence on the inalienable dignity before God of each human person reiterates somewhat more abstractly Jesus' own insistence that His disciples' love imitate **Abba**'s by reaching out indiscriminately to all, saint and sinner alike. The universal sharing of material supports of life which Jesus enjoins upon His followers undergirds traditional Catholic teaching that God intends the goods of creation for the benefit of all and not just of the economically privileged. The same teaching justifies traditional Catholic concern that cultural, economic and political structures promote the common good by creating the conditions under which all can contribute to and benefit from social benefits and security.

When, then, one reads the documents of Vatican II in the light of a contemporary theology of five-fold conversion, they summon contemporary Christians not only to personal but to socio-political conversion. That same theology of conversion also endorses the soundness of other conciliar teachings. Vatican II holds that the lay apostolate flows from Christian initiation, that it expresses the universal mission of the Church, and that it consecrates lay Christians not only to service in the church but to the immense challenge of Christianizing secular society. All three teachings lie grounded in the moral consequences of Christian conversion which transvalue in faith affective, intellectual, moral, and socio-political conversion. As we saw in the preceding section of this essay, the transformation of affective, intellectual, and moral conversion into Christian faith, hope, and love introduces Christian converts into that graced social process we call the church and makes them into charismatically active contributors to to the Christian community's shared life. As consent to Jesus' moral vision informs socio-political conversion, it consecrates lay Christians to the search for a social order that incarnates the justice of God. Both forms of the lay apostlate flow from Christian initiation because they express the moral consequences of the initial conversion to Christ which the rites of initiation solemnize.

(d) **Christian discipleship transforms Christian families into apostolic communities of hope, faith, love, and service.** Jesus did not begin the institution of marriage; but He transformed the institution He found in three ways. He repudiated Mosaic divorce practices. He demanded that all His disciples, including therefore those who marry, should relate to one another with a certain quality of hope, faith, and love. Finally, He sent the Christian community his Breath to anoint Christians to the ministry of marriage by sanctifying their union with one another. In virtue of these interrelated actions, Jesus Christ may legitimately be said to have instituted marriage as a Christian ritual. Moreover, as we have seen , consent to Jesus' moral vision helps define the specifically Christian character of hope, faith, and love. Because Christian families are called by God to grow individually and collectively in hope, faith, and love, that same ethic must inform their lives together.

The mutual sharing of the material supports of life in Christian families should create a graced environment of religious hope that nurtures the hope of each family member. Such sharing must advance on the basis of need, not of merit. It should express a filial trust in the father's providential care not only on the part of each family member but also on the part of the family as a whole. The sharing which expresses the hope of Christian families must, if authentic, also express the universality and gratuity of Christian love. Christian families need to reach out individually and collectively to those who experience the greatest need. Their hospitality should as far as possible imitate Jesus's table fellowship with sinners. The Christian family's active concern to succor the needy should express and instill a hope that transcends this world and looks to the God who rewards the compassionate in the life to come.

Not only does Vatican II portray Christian marriage as an important form of the lay apostolate, but it also insits on the charismatic inspiration of Christian marriage. The Breath of Jesus calls Christian spouses charismatically to marital union. Moreover, their mutual service to one another within the family creates the context of faith which nurtures the personal faith of their children to charismatic maturity. The sharing of the charisms within Christian families imitates on a smaller scale the sharing of the charisms within the church as a whole. The shared faith of the Christian community as a whole results from the sharing of the charisms of the holy Breath, for each charism contributes something to the shared faith consciousness of the Christian community as a whole. Gifts of prayer summon the Church to repentance and to hope. Together gifts of prophecy and of teaching instill an understanding of the Christian community's origin and identity. They also help the church reach a consensus concerning the kind of future to which God is calling it. Discernment enables the community to discriminate between hopes, beliefs, and paths of action which express the mind of Christ and those which do not. Action gifts mobilize the other charisms in order to actualize the community's shared aspirations. Although Christian families, because of their size, will never boast the rich diversity of charisms present in the church as a whole, nevertheless, gifts of prayer, words that summon to repentance and to hope, teaching, discernment, and practical ministry both within the family and to those outside it, all shape the family's shared faith awareness. That shared faith nourishes in turn the charisms of the parents and creates the environment of faith in which children can advance to adult conversion and active charismatic ministry.

Christian families also discover in the Jesus' filial ethics of discipleship the concrete meaning of Christian love. That ethical vision becomes Christian love when it motivates Christian practice. It teaches parents and children alike to love one another with the atoning, forgiving love of Christ and to measure the authenticity of their shared prayer by their capacity to forgive as God forgave us in Jesus.

An insight into the way in which the dynamics of Christian conversion transforms and transmutes the experience of family life both validates and illumines Vatican II's teaching concerning Christian marriage. It also spells out in more concrete detail than the council itself the practical meaning of growth in holiness within the context of family life.

(e) **The vows of religion seek to express one legitimate way of living out the moral consequences of Christian discipleship.** As we have seen Vatican II presents the three traditional vows of poverty, chastity, and obedience as distinguishing marks of religious life. The three vows of religion did not take their present more or less standardized form until the eleventh century, but the remote origins of vowed living extend back to the fourth century, when Christian hermits banded together to form cenobitic communities dedicated to a life of work and contemplation.

We have already seen how a Christian ethics of discipleship motivates the apostolic involvement of lay Christians both in ecclisial ministry and in the Christianization of secular society. We have also seen how Jesus' moral vision Christianizes and scramentalizes the institution of marriage. The vows of religion represent yet another attempt to bring the moral vision of Jesus to institutional embodiment.

Not only do vowed religious renounce the personal ownership of property but they also commit themselves to participate in the common life of the religious community they join. That promise expresses the same trust in God's providential care which faith sharing in the church or in Christian families incarnates. The vow of poverty seeks then to bring into existence a community of Christian hope committed to sharing the physical supports of life among its members and also with others in physical need. A willingness to share gratuitously, on the basis of need rather than of merit, testifies to the eschatological character of that hope, for it reaches out to those least capable of responding in kind. As a consequence, such sharing looks for its reward more in the next life than in this one.

If Christian hope contextualizes and gives meaning to the first vow of religion, Christian faith performs a similar function for the vow of obedience. The faith of individual Christians, as we have seen, is nurtured by the shared faith consciousness of the church as a whole. The shared faith consciousness of the Christian community, however, results, as we have seen, from the active sharing of the charisms of the Holy Breath. In such a community the obedience of faith consists in discerning and responding to one's charism of service by recognizing and using one's competence in faith to contribute to the shared life of the Christian and human communities. For religious, the vow of obedience provides a supportive institutional structure which attempts to facilitate that process of discernment. Through the vow of obedience religious renounce their own wills and promise to submit to the decisions of their superiors in accord with their specific institute. Religious superiors, however, relate to their communities in a way analogous to the relationship between the hierarchy and the church as a whole. Both religious superiors and the church's hierarchy serve by aiding those over whom they exercise authority to discern and respond actively to the Breath's enabling, charasmatic call. The vow of obedience also contextualizes that process of discernment, for it consecrates a religious to promote the pastoral aims and goals of a specific ministerial community within the church. As a consequence, the vow of obedience endows the vowed religious' practical, charismatic profession of faith with public institutional visibility.

Christian love contextualizes the vow of chastity. Religious bind themselves by vow to love others as celibates. Christian celibate love, however, involves much more than the renunciation of marriage and of the genital uses of human sexuality. Christian celibacy seeks to incarnate a certain quality of love. All Christian love derives its moral content from Jesus' filial ethics of discipleship.

We can, however, understand better the distinctive nature of celibate love if we compare and contrast it with married love. Every attempt to love others in the name and image of Jesus engages four values: concreteness, reciprocity, gratuity, and universality. Incarnational love always reaches out ultimately to concrete pesons, whether as individuals or as communities, and attempts to minister to concrete human needs. Because Christian love seeks to bring into existence a community whose members minister to one another's needs, it always commits those who practice it to reciprocal service. Because it attempts to incarnate the forgiving, atoning, love of Christ, Christian love reproduces the gratuity of divine love. It follows need, not merit. It forgives in advance every wrong. Because it excludes no one in principle from its practical concern, Christian love expresses in a finite human manner something of the universality of God's love.

These four values of concreteness, reciprocity, gratuity, and universality characterizes, then, every authentic expression of Christian love.

In married love, however, concreteness and reciprocity tend to be valued up, while gratuity and universality tend to be valued down. In celibate love, by contrast, gratuity and universality tend to be valued up, while concreteness and reciprocity tend to be valued down. Let us reflect on how this occurs.

In married love two concrete individuals commit themselves to one another with the unconditioned, atoning love of Christ. They commit themselves to the children that will result from their union with a similar Christlike love. When Christian marriage succeeds, then, the love it embodies expresses in a special way the concreteness of reciprocity of charity, even though both within the family and in its apostolic outreach to others married love continues in other ways to incarnate the gratuity and universality of Christian love. Celibates renounce marriage but not Christian love. They renounce marriage out of loving concern for others. By the vow of celibacy they commit themselves to reach out actively in every situation to those in greatest need. Every celibate's ability to live such a commitment remains, of course, humanly conditioned, but in its desire to reach out to the marginal and alienated in human society celibate love expresses with heightened visibility the gratuity and universality of Christian love. Still, celibates experience human neediness. They need not only to minister to others but to be ministered to. They must still minister to concrete individuals or communities. Their love, then, still incarnates concreteness and reciprocity but with less social and institutional visibility than does the successful Christian marriage.

The history of religious life suggests, moreover, that religious communities come into existence out of the shared desire to minister to some pressing need in the church or in society at large. Pressing needs demand special sacrifice. Celibacy, as the apostle Paul saw clearly, brings with it in principle greater apostolic availability. The precise character of that availability will vary with different religious institutes. Some institutes consecrate religious in a special way to the ministry of prayer and to the creation of spiritual centers of service within the church. Others consecrate their members to a more pastorally active ministry of proclamation or of practical compassion and concern with crying human needs. Religious life gives social and communal expression to the apostolic thrust of the vow of celibacy.

These insights derived from a Christian theology of conversion not only validate Vatican II's description of the scope and purpose of vowed ministry but also allow us to develop a number of council's insights even further than the council itself. Vatican II teaches that the vows of religion flow from and express Christian initiation. As we have seen, the sacraments of initiation commit Christians collectively and individually to a life of hope, faith, love, and mutual charismatic service. When understood in the light of the dynamics of Christian conversion, the vows of religion, as we have seen, clearly attempt to incarnate in a specific manner the hope, faith, love, and mutual service to which the rites of initiation consecrate the disciples of Jesus.

Vatican II does not itself speak of religious life as charismatic. Papal teaching subsequent to the council has, however, correctly insisted not only on the charismatic but on the prophetic character of religious life. In so teaching both Paul VI and John Paul II have explicated insights latent in the council's documents. Those documents insist on the charismatic inspiration of the ministry of both the laity and the hierarchy. If religious life expresses a legitimate way of exercising both apostolates in the church, it cannot lack charismatic inspiration.

Moreover, the vows of religion make a public, countercultural statement that sets the vowed Christians in open, prophetic opposition to the ambition, materialism, and sensuality of much of human society. Religious life may be legitimately described as prophetic for yet another reason. The renunciation of property and of family which the first two vows of religion express frees religious to respond with greater flexibility to pressing needs in the church and in the human community. At the same time, the vow of obedience endows the ministry of religious with a certain quality of selflessness and with a public visibility that results from membership in a specific ministerial community.

The vows of religion stand in judgment, then, over religious who in the course of their ministry prefer their own security to concern for the needy. The vows also judge communities which allow their institutions to deprive them of the kind of apostolic flexibility to which religious consecration aspires.

When, however, religious communities live their vows, they will tend to exhibit a greater capacity than, for example, the more specialized institution of the family to respond with apostolic flexibility to pressing human and ecclesial needs. In so acting, lay religious should follow the charismatic anointing of the Breath of God rather than wait always for explicit directives from the hierarchy, even though as lay apostles they collaborate with the ordained and should respond to the initiatives of the ordained leadership of the church. This flexible capacity to respond publicly to pressing pastoral needs which religious life at its best represents not only justifies calling it charismatic but also endows the ministry of religious with a prophetic character by publicly focusing the church's attention on situations of great human and pastoral need.

The insights of Vatican II also justify characterizing the ministry of lay religious as secular, in the council's sense of that term. Lay apostles with religious vows not only collaborate in intraecclesial church ministry but also consecrate themselves to the Christianization of secular society. Like other lay apostles, they bear a special responsibility to confront the principalities and powers of this world in Jesus' name and summon them to repentence.

I have been attempting to use a theology of Christian conversion in order to validate the teachings of Vatican II concerning lay ministry in the church. The validity of the council's insights suggests that those who resist its reforms act not from authentic faith but from an unacknowledged lack of conversion that they have piously rationalized. A theology of conversion has also allowed us to clarify, and in some instances, to expand conciliar teaching. It has, moreover, allowed us to understand the council's vision of the apostolic role of the laity, whether vowed or not, as a spirituality, as a practical way of approaching God. Our insights, however, like the teachings of the council itself will remain only ideals until lay Christians under the guidance of the Breath of God translate them into deeds.